SCIENCE
ENCYCLOPEDIA

SCIENCE
ENCYCLOPEDIA

First published in 2004 by Miles Kelly Publishing Ltd
Bardfield Centre, Great Bardfield, Essex, CM7 4SL

Copyright © Miles Kelly Publishing Ltd 2004

This edition printed in 2008

2 4 6 8 10 9 7 5 3

Editorial Director Belinda Gallagher
Art Director Jo Brewer
Editor Jenni Rainford
Editorial Assistant Teri Mort
Design Concept Debbie Meekcoms
Lenticular Designer Warris Kidwai
Design Stonecastle Graphics
Copy Editor Rosalind Beckman
Consultants Sue Becklake, Robert Birke, John Farndon, Steve Parker,
Chris Pellant, Helen Pellant, Dr Kristina Routh, Richard Tames
Proofreaders Margaret Berrill, Hayley Kerr
Indexer Hilary Bird
Reprints Controller Bethan Ellish
Production Manager Elizabeth Brunwin
Reprographics Anthony Cambray, Liberty Newton

ISBN 978-1-84236-913-5

Printed in China

British Library Cataloguing-in-Publication Data
A catalogue record for this book is available from the British Library

www.mileskelly.net
info@mileskelly.net

www.factsforprojects.com

Third-party website addresses are provided by Miles Kelly Publishing
in good faith and for information only, and are suitable and accurate at the time of going to press.
Miles Kelly Publishing Ltd disclaims any responsibility for the material contained therein.

Contents

Plants

Wild Animals

How Animals Live

Human Body

How Things Work

Inventions

Great Scientists

How to use this book

CHILDREN'S SCIENCE ENCYCLOPEDIA is packed with information, colour photos, diagrams, illustrations and features to help you learn more about all aspects of science. Do you know what the Earth is made of or which animal develops from eggs inside the male? Did you know that skin is the heaviest organ in the human body or that time is the fourth dimension? Enter the fascinating world of science and learn about why things happen, where things come from and how things work. Find out how to use this book and start your journey of scientific discovery.

Main text
Each subject begins with an introduction to the different subject areas.

It's a fact
Key statistics and extra facts on each subject provide additional information.

Main image
Each topic is clearly illustrated. Some images are labelled, providing further information.

Check it out!
Find out more by surfing the Internet.

26

Energy and work

ENERGY IS the ability to make something happen. It is not just the light that comes from the Sun, or the heat that comes from a fire. Scientists say that energy is the capacity to do work. It is involved in everything that happens everywhere in the universe, however tiny or gigantic, from grass growing to stars exploding. All substances have energy locked up inside their atoms and molecules. Energy comes in many different forms and it can change from one form to another.

BRIGHT SPARKS

• Energy can never be created or destroyed; it can only be changed from one form to another. So all the energy in the universe has always existed no matter what form it is in now.

• Scientists define work as a force multiplied by the distance a load moves when the force acts on it. In the metric system, the unit of energy is called the joule. One joule is the work done when a force of 1 newton moves an object a distance of 1 metre, or a metre-newton. The foot-pound is the imperial energy unit used in countries such as the USA.

IT'S A FACT

• All the energy in the universe may eventually turn to heat. This is called the 'Heat Death of the Universe' theory.

• Walking needs about five times as much energy as sitting still; running needs about seven times more energy.

● Movement energy

A moving object has a type of energy called kinetic energy. The more massive the object is and the faster it moves, the more kinetic energy it has. When runners set off at the beginning of a race, they convert chemical energy in their muscles to kinetic energy. The faster they can change chemical energy into kinetic energy, the faster they run. At the end of the race they stop producing kinetic energy. Air resistance and friction between their shoes and the ground slow them down.

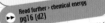

Read further > chemical energy
pg16 (d2)

▶ At the end of the race, the runners quickly lose their kinetic energy and come to a halt.

▶ For a split second as the sprinters come away from the starting blocks, they accelerate faster than an average sports car.

Check it out!
• http://www.eia.doe.gov/kids/
• http://www.energyquest.ca.gov

▶▶ SUN see pg42 (k2) ▶▶

1   2   3   4   5   6   7   8   9   10   11   12   13   14   15   16   17

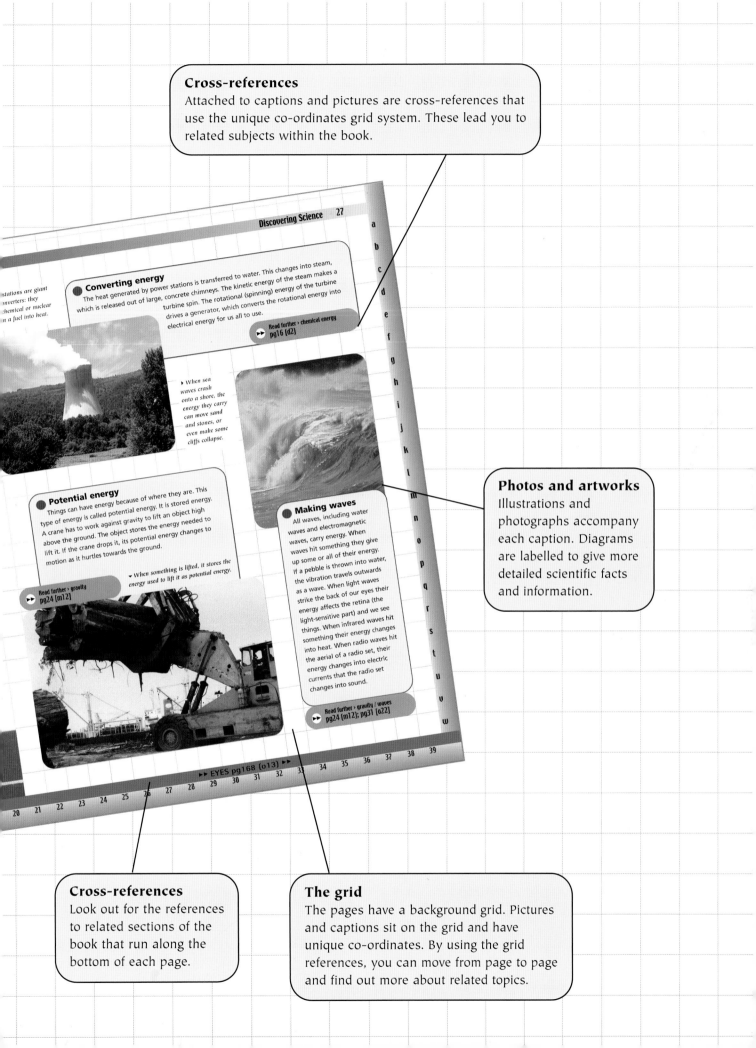

Cross-references

Attached to captions and pictures are cross-references that use the unique co-ordinates grid system. These lead you to related subjects within the book.

Converting energy

The heat generated by power stations is transferred to water. This changes into steam, which is released out of large, concrete chimneys. The kinetic energy of the steam makes a turbine spin. The rotational (spinning) energy of the turbine drives a generator, which converts the rotational energy into electrical energy for us all to use.

Read further › chemical energy
pg16 (d2)

stations are giant converters: they chemical or nuclear n a fuel into heat.

▸ When sea waves crash onto a shore, the energy they carry can move sand and stones, or even make some cliffs collapse.

Potential energy

Things can have energy because of where they are. This type of energy is called potential energy. It is stored energy. A crane has to work against gravity to lift an object high above the ground. The object stores the energy needed to lift it. If the crane drops it, its potential energy changes to motion as it hurtles towards the ground.

▾ When something is lifted, it stores the energy used to lift it as potential energy.

Read further › gravity
pg24 (m12)

Making waves

All waves, including water waves and electromagnetic waves, carry energy. When waves hit something they give up some or all of their energy. If a pebble is thrown into water, the vibration travels outwards as a wave. When light waves strike the back of our eyes their energy affects the retina (the light-sensitive part) and we see things. When infrared waves hit something their energy changes into heat. When radio waves hit the aerial of a radio set, their energy changes into electric currents that the radio set changes into sound.

Read further › gravity / waves
pg24 (m12); pg31 (o22)

Photos and artworks

Illustrations and photographs accompany each caption. Diagrams are labelled to give more detailed scientific facts and information.

▸▸ EYES pg168 (o13) ▸▸

20 21 22 23 24 25 26 27 28 29 30 31 32 33 34 35 36 37 38 39

Cross-references

Look out for the references to related sections of the book that run along the bottom of each page.

The grid

The pages have a background grid. Pictures and captions sit on the grid and have unique co-ordinates. By using the grid references, you can move from page to page and find out more about related topics.

Solids, liquids and gases

NEARLY EVERY substance in the universe is either a solid, a liquid or a gas. These are called states of matter. For example, rock is solid, water is liquid and oxygen is a gas. A substance can change from one state to another by gaining or losing energy. Heating water gives it more energy. The extra energy makes the water particles move about faster. If they have enough energy, they can escape from the water and form a gas – steam.

Some of the substances in lava (liquid rock) are heated so much that they change to gas

Warm air rises and cools

Gas (atoms or molecules) can move fast. They spread out to fill the space they are in

Water (liquid) cools and freezes as it becomes ice (solid)

Gas

Liquid (atoms or molecules) can move about enough to flow past each other

Liquid

● Rock, air and water

Solids, liquids and gases are everywhere in the world. The land is made of solid materials, such as rock and earth. Oceans and rivers are water, which is liquid. The air consists of many different gases (*see pg35 [h25]*). They may seem fixed, but they can all alter their state with a change in temperature or pressure.

Solid (atoms or molecules) stay in the same positions

Solid

▶▶ **Read further › air / water / gases**
pg34 [m11]; pg35 [b22; b34]

▶▶ RIVERS see pg74 (d2) ▶▶

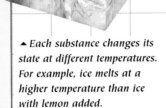

So solid

Nearly every substance is made of tiny particles called molecules – too small to see with the eye alone. Solids have strength and a definite shape. The molecules are firmly bonded together in a regular framework. All molecules move non-stop, but in a solid they simply vibrate on the spot. The hotter the solid becomes, the more they vibrate. If it gets hot enough the molecules vibrate so much that the framework breaks down and the solid melts, such as ice turning to water.

▲ *Each substance changes its state at different temperatures. For example, ice melts at a higher temperature than ice with lemon added.*

Read further › molecules
pg12 (j15); pg28 (n2)

Boiling and melting

The temperature at which a substance melts from a solid to a liquid is called its melting point. The highest temperature a liquid can reach before turning to a gas is called its boiling point – although some of the liquid may evaporate (turn to gas) before it reaches this point. Each substance, such as water or chocolate, has its own melting and boiling point. Water melts at 0°C and boils at 100°C. When a gas cools down enough, it condenses to a liquid, such as when steam turns to water. When a liquid cools down enough, it turns solid or freezes, such as when water turns to ice.

Read further › heat
pg28 (d2)

Going liquid

Unlike solids, liquids such as water have no shape of their own and therefore flow into the shape of any container they are poured into. The molecules in liquids are partly bound together in clusters. Liquids flow because these bonds are loose enough for the molecules to move about. The clusters roll over each other like dry sand, allowing the liquid to flow freely and quickly.

▲ *Water, like all liquids, takes the shape of whatever it is poured into.*

▸ *The particles in solid chocolate gain energy as they are heated – breaking away from each other as the solid melts.*

Read further › moving molecules
pg12 (j15)

◂ *The molecules in water flow freely over each other allowing liquids to pour quickly, such as the water in this waterfall.*

What a gas

Like liquids, gases have no shape or strength of their own. Unlike liquids, they have no fixed volume (mass or amount of space taken) either so they spread out to fill the space they are put in. In the same way, they can be squeezed into a much smaller space.

◂ *Airships float because the gas (helium) inside is lighter than the air outside.*

Read further › gases / air
pg15 (d29); pg33 (b22)

a
b
c
d
e
f
g
h
i
j
l
m
n
o
p
q
r
s
t
u
v
w

▸▸ FLOATING see pg189 (b31) ▸▸

22 23 24 25 26 27 28 29 30 31 32 33 34 35 36 37 38 39

The tiniest bits of all

MATTER IS every substance in the universe – everything that is not just empty space. Yet matter itself, even the most solid rock, is largely empty space. All matter is made of tiny particles, atoms, with empty space between them. Atoms, and the spaces between them, are far too small to see except with the most amazingly powerful microscopes. You could fit two billion atoms on this full stop. Even atoms are not solid, though. They are more like clouds of energy, dotted with tinier particles called sub-atomic particles.

● **IT'S A FACT**

• By smashing atoms together at great speeds, scientists have found over 200 sub-atomic particles, but few last for more than a fraction of a second.

• Among the tiniest particles of all are neutrinos. They are thousands of times lighter than electrons.

▶▶ **Read further › compounds / elements**
pg15 (b22; l29); pg17 (c22)

● **Atomic partners**
Atoms usually bond (join) together in groups to form combinations called molecules. A molecule is the smallest particle of a substance that can exist on its own. For example, a molecule of oxygen, the gas we breath in in order to live, occurs as a pair of oxygen atoms bonded together. Water, also essential for life, is a molecule of two atoms of hydrogen and one of oxygen joined together.

▸ *Particles with opposite electrical charges (positive and negative) attract each other. A proton has a positive electrical charge. An electron has an equal but opposite (negative) electric charge. Atoms contain protons and electrons, which attract each other, holding the whole atom together.*

▲ *In a hydrogen atom, one electron whizzes around one proton nucleus.*

▲ *In a helium atom, two electrons whizz around a nucleus of two protons and two neutrons.*

● **Atomic**
At the centre of an atom is a nucleus (dense cluster) of two kinds of particle: protons and neutrons. Even tinier particles, called electrons, zoom around the nucleus (see pg13 [q33]). The various sub-atomic particles are just concentrations of energy that are likely to occur in certain places. Protons have a positive electrical charge, electrons have a negative electrical charge and neutrons have no charge.

 Electron
 Proton
Neutron

▸ *In an oxygen atom, eight electrons whizz around a nucleus of eight protons and eight neutrons.*

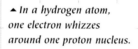

▾ *A carbon dioxide molecule (waste product when we breathe out) is a chemical compound that consists of one carbon atom and two oxygen atoms. Carbon dioxide has the chemical formula CO_2.*

▶▶ **Read further › electricity**
pg20 (l9); pg21 (e22)

 Check it out!
• http://www.chem4kids.com/files/atom_intro.html
• http://www.pbs.org/wgbh/aso/tryit/atom/

Crystal gazing

Most naturally occurring solids form crystals. Crystals are hard, shiny chunks that form in uniform geometric shapes. Each crystal is made from a regular framework or lattice of atoms or molecules. Grains of sugar (*see pg35 [r28]*) and salt are crystals. So, too, are most gems, such as diamonds and emeralds. Most rocks and metals are built up from crystals, too, although the individual crystals are often far too small to see with the naked eye.

▲ *Diamond, made of carbon atoms linked together in a rigid structure, is the hardest natural material.*

▶▶ **Read further › metals / carbon**
pg16 (i14); pg18 (i13)

BRIGHT SPARKS

• Most of an atom is empty space. The distance from its nucleus to the closest electron is about 5000 times the size of the nucleus. If the nucleus was 1 cm wide, the closest electron would be about 50 m away.

• Protons normally push each other away because they are all positively charged. Inside an atom a powerful force, called a strong nuclear force, holds them togehter and stops the nucleus from flying apart.

Different atoms

Each of nature's 100 or so basic chemicals or elements is made up from an atom with a certain number of protons in its nucleus. A uranium atom has 92 protons, the most in any element found in large amounts in nature. In each atom, the number of protons is usually matched by the same number of electrons, which are arranged in rings or 'shells' around the nucleus. The way an atom reacts with other atoms (its chemical character) depends on how many electrons there are in its outer shell.

▶▶ **Read further › electron shells**
pg14 (d2; h9)

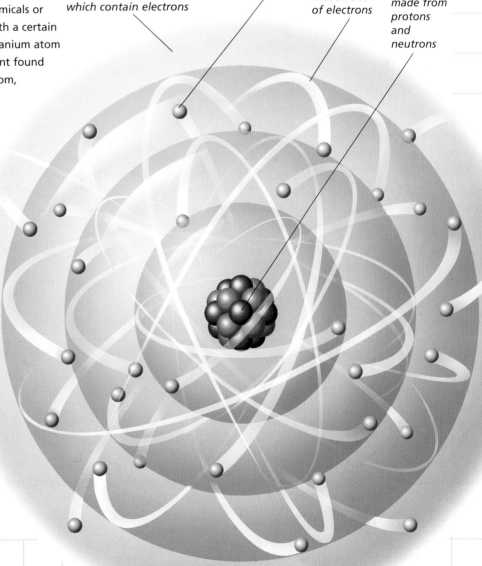

Spherical (round) shells which contain electrons

Electrons

Movement of electrons

Nucleus made from protons and neutrons

● Neutron

● Proton

● Electron

▸ *In the centre of the atom is the nucleus, which is made up of equal numbers of protons and neutrons. These are held together by a very strong force, which can be used to create nuclear energy.*

▶▶ URANIUM ATOMS see pg 231 (i32) ▶▶

a b c d e f g h i j k l m n o p q r s t u v w

Key substances

A LL THE substances in the universe can be split into smaller pieces until they become the simplest known substances, chemical elements. Examples are gold, carbon, and oxygen. Each element has unique chemical and physical features because it is made up from its own kind of atoms. All the atoms of an element are the same, with the same number of protons and other parts (*see pg13 [n33]*), and different from the atoms of all other elements.

IT'S A FACT

• The most recently identified elements were not found in nature – they were created by scientists.

• New elements created by scientists are often very unstable and last for only a fraction of a second before they break down. That is why they are not found in nature.

Arranging the elements

An element's atomic number is the number of protons in its nucleus. Elements can be listed from the lightest, hydrogen (atomic number 1), to heavier elements, such as lawrencium (atomic number 103). Russian chemist Dimitri Mendeleév arranged them in the Periodic Table. The elements in a vertical column, or Group, are similar to each other in chemical and physical features, but get heavier in 'jumps' downwards. The elements in a horizontal row, or Period, are heavier from left to right by one each time. Each also becomes less reactive or able to join with other elements, depending on the number of electrons and gaps for electrons in its outermost shell (*see pg13 [k31]*). The most reactive elements are on the left side, and the least reactive on the right side (*see pg15 [k26]*).

▼ *Elements also change their characteristics out of step with the Groups/Periods in two subsets: A and B.*

Period or row 1A is a 'special case' with just the two lightest elements: hydrogen and helium

Group or column 2A elements (green), called alkaline-earth metals, are fairly soft and reactive

Elements in Groups 3B onwards (purple) are mostly hard and shiny, known as transition metals

▶▶ Read further > atoms / metals
pg13 (i22); pg17 (c22)

Group 1 elements (blue) are soft and react readily, known as alkali metals

These two rows, (orange and green) lanthanides and actinides, each fit into one position in the main table

H Hydrogen 1															
Li Lithium 3	Be Beryllium 4												B Boron 5	C Carbon 6
Na Sodium 11	Mg Magnesium 12												Al Aluminium 13	Si Silicon 14
K Potassium 19	Ca Calcium 20	Sc Scandium 21	Ti Titanium 22	V Vanadium 23	Cr Chromium 24	Mn Manganese 25	Fe Iron 26	Co Cobalt 27	Ni Nickel 28	Cu Copper 29	Zn Zinc 30	Ga Gallium 31	Ge Germanium 32
Rb Rubidium 37	Sr Strontium 38	Y Yttrium 39	Zr Zirconium 40	Nb Niobium 41	Mo Molybdenum 42	Tc Technetium 43	Ru Ruthenium 44	Rh Rhodium 45	Pd Palladium 46	Ag Silver 47	Cd Cadmium 48	In Indium 49	Sn Tin 50
Cs Caesium 55	Ba Barium 56		Hf Hafnium 72	Ta Tantalum 73	W Tungsten 74	Re Rhenium 75	Os Osmium 76	Ir Iridium 77	Pt Platanium 78	Au Gold 79	Hg Mercury 80	Tl Thalium 81	Pb Lead 82
Fr Francium 87	Ra Radium 88		Rf Rutherfordium 104	Db Dubnium 105	Sg Seaborgium 106	Bh Bohrium 107	Hs Hassium 108	Mt Meitnerium 109	Uun Ununnilium 110	Uuu Unununium 111	Uub Ununbium 112		

La Lanthanum 57	Ce Cerium 58	Pr Praseodymium 59	Nd Neodymium 60	Pm Promethium 61	Sm Samarium 62	Eu Europium 63	Gd Gadoloinium 64	Tb Terbium 65	Dy Dysprosium 66	Ho Holmium 67
Ac Actinium 89	Th Thorium 90	Pa Protactinium 91	U Uranium 92	Np Neptunium 93	Pu Plutonium 94	Am Americium 95	Cm Curium 96	Bk Berkelium 97	Cf Californium 98	Es Einsteinium 99

▶▶ ELEMENTS OF THE EARTH see pg59 (c28) ▶▶

1 2 3 4 5 6 7 8 9 10 11 12 13 14 15 16 17 18 19

BRIGHT SPARKS

• In addition to the atomic number, each element also has an atomic mass. This is the relative 'weight' of the atom's whole nucleus – the protons and neutrons added together. Lead's atomic number is 82 but its atomic mass is 207.

• Scientists give each element a symbol. This is usually the first letter of its name, like O for oxygen and C for carbon. If two or more elements begin with the same letter, a second small letter may be added. So hydrogen is H and helium is He.

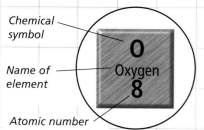

Chemical symbol

O
Oxygen
8

Name of element

Atomic number indicating number of protons in atom's nucleus

Gases most noble

The Group 8 elements down the furthest right of the Periodic Table is a very special Group. It is also called Group 8 or 0, because the atoms of these elements have no electrons missing from their outer shells. With a full outer shell of electrons, their atoms have no need to share electrons with other atoms. They are therefore extremely stable and unreactive. They are also called the noble gases, because they stay noble (apart from) other chemicals. Noble gases such as argon and krypton are used in light bulbs just because they are so unreactive, so will not burn out the filament – the tiny, thin coiled wire inside the bulb. Neon is used to make neon lights for the same reason, so it can burn brightly without reacting.

Read further › gases
pg11 (q31); pg35 (b22)

▲ An electric current sent to the lightbulb makes the filament glow to create light. Argon inside the bulb saves the filament from burning out.

He
Helium
2

Group 8 elements (light blue) are known as noble gases and hardly ever react with other elements

N	O	F	Ne
Nitrogen 7	Oxygen 8	Flourine 9	Neon 10
P	S	Cl	Ar
Phosphorus 15	Sulphur 16	Chlorine 17	Argon 18
As	Se	Br	Kr
Arsenic 33	Selentium 34	Bromine 35	Krypton 36
Sb	Te	I	Xe
Antimony 51	Tellurium 52	Iodine 53	Xenon 54
Bi	Po	At	Rn
Bismuth 83	Polonium 84	Astatine 85	Radon 86

Some elements in Groups 3A to 7A (green) are called poor metals

The other elements in Groups 3A to 7A (brown) are called non-metals

Er	Tm	Yb	Lu
Erbium 68	Thulium 69	Ytterbium 70	Lutetium 71
Fm	Md	No	Lr
Fermium 100	Mendelevium 101	Nobelium 102	Lawrencium 103

Compounds

Pure elements are quite rare in the world. Most substances are made of two or more elements joined together in a compound. A compound is not just a mixture of the elements. When the elements combine they are changed chemically to make an entirely new substance. Sodium, for instance, is an element that fizzes violently when dropped in water, while chlorine is a thick, green gas, but they combine to make a compound called sodium chloride, which is ordinary table salt.

▲ Eggs are a compound of sulphur, carbon, nitrogen, phosphorus, hydrogen and oxygen.

▼ Citric acid, found in lemon juice, is a compound of hydrogen, oxygen and carbon mixed with water.

Read further › ores /salt
pg16 (i14); pg17 (k31)

Check it out!
• http://www.funbrain.com/periodic/
• http://www.chem4kids.com/files/elem_pertable.html

▶ When food products such as eggs, butter and sugar are mixed together and cooked, the heat bonds the different compounds together into a new compound.

Chemicals and materials

THE UNIVERSE is made up from millions of different substances that we know about – and probably millions more that have not yet been discovered. Barely 100 of these are pure chemical elements consisting of identical atoms. Most are compounds made from different combinations of these atoms. Many natural substances, such as wood, soil and rocks, are a mixture of two or more compounds. Metals exist naturally as compounds and pure water is a compound of the elements hydrogen and oxygen. Tap water and sea water are mixtures, for there are always other substances mixed in with them. Some substances, when mixed with water, form an acid.

● IT'S A FACT

- The oldest known alloy is bronze, made at least 5000 years ago, by mixing copper and tin.

- Mercury is the only metal that is liquid at normal temperatures. It freezes when the temperature drops to -38.87°C.

● Mixed metals

Metals are very rarely pure. Most occur naturally in the ground in compounds called ores, and the metal must be extracted by heating and other processes. Even then, metals usually contain some impurities. Sometimes impurities are added deliberately to create an 'alloy', which gives the metal a particular quality, such as resistance to corrosion or extra strength. Carbon is added to iron to make an incredibly tough alloy called steel, and chromium is added to steel to make stainless steel, which does not rust or stain.

◀ *Alloys of aluminium and magnesium are very strong and corrosion-resistant. This makes them ideal for producing vehicle frames and buildings that have to withstand the weather and environmental pollution.*

▶▶ **Read further ‣ carbon**
pg18 (d2; i13)

▶ *Metals such as steel are used in building tough structures such as cars.*

Metallic

Three out of every four elements is a metal, such as gold or iron. Most metals are shiny, hard substances that ring when you hit them. They are mostly tough, yet can often be easily shaped – either by hammering or by melting into moulds. This makes them wonderful materials for making everything from spoons to cars and space-rockets. The atom of metals knit together into a strong framework or lattice. Atoms within the lattice share their electrons freely. The freely dancing electrons make metals great conductors of heat and electricity, since the moving electrons pass them on like batons in a relay race.

▶▶ **Read further › conduction**
pg29 (c22; r30)

▶ *Anybody can float easily in the Dead Sea in Israel. The very high salt content gives greater upward force than fresh water.*

▶▶ **Read further › hydrogen**
pg14 (d2); pg35 (b22; b34)

Liquids that burn

When some substances dissolve in water they create a special liquid called an acid. A drink that tastes sour, such as lemon juice, is a weak acid. Strong acids, such as sulphuric acid, are highly corrosive, attacking clothes and skin, and dissolving metals. All acids, both weak and strong, contain hydrogen. When mixed with water, the hydrogen atoms lose their one electron, and become ions – electrically charged atoms. It is these ions that make acids sour tasting and corrosive.

▶ *The chemical opposite of an acid is a base. Strong bases, such as caustic soda, are so corrosive that they are dangerous so protective gloves and clothing is worn when they are handled. Weak bases, such as baking powder, taste bitter or may have a soapy feel.*

BRIGHT SPARKS

• Tap water often has traces of dissolved salts such as calcium carbonate, which make water 'hard'. Hard water can create limescale around taps and make soap slow to lather.

• Acids play a crucial role in the human body. Amino acids make protein. The acid DNA, found in cells inside the body, provides instructions for life.

Salt of the earth

Table salt is just one of many substances called salt. Many of the minerals that make up the rocks of the Earth's surface are salts. Salts are a special kind of solid made of crystals that can take a variety of shapes. Salt is obtained from sea water in hot countries. Some sea water has a high salt content. The water is held in shallow pools and the salt gathered when all the water has evaporated in the heat. A salt forms when an acid and a base react together. For example, table salt forms when the base sodium hydroxide reacts with hydrochloric acid. Most salts dissolve in water, which makes them very useful materials for living things. Salts in the body maintain water balance and keep nerve signals healthy.

▶▶ **Read further › crystals / dissolving**
pg13 (b22); pg35 (m22)

Check it out!

• http://www.miamisci.org/ph/phpanel.html

▶▶ NERVOUS SYSTEM see pg172 (m8) ▶▶

a b c d e f g h i j k l m n o p q r s t u v w

Carbon chemicals

CARBON IS a very special element. The hardest known substance, diamond, is carbon. So is coal and the graphite in pencils. Carbon has an ability to form compounds easily because of the structure of its atom. There are more than 1 million known carbon compounds, from limestone to diesel oil. With four out of the full eight electrons in its outer shell, a carbon atom can form compounds either by gaining electrons or by losing them. This means it will join up with just about anything to make a wide variety of products, from oil-based paints to parachutes.

● **Carbon**

Pure carbon occurs in four allotropes (forms): diamond, graphite, soot and charcoal and a special manufactured form called fullerene. Graphite can be stretched out into long fibres called carbon fibres.

◄ *When bonded together, carbon fibres make an incredibly light but tough material, ideal for making items, such as oars used for rowing.*

Diesel *Graphite*

Carbon

Diamond *Charcoal*

◄ *Carbon and its compounds can be used for many things: diesel to run vehicles; graphite in pencils; diamonds in jewellery; and charcoal burnt to produce energy.*

▶▶ **Read further > alloys pg16 (i14)**

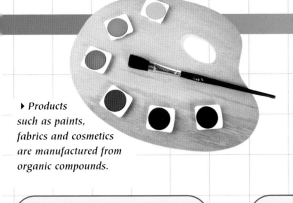

▸ *Products such as paints, fabrics and cosmetics are manufactured from organic compounds.*

▸ *The bow shape of this parachute is created by the air pushing up against it, which helps to slow down the speed at which the forces of gravity pull the parachutist down to the ground.*

● Organic chemicals

Carbon has an almost unique ability not only to form compounds with other elements, but also to join together with other carbon atoms as well to form complex chains and rings. Complex carbon chain and ring molecules are the basic chemicals that life itself depends on. For example, the proteins from which the body is built are all carbon compounds. There is such a huge variety of carbon compounds that there is an entire branch of chemistry called organic chemistry devoted to their study.

▶▶ Read further › compounds
pg15 (l29)

● Plastic world

Plastics are among the most amazing of all materials, used for everything from drinks bottles to car bodies. Light and easy to shape into any form, they can be made as soft as silk or as strong as steel. They are entirely manufactured: the secret is to get molecules of carbon compounds – mainly carbon and hydrogen – to link up in long chains called polymers. In some plastics, the chains are tangled together like spaghetti to make them strong yet flexible. These are ideal for making items such as parachutes, which need to be strong enough to support weight and yet flexible enough to glide in the air. Chains that are held rigidly together make stiff plastic, used for items such as window frames.

▶▶ Read further › molecules / steel
pg12 (i14); pg16 (i14)

● The carbon cycle

Most carbon atoms have existed since the beginning of the Earth and, through a process called the carbon cycle, circulate through animals, plants and the air. The leaves and stems of every plant are built largely from a natural material called cellulose. Like plastic, cellulose is a polymer – a long chain of carbon-based molecules. Plants put these chains together from sugar molecules called glucose, which they make with water and carbon dioxide from the air using energy from the Sun. Animals eat plants, using the carbon compounds taken in.

▶▶ Read further › the Sun's energy
pg23 (b22)

● BRIGHT SPARKS

• Plastic's durability makes it hard to dispose of, so scientists have developed kinds that can be degraded (broken down) by light or bacteria. However, the world still faces increasing problems with plastic waste.

• Fullerenes are molecules between 32 and 600 carbon atoms linked together in a ball shape. The first fullerene was a ball of 60 carbon atoms. It was named Buckminsterfullerene, or the 'Bucky Ball', after the architect R. Buckminster Fuller who made domes that the Bucky Ball looked like.

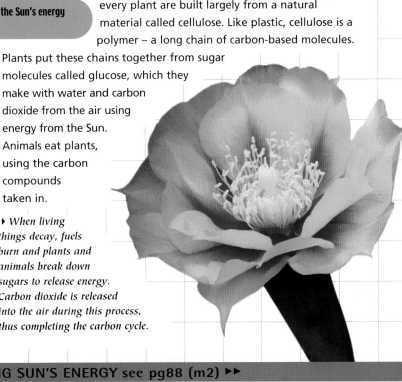

▸ *When living things decay, fuels burn and plants and animals break down sugars to release energy. Carbon dioxide is released into the air during this process, thus completing the carbon cycle.*

▶▶ PLANTS USING SUN'S ENERGY see pg88 (m2) ▶▶

a b c d e f g h i j k l m n o p q r s t u v w

Electricity and magnetism

● **IT'S A FACT**

• Lightning is the sudden release of a giant charge of static electricity that builds up inside storm clouds.

• The best conductors of electricity are materials that contain lots of free electrons, such as copper and silver.

ELECTRICITY IS one of the most useful of all forms of energy, providing us with everything from heat and light to the tiny pulses that make computers work. Electricity is closely linked with magnetism – the invisible force between magnetic materials. When electricity moves, magnetism is created. When magnets move, electricity is created. Together, electricity and magnetism form one of the forces that holds the universe together – electromagnetism.

▾ *Pylons carry electric cables from power stations through a distribution grid. Electricity can travel safely, high above ground.*

Cables carry flo[w] of electricity

High pylons hold electric cables safely above ground

● BRIGHT SPARKS

• The Earth is a giant magnet. If a magnet is left to move freely, the Earth's magnetic field ensures that it always points with one end aimed at the North Pole and the other at the South Pole.

• Materials that do not conduct electricity very well are called insulators. Plastic and rubber are good insulators.

▾ *Electricity is made from atoms that move along a wire.*

● Electric currents

When a magnet and a coil of wire move near each other, the magnet induces (creates) an electric current in the wire by pushing electrons along it. Power stations use this to make electricity. Flowing water or a jet of steam spins coils of wire around powerful magnets. Electric currents are induced in the coils. The electricity then flows along wires to our homes, schools and workplaces. The wires are either held above ground on top of tall pylons or are buried underground.

►► **Read further › currents**
pg21 (m22)

Atom

Electrons can be pushed from one atom to the next and when billions do this every second, electricity flows

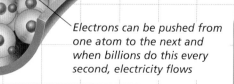

● **Check it out!**

• http://www.mos.org/sln/toe/toe.html
• http://www.factmonster.com/ce6/ sci/A0831162.html

Electron

▸ *Charged particles such as those generated by a Van de Graaf generator, can make hair stand on end. All the hairs have the same charge (all positive or all negative) and so repel (push apart) each other. They stand on end to get away from each other.*

Static electricity

Electricity is caused by the behaviour of electrons, which are electrically charged particles. If a material gains extra electrons it becomes negatively charged. If a material loses electrons it becomes positively charged. When two materials rub together, electrons may rub from one onto the other. They both become electrically charged, one positive and the other negative. This is called static electricity, because the electric charges on the charged material do not move – they are static (stationary).

Read further > protons / electrons
pg12 (o2); pg13 (i22)

Electric currents

Electrons move easily through material called conductors. Metals, such as copper and gold, are used as connectors in electric circuits because they are very good electrical conductors. They have many electrons, which can move easily through wires. When lots of electrons move in the same direction an electric current is produced. These flow around loops, or circuits. Batteries provide the energy to drive these electrons around a closed loop. They produce currents that flow instantly in one direction – direct currrent (DC).

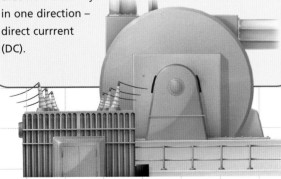

▲ *Power stations generate currents that reverse many times every second. Unlike the currents in batteries, power station currents are called alternating currents (AC).*

Magnetic attraction

Magnets are special pieces of metal – usually iron – that have the power to attract magnetic materials such as iron and steel. Around each magnet is a region or 'field' where its effect is felt. The field is strongest at the two ends or 'poles' of the magnet, and gets weaker further away. The magnet's power works in opposite directions at each pole, so one is called a north pole and the other a south pole. While opposite poles on two magnets attract each other, identical poles repel (push each other apart). So north poles attract south poles but repel north poles.

Read further > iron / water
pg17 (c22); pg35 (b34)

▸ *Objects containing iron, such as nails or screwdrivers are affected by magnetic fields.*

Magnetic field

Magnetic lines of force

Electric magnets

When an electric current flows through a wire, it produces a magnetic field around the wire. The magnetic field is stronger when the wire is coiled around a piece of iron. This type of 'electric magnet' is called an electromagnet. Unlike a bar magnet, an electromagnet can be switched on and off. The magnetic field disappears when the electric current is switched off.

▸ *An electromagnet can lift a car into the air by attracting the iron-based steel of the car's body.*

Read further > electrical charges
pg12 (o2)

Electromagnetic radiation

LIGHT BEAMS, radio signals, microwaves used for cooking, heat rays from fires and X-rays used in hospitals are all part of the same family of electromagnetic radiation. They are called electromagnetic waves because they are partly electric and partly magnetic. They travel in straight lines and at the same speed – the speed of light. In the vacuum of space, electromagnetic waves travel at 300 million metres per second. At that speed, they could travel around the world in about one-tenth of a second. The difference between electromagnetic waves is the length of each wave.

IT'S A FACT

• Glass lets visible light pass through, but not infra-red (heat) rays. Greenhouses are warm inside because light can enter and warm the contents, but the heat rays produced inside the greenhouse are trapped by glass.

• Nearly all the fuels we use today, including oil and wood, were produced by the action of electromagnetic radiation from the Sun on plants.

BRIGHT SPARKS

• Scientists can track the movements of all sorts of creatures, from whales and polar bears to tigers and elephants, by fitting them with radio collars. A radio collar transmits (sends out) a radio signal that can be received a long way away, even by satellite, allowing the animal's position to be marked on a map.

• Weather satellites can take pictures of the world's weather at night by using infra-red cameras.

Energy waves

Electrons emit a huge range or 'spectrum' of electromagnetic waves. The light we see, called visible light, is just a small portion in the middle of the spectrum. At one end of the spectrum are waves too long for our eyes to see, including radio waves and microwaves. At the other end are waves too short for us to see, including ultraviolet light and X-rays.

◀ *The varying lengths of electromagnetic waves are each useful for different purposes.*

▶▶ Read further › electromagnetism pg20 (f2)

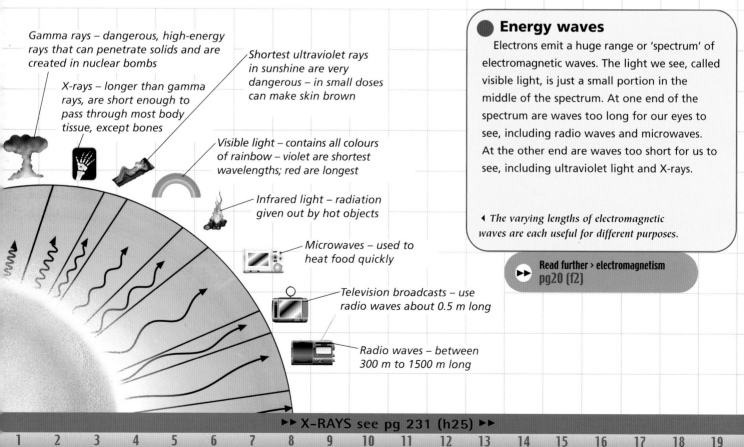

Gamma rays – dangerous, high-energy rays that can penetrate solids and are created in nuclear bombs

X-rays – longer than gamma rays, are short enough to pass through most body tissue, except bones

Shortest ultraviolet rays in sunshine are very dangerous – in small doses can make skin brown

Visible light – contains all colours of rainbow – violet are shortest wavelengths; red are longest

Infrared light – radiation given out by hot objects

Microwaves – used to heat food quickly

Television broadcasts – use radio waves about 0.5 m long

Radio waves – between 300 m to 1500 m long

▶▶ X–RAYS see pg 231 (h25) ▶▶

1 2 3 4 5 6 7 8 9 10 11 12 13 14 15 16 17 18 19

Sun

Most of the radiation hitting the Earth comes from the Sun, which pushes out huge amounts of energy. Some of the Sun's radiation is waves, such as light and X-rays. Fortunately, Earth's atmosphere only lets through the light and warmth that we need, and shields us from the most harmful waves, such as extreme ultraviolet and X-rays.

▶▶ **Read further › magnetic fields**
pg21 (b31)

▲ *The Earth's atmosphere is vital, allowing for humans and animals to breathe, and keeping out the most harmful radiation from the Sun.*

Radiation hazard

Some electromagnetic radiation can be dangerous. Even low energy radiation from the Sun can cause harmful diseases, such as skin cancer, after prolonged exposure from sunbathing. But it is short wave, high-energy rays, such as X-rays and gamma rays that are the main hazards. Rays like these damage living tissues by 'ionizing' the atoms in them – that is, knocking electrons off. This can cause damage to the biological mechanisms of the body. This is why people who work with X-rays in hospitals are protected behind screens.

◀ *Prolonged exposure to ultraviolet (UV) rays can cause serious damage. Suntan lotions containing a block against these UVA and UVB rays help to prevent sunburn and diseases such as skin cancer.*

▶▶ **Read further › atoms / electrons**
pg12 (i22)

Heat pictures

Hot objects emit (give out) electromagnetic waves. We are unable to see them, but thermal cameras can detect them and make pictures from them. In a thermal picture the hottest things are the brightest and the coldest things are the darkest. Thermal cameras can take pictures in total darkness because they do not rely on light. They can be useful in showing how animals behave in the wild at night, without having to shine bright lights on them.

▶ *Thermal cameras are used to to diagnose illnesses by highlighting different parts of the body according to temperature. The yellow areas show heat, and possibly disease, blue areas show cooler parts of the body.*

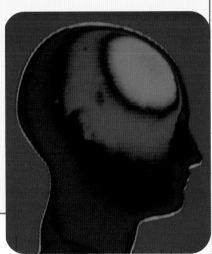

▶ *Satellites and spacecraft use radio waves to send pictures and other information to Earth.*

Space waves

Unlike sound waves, which need something to travel through, electromagnetic waves can travel through empty space. This property is very useful. It lets us see distant stars at night – the light from them has to travel through empty space to reach us. It also lets us speak to astronauts in space and communicate with satellites by radio.

▶▶ **Read further › waves**
pg27 (m34)

a
b
c
d
e
f
g
h
i
j
k
l
m
n
o
p
q
r
s
t
u
v
w

Force and motion

• The force of gravity on Earth is six times stronger than on the Moon because the Earth is much bigger and contains more matter.

• A jumping flea can accelerate at up to 140 g (140 times the acceleration of gravity towards Earth), or 50 times the acceleration of a space shuttle taking off.

FORCES ARE pushes and pulls. They change the speed, direction or shape of things. Some forces act only when things touch each other, like kicking a football. Other forces, including gravity and magnetism, act at a distance. Forces always occur in pairs – a force acting in one direction always creates an equal force acting in the opposite direction. The two forces are called the action and the reaction. When you push against a wall, the wall pushes back equally hard. If it did not, your hand would go through it. The main types of forces in nature are gravitational (gravity), electrical, magnetic and nuclear.

▲ When sky-divers open their parachute, its air resistance force acts in the opposite direction to gravity, slowing them down.

Rollercoaster ride

A rollercoaster has no motor. It gets its thrilling speed from gravity. It is towed up high and released. As it hurtles downhill, the constant pull of gravity makes it go faster and faster. When it reaches the bottom of a slope it is travelling so fast that it carries on uphill to the top of the next slope. The tendency of a moving body to keep moving is called momentum.

▶▶ Read further › gravity
pg25 (j28)

Falling down forcefully

One of Newton's most startling discoveries was that things do not just fall of their own accord: they fall because they are pulled down by a force called gravity. Gravity is the force of attraction that pulls everything towards the centre of the Earth. Every single bit of matter in the universe, no matter how tiny, exerts its own gravitational pull on other matter. The strength of the pull depends on the mass (matter) of the object. More massive objects exert a stronger pull of gravity. The further apart things are, the weaker their pull of gravity on each other.

▶▶ Read further › Newton / black holes
pg25 (q30); pg37 (m22)

Check it out!

• http://www.funderstanding.com/k12/coaster

Ice dancer being lifted does 'work' by moving and holding her body in correct position

Work, effort and load

Work, effort and load are important concepts in physics, especially in relation to machines, which usually move something. Load describes the size of the object moved, measured in kilograms or pounds. Effort describes the force used to move it, measured in newtons or pounds. Work describes just how long the effort is applied for – or more specifically the force used times the distance moved by the load. In the metric system, the unit of work is the joule – the work done when a force of 1 newton moves something 1 metre. One joule equals 1 newton-metre. In the US, the unit of work is a foot-pound. This is the work done when a force of 1 lb (pound) moves something 1 ft (foot).

Energy is being used as effort to lift ice dancer

►► Read further › gravity
pg24 (m12)

▶ *The lifting force of the ice dancer overcomes the force of gravity as he lifts the load.*

Ice dancer being lifted is affected by force of gravity

►► Read further › energy
pg26 (d2)

Acceleration and mass

In the 17th century, English scientist Isaac Newton realized that forces work the same way everywhere in the universe, and that their effect can be predicted. A force makes objects accelerate. Just how much they accelerate depends on how strong the force is and how great the object's mass is – how much matter it contains. The bigger the force, the greater the acceleration. More massive objects need a bigger force to give them the same acceleration.

◀ *A heavy cannon ball needs a very strong force to give it the required amount of acceleration.*

BRIGHT SPARKS

• Like all forces, gravity makes things accelerate. Anything falling towards the Earth accelerates, gaining speed at the rate of 9.8 m/sec, when near the Earth. This is called acceleration due to gravity, or g.

• Objects resist changes of motion. The more mass (matter) a substance contains, the more it resists changes. The resistance is called inertia.

The Laws of Motion

In the late 17th century, Isaac Newton summed up the link between force and motion with three laws: Law one: an object only accelerates (changes speed or direction) when a force acts on it. Law two: acceleration increases as the force increases, but decreases as the mass increases. Law three: every action (force) is matched by an equal and opposite reaction (opposing force). These three laws apply to everything from kicking a ball to flying a spacecraft.

►► Read further › Newton
pg24 (m10)

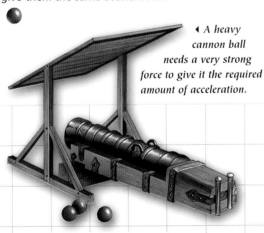

▼ *Without gravity or air resistance a kicked football would continue on its path.*

Air resistance slows down the ball

Force is applied when the ball is kicked

Gravity pulls down the ball

Air resistance and gravity combine to bring the ball back down to the ground

►► NEWTON see pg 220 (l2) ►►

a b c d e f g h i j k l m n o p q r s t u v w

Energy and work

ENERGY IS the ability to make something happen. It is not just the light that comes from the Sun, or the heat that comes from a fire. Scientists say that energy is the capacity to do work. It is involved in everything that happens everywhere in the universe, however tiny or gigantic, from grass growing to stars exploding. All substances have energy locked up inside their atoms and molecules. Energy comes in many different forms and it can change from one form to another.

BRIGHT SPARKS

• Energy can never be created or destroyed; it can only be changed from one form to another. So all the energy in the universe has always existed no matter what form it is in now.

• Scientists define work as a force multiplied by the distance a load moves when the force acts on it. In the metric system, the unit of energy is called the joule. One joule is the work done when a force of 1 newton moves an object a distance of 1 metre, or a metre-newton. The foot-pound is the imperial energy unit used in countries such as the USA.

IT'S A FACT

• All the energy in the universe may eventually turn to heat. This is called the 'Heat Death of the Universe' theory.

• Walking needs about five times as much energy as sitting still; running needs about seven times more energy.

Movement energy

A moving object has a type of energy called kinetic energy. The more massive the object is and the faster it moves, the more kinetic energy it has. When runners set off at the beginning of a race, they convert chemical energy in their muscles to kinetic energy. The faster they can change chemical energy into kinetic energy, the faster they run. At the end of the race they stop producing kinetic energy. Air resistance and friction between their shoes and the ground slow them down.

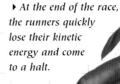

Read further › chemical energy
pg16 (d2)

▼ *For a split second as the sprinters come away from the starting blocks, they accelerate faster than an average sports car.*

▶ *At the end of the race, the runners quickly lose their kinetic energy and come to a halt.*

Check it out!

• http://www.eia.doe.gov/kids/
• http://www.energyquest.ca.gov

►► SUN see pg42 (k2) ►►

1   2   3   4   5   6   7   8   9   10   11   12   13   14   15   16   17   18   19

▾ Power stations are giant energy converters: they convert chemical or nuclear energy in a fuel into heat.

● Converting energy

The heat generated by power stations is transferred to water. This changes into steam, which is released out of large, concrete chimneys. The kinetic energy of the steam makes a turbine spin. The rotational (spinning) energy of the turbine drives a generator, which converts the rotational energy into electrical energy for us all to use.

▸▸ Read further › chemical energy
pg16 [d2]

▸ When sea waves crash onto a shore, the energy they carry can move sand and stones, or even make some cliffs collapse.

● Potential energy

Things can have energy because of where they are. This type of energy is called potential energy. It is stored energy. A crane has to work against gravity to lift an object high above the ground. The object stores the energy needed to lift it. If the crane drops it, its potential energy changes to motion as it hurtles towards the ground.

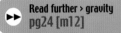

▸▸ Read further › gravity
pg24 [m12]

▾ When something is lifted, it stores the energy used to lift it as potential energy.

● Making waves

All waves, including water waves and electromagnetic waves, carry energy. When waves hit something they give up some or all of their energy. If a pebble is thrown into water, the vibration travels outwards as a wave. When light waves strike the back of our eyes their energy affects the retina (the light-sensitive part) and we see things. When infrared waves hit something their energy changes into heat. When radio waves hit the aerial of a radio set, their energy changes into electric currents that the radio set changes into sound.

▸▸ Read further › gravity / waves
pg24 [m12]; pg31 [o22]

a b c d e f g h i j k l m n o p q r s t u v w

Heat

HEAT IS another name for 'internal energy' or energy that is stored inside a substance. It is a form of energy that moves from one place to another when its temperatures are different. You can give extra internal energy to a substance by heating it or doing work on it. A bicycle pump warms up when you use it because the air inside it is squashed every time you push the handle. The work put into squashing the air gives it more energy, which makes its atoms and molecules move around faster. Every time energy changes from one form to another, some of it turns into heat, which then spreads to its surroundings. That is why computers, television sets and all sorts of machines often heat up when they are working.

▼ A refrigerator is a heat pump – it pumps heat energy from cold to hot, opposite to the way it flows in nature.

● Expansion and contraction

When things heat up they expand because their molecules vibrate more and move further apart. When they cool down, they contract because the molecules vibrate less and move closer together. With solids, the expansion and contraction is often too small to see. For example, a steel bar becomes only 0.0001 per cent longer for every degree rise in temperature. But the force of expansion is so powerful that extreme heat can make, for example, railway tracks buckle or doors jam.

Iron

Copper

Heating element

►► Read further › solids
pg11 (b22)

● Hot and cold

Heat always flows from hot to cold in nature, but it can be made to flow in the opposite direction by using a refrigerator. Heat from food inside the refrigerator warms a special liquid flowing through pipes in the fridge. The heat makes the liquid evaporate (change from a liquid to a gas). The gas is piped outside the refrigerator, where it is first cooled and then compressed (squashed) to change it back to a liquid. It goes back inside the refrigerator where it collects more heat from the food and evaporates.

►► Read further › changing states
pg10 (d2)

◄ Bimetallic strips used in thermostats to respond to a change in temperature consist of iron and copper bonded firmly together. The strip bends when heated because the copper expands more than the iron.

▶▶ **Read further › radiation**
pg23 (b22)

● Moving heat

Heat spreads in three ways: conduction, convection and radiation. Conduction is the spread of heat from atom to atom. The atoms in a hot substance move fast and hit each other. These collisions pass energy on to nearby atoms, and those atoms pass their energy on to the next atoms, and so on. Convection spreads heat in gases (and liquids). When they are heated their molecules speed up, collide more often and spread out further apart. The gas (or liquid) becomes lighter than the surrounding, cooler gas (or liquid) and floats upwards. Convection currents carry warm air up from a radiator. Radiation spreads heat by means of invisible infrared (heat) rays.

◀ *Hot liquid heats a metal spoon by conduction.*

▲ *Radiation is one of the ways that heat spreads from a flame.*

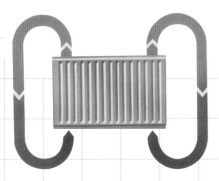

◀ *Air warmed by a radiator gets lighter and rises. Cold air moves in from below to replace it, and this is heated up too.*

▶▶ **Read further › temperature**
pg11 (b33)

BRIGHT SPARKS

• Heat is not the same as temperature. Temperature is a measure of how fast molecules are moving. Heat is the movement energy of all the molecules added together.

• Temperature is measured by a thermometer. When a thermometer is dipped in something hot, it quickly reaches the same temperature. A liquid (usually mercury or alcohol are used) inside the thermometer expands as it heats up and spreads out along a channel inside the thermometer. The hotter the liquid, the more it spreads.

● IT'S A FACT

• Temperature is measured in degrees on a temperature scale. The most common temperature scales are Celsius (Centigrade) and Fahrenheit. On the Celsius scale, the freezing point of water is 0°C and its boiling point is 100°C. On the Fahrenheit scale, these two points are at 32°F and 212°F.

• A hot-air balloon flies because the air trapped inside it is warmer than the surrounding air. The trapped air floats upwards, carrying the balloon with it.

▼ *Double glazed windows are used in most commerical buildings to slow down the loss of heat energy.*

● Stopping the flow

Sometimes it is necessary to stop heat moving and keep it in one place. When a building is heated during winter the heat tries to flow out to make the building the same temperature as the air outside. Glass conducts heat faster than walls and roofs so a lot of heat escapes through windows. Therefore, some buildings are fitted with double-glazed windows to help keep the heat in. Double-glazed windows have two sheets of glass instead of one, with a small gap between them. The air in the gap is a poor conductor of heat.

▶▶ HOT–AIR BALLOON see pg189 (b31) ▶▶

a b c d e f g h i j k l m n o p q r s t u v w

22 23 24 25 26 27 28 29 30 31 32 33 34 35 36 37 38 39

Light

LIGHT IS the only kind of electromagnetic radiation to which our eyes are sensitive. We are surrounded by light most of the time but surprisingly few things actually give out light. The Sun is our main source of light *(see pg22 [t5])*. Light also comes from stars, candles, electric lights and even small insects, such as glow-worms. But most things are only visible because they reflect light from other sources.

IT'S A FACT

- All the colours of the rainbow can be made by mixing just three 'primary' colours of light: red, blue and yellow.

- Light waves are so short that 2000 of them would easily fit on a pinhead.

►► Read further › waves
pg27 (m34)

Light and shade

When light rays hit an object, they bounce off, are absorbed or pass through. Substances, such as clear glass, which lets light through without breaking the direction of the rays, are transparent. Substances that jumble the light on the way through, such as frosted glass, are translucent. Those that stop the light altogether are opaque.

Clear glass is transparent

Casting a shadow

Light travels in straight lines. Different substances allow different amounts of light to pass through them. When light hits an opaque object, it does not bend around it. Opaque objects cast two types of shadow: if no light reaches an area, a dark shadow called an umbra is formed. If some light reaches an area, a grey shadow called a penumbra is formed.

▼ *The pillars at Stonehenge are opaque, so when sunlight falls on them, the area behind them receives no light and is left in shadow as light cannot pass through.*

Frosted glass is translucent

China objects are opaque

▶ *Not all light gives off heat. Glow-worms and fireflies attract a mate by making a part of their body glow using chemical reactions inside their bodies.*

►► INSECTS see pg118 (d2) ►►

1   2   3   4   5   6   7   8   9   10   11   12   13   14   15   16   17   18   19

a
b
c
d
e
f
g
h
i
j
k
l
m
n
o
p
q
r
s
t
u
v
w

Reflection and refraction

When light strikes a surface, some or all of it is reflected. From most surfaces it is scattered in all directions. On mirrors and other smooth shiny surfaces every ray may bounce off in exactly the same pattern as it arrives. The result is a perfect reflection of the light source or a mirror image. When light passes through something transparent, such as water, the rays are bent or refracted as the light slows down. This is why swimming pools sometimes look shallower than they really are, and straws appear bent when standing in a glass of water.

◄ Refraction makes a straw look bent. It is not really bent: the light rays bend when they pass through the water.

►► Read further › solar rays
pg23 (n22)

Colours of light

When we see different colours, we are seeing different wavelengths of light. Sunlight appears colourless but it is called white light, which is actually a mixture of all colours. When it hits raindrops in the sky it can be split up into all the different colours to form a rainbow. They are split because the raindrop refracts (bends) each wavelength of light differently, fanning out the colours in a particular order, from red (the longest waves) at one end, to violet (the shortest) at the other.

►► Read further › Sun's rays
pg23 (b22; n22)

◄ The whole band of colour is called the spectrum. The individual colours are created by splitting white light.

How light travels

Light is the fastest thing in the universe. In space, it travels at 299,792,458 m/sec and takes just eight minutes to reach Earth from the Sun. It travels slightly slower in air, and slower still in water, but still travels very fast. Light always travels in tiny waves. But these waves are tiny vibrations of energy, not a bit like ripples in a pond. Every beam of light is a stream of tiny packets of these vibrations called photons, each with its own wavelength. Photons are particles like electrons, but so small they have no mass at all.

BRIGHT SPARKS

• Fluorescent lights can be made from a tube filled with a gas called neon. When electricity passes through the tube, energy is given to particles in the gas, which transfer this into light – neon light.

• Scientists think the human eye is so sensitive that a single photon falling on the eye can trigger a signal to the brain.

▼ The waves in the electromagnetic spectrum all differ in length, but all produce the same form of energy – just at different levels.

Long radio waves   Microwaves   X-rays   Gamma rays

Shorter radio waves (TV)   Light waves   Short X-rays

►► Read further › light
pg27 (m34)

Check it out!
• http://unmuseum.mus.pa.us/speed.htm

►► SPLITTING WHITE LIGHT see pg220 (l2) ►►

Sound

E VERY SOUND you hear, from a child's cry to the roar of an engine, is created by a vibration. Sometimes you can see the vibration – such as a guitar string twanging quickly back and forth. Often the movement is invisible, but the vibration is always there, and as the sound source moves to and fro it pushes the air around it to and fro as well. The air is alternately squeezed and stretched to create waves that spread out in all directions. When these sound waves reach you, the sensitive mechanisms in your ears respond to the air vibrations, and so you hear sound.

● Waves of sound

Sound waves radiate in all directions from the sound source. Sound can travel through liquids, such as water, and many hard solids too. But a vacuum – completely empty space – is completely silent, because there is nothing to transmit the sound waves.

▶▶ Read further › solids / waves
pg10 (d2); pg27 (m34)

● Echoes and acoustics

If you shout in a large empty hall you may hear the sound ringing out momentarily afterwards. This is because the sound of your voice bounces back to you off the hard walls. Every smooth, hard surface, such as a wall, bounces sound back, but you only hear echoes in big, empty spaces where the walls are far enough away for there to be a gap between the original sound and its return. Although you may not always hear a distinct echo, sound reflections always affect the quality of the sound you hear. Concert halls must be designed carefully so that the internal surfaces of the hall create the right acoustics – sound vibrations – for the musicians and orchestras playing.

▶▶ Read further › reflection
pg31 (b22)

▸ Whales and dolphins make high-pitched squeaks, clicks and whistles that bounce off the seabed and surrounding fish or rocks. The echo that returns to the whale or dolphin helps it to find food.

● Check it out!

• http://www.physicsclassroom.com/Class/sound/soundtoc.html

▶▶ EARS see pg169 (b22) ▶▶

1   2   3   4   5   6   7   8   9   10   11   12   13   14   15   16   17   18   19

◄ The sound of a jet plane moving through the air is created by sound waves that move slower than light waves. Therefore we see the plane before we hear it, as the light waves reach us first.

▶▶ **Read further › vibrations** pg36 (r2)

● Loudness (volume) and frequency (pitch)

Sounds can be soft or loud, high-pitched or low-pitched. It all depends on the energy and frequency of the sound waves. Big, energetic waves move your eardrums a long way within the ear and sound loud; small, low energy waves sound quieter. Loudness (volume) is measured in 'bels', or tenths of bels, called decibels. The pitch of a sound depends on the frequency of the waves (the number of waves that reach your ears every second). The greater the frequency, the higher the pitch of the sound. Frequency is measured in hertz (Hz), waves per second.

Atomic explosion – 180 dB

Jet plane taking off – 110 to 140 dB

◄ Sounds that are too loud can damage the ears. Sounds of 130 dB or over are painful, and prolonged exposure to sounds of between 90 to 100 dB can cause deafness. People who work with loud machinery in factories or workshops must wear ear protectors to guard them against the noise.

Express train – 80 dB

Whispering – 20 to 50 dB

● Speed of sound

Sound takes time to travel through air. In a thunderstorm, you hear the thunder just after the flash of lightning that caused it, because light travels faster than sound. Sound travels slightly faster in warm air than cold. In icy air at 0°C, sound travels only 331 m/sec. In milder air at 21°C, sound travels at 343 m/sec. In hot air at 40°C, the speed of sound is 354 m/sec. In liquid, the speed of sound is four times faster, and in hard solids such as wood and steel it travels even faster still.

▶▶ **Read further › light** pg31 (o22)

▼ When an orchestra stops playing in a concert hall, the sound can be heard for about two seconds afterwards. This is called the reverberation time.

BRIGHT SPARKS

• A supersonic jet plane flies faster than sound. Its speed is given as a Mach number. The Mach number is the speed of the plane divided by the speed of sound in the air the plane is flying through. Mach 1 is the speed of sound, Mach 2 is twice the speed of sound.

• Most sounds contain lots of different frequencies jumbled together – some are louder than others. A guitar and a violin playing the same note sound different, because they produce a different mix of strong and weak frequencies.

▶▶ THUNDERSTORMS see pg80 (d2) ▶▶

Air and water

A IR AND water are the two most important substances in the world. Without air and water, life on Earth would be impossible. Air not only provides living creatures with the oxygen they need to breath, but also a place to move around easily, too. The Earth's blanket of air, called the atmosphere, provides vital protection against the harmful radiations from space and helps to maintain a stable environment in which life can flourish.

▾ *Plants need water to grow and survive. Rainforests receive a lot of rain annually, and so are abundant with plant life and animals. In an ecosystem, each organism (living thing) is dependent on the other organisms living there.*

IT'S A FACT

• At the temperature called the triple point (0°C), water can exist in all three states (solid, liquid and gas) at the same time.

• Only 2 per cent of the world's water is permanently frozen in ice caps and glaciers.

BRIGHT SPARKS

• Water is less dense as a solid (ice) than as a liquid, which is why ice floats. Water actually expands as it freezes, which is why pipes burst in cold winters and frost can split rock.

• Carbon dioxide (CO_2) makes up 0.03 per cent of the air, but the proportion is continually changing as it is breathed out by animals and taken in by plants as they grow. Extra gas pumped out by industries and vehicles burning oil boosts CO_2 levels dramatically.

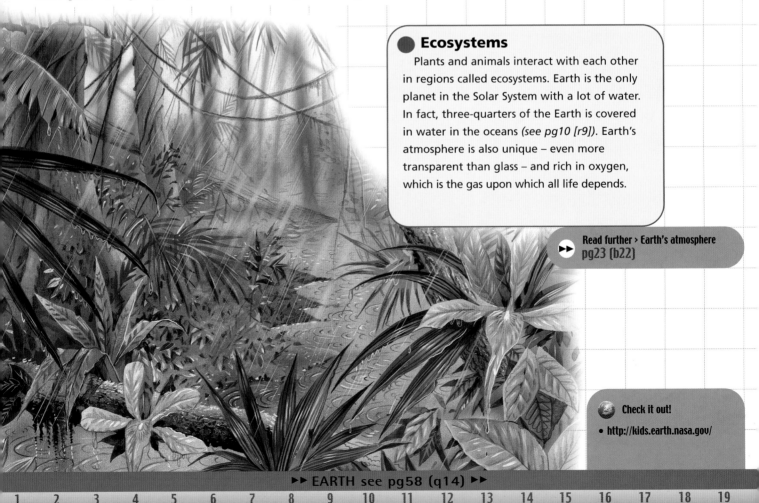

Ecosystems

Plants and animals interact with each other in regions called ecosystems. Earth is the only planet in the Solar System with a lot of water. In fact, three-quarters of the Earth is covered in water in the oceans *(see pg10 [r9])*. Earth's atmosphere is also unique – even more transparent than glass – and rich in oxygen, which is the gas upon which all life depends.

▶▶ Read further › Earth's atmosphere pg23 (b22)

Check it out!
• http://kids.earth.nasa.gov/

What are air and water?

Water is a compound in which two atoms of hydrogen gas (H_2) combine with one atom of oxygen gas (O) to form a colourless, odourless, tasteless liquid (H_2O). Sometimes, though, it may contain dissolved traces of other chemicals. Air, however, is always a mixture – not a compound – containing a variety of gases that are mixed but not chemically linked. More than three-quarters of the air is nitrogen (about 78 per cent), and most of the rest is oxygen (about 21 per cent). The remaining 1 per cent consists of carbon dioxide, water vapour and traces of other gases such as neon, helium, ozone and krypton.

Nitrogen
78.08%

Oxygen
20.94%

Carbon dioxide
0.03%

Argon and other gases
0.95%

▶▶ **Read further › gases**
pg11 (q31); pg15 (b29)

◂ *Air is a unique mixture that exists on Earth and nowhere else in the Solar System.*

▶▶ **Read further › attraction**
pg21 (b31)

What is a solution?

A remarkable property of water is its ability to make solutions with other substances. A solution is formed when a substance is added to a liquid and instead of just floating in the liquid, the substance breaks up entirely, so that its atoms and molecules completely intermingle with those of the liquid. This happens when coffee is added to water. The substance dissolved is called the solute; the liquid is called the solvent.

▸ *When sugar dissolves in coffee, the sugar is the solute and the coffee is the solvent.*

▶▶ **Read further › crystals / salt**
pg17 (k31)

Why is water liquid?

Water is the only substance that can be solid, liquid or gas at everyday temperatures. As a water molecule consists of two hydrogen atoms and one oxygen atom, the hydrogen atoms at one end of the molecule have a positive electrical charge; the oxygen atom at the other end has a negative charge. Molecules like this are called polar molecules. The positive and negative charges attract each other and hold water molecules together. Without them the molecules would come apart from each other more easily and water would change to steam at a lower temperature.

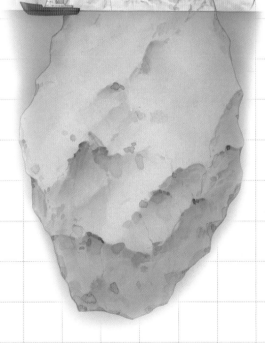

▴ *Ice is slightly less dense than water, which is why icebergs float in water, often partially above the surface depending on the volume (size) of the iceberg.*

◂◂ POSITIVE AND NEGATIVE CHARGES see pg21 (b31) ◂◂

a b c d e f g h i j k l m n o p q r s t u v w

Time

BEFORE THE invention of clocks, people measured time by the natural rhythm of the Earth – by watching the movements of the Sun, Moon and stars in the sky. Now we can see time passing as hands move or figures change on a clock. Modern atomic clocks can measure time with astonishing accuracy. Yet scientists and philosophers still find it hard to agree on what time is. Scientists say time is a dimension (like length and width) and that we move through time just as we can move sideways or backwards and forwards, or up and down. Time is said to be the fourth dimension: the other three are length, width and depth. But time only runs one way: a candle cannot be unburned, or your life lived backwards.

IT'S A FACT

- All living things have their own 'biological' clocks to control their lives and stimulate certain behaviour at specific times.
- The shortest time that can be measured is a pico-second – one trillionth of a second.

Detector counts the atoms

Magnet separates atoms

Microwave source

▶ Atomic time is measured by how many electromagnetic waves are absorbed by atoms.

Oven where atoms 'boil off'

Frequency divider

Computer adjusts microwaves

17:00:1070

Digital display to show time

Atomic time

Just as a guitar string vibrates at a certain pitch or frequency, so do atoms and molecules. Atomic vibrations are so regular that they can be used to make the world's most accurate clocks – atomic clocks. These special clocks, all housed in special laboratories, mostly use the caesium-133 atom (see pg14 [r2]). Since 1967, 1 second has been defined as 9,192,631,770 vibrations of a caesium-133 atom. Atomic clocks are also used to set the world's standard time, called Co-ordinated Universal Time (UTC), set by the United States National Institute of Standards and Technology (NIST) agency.

Read further > vibrations pg32 [d2]

Check it out!

- http://www.mrdowling.com/601-time.html

▶▶ TIME AND SPACE see pg232 (d2) ▶▶

1 2 3 4 5 6 7 8 9 10 11 12 13 14 15 16 17 18 19

Natural clock

Sundials work well in the sunshine, but they do not work at night or in cloudy weather. Other ways of measuring time that did not depend on sunshine were invented in the ancient world. A candle burns down steadily, so time can be measured by the changing length of a burning candle. Water or sand running steadily from one container to another can also mark the passing of time. Then in the 17th century, the great Italian scientist Galileo Galilei noticed that a pendulum of a certain length (a weight on the end of a wire or rod) always swings at the same rate. This discovery made it possible to build accurate clocks by linking the swinging pendulum to pointers (hands) that showed the time on a dial (clock face).

▲ As the Sun moves from east at the beginning of the day to west at the end of the day, the position of the shadow cast on the sundial moves, showing what time of day it is.

Read further › shadows
pg30 (k2)

BRIGHT SPARKS

• The length of a day on Earth has not always been the same. In the past, days were shorter and in the future, days will be longer because the Earth is spinning more slowly as time goes on. The average day is 1.6 milliseconds (thousandths of a second) longer every 100 years.

• Einstein showed that the faster things travel, the slower time runs. When *Apollo 11* went to the Moon, an accurate clock on board lost a few seconds, not because of any fault but because time ran slowly in the speeding space ship.

▼ Time travel has been the subject of many books and films. The machine in H.G. Wells' classic novel The Time Machine is portrayed on screen as being able to withstand the immense pressure of wormholes.

Time travel

The brilliant scientist Albert Einstein suggested that time does not exist on its own but is part of something called space-time, which includes the whole universe. When we move about, we are not moving through space while time passes separately. We move through space-time. If time is linked to space, some scientists wonder if we might be able to move through the time part of space-time into the past or future. Objects in space called black holes have such a strong force of gravity that they might be able to bend space-time enough to create pathways called worm-holes that link to other places or times. If wormholes do exist then they are understood to be even smaller than an atom. Some scientists believe it might be possible to enlarge them using an extremely powerful electric field, holding them open long enough to make a tunnel through space-time and thus travel through time.

Read further › gravity
pg24 (m12)

a b c d e f g h i j k l m n o p q r s t u v w

What is space?

SPACE IS everything in the universe that lies outside the Earth's atmosphere. Looking at the night sky, space seems filled with stars. Yet the distances between the stars are unimaginably vast, and there is almost nothing between them but clouds of stardust. Much of space is a vast, empty void, which is how it gets its name. No one knows how large space is, and much of it is too far away to see, but using modern technology astronomers are discovering more and more.

ABOVE AND BEYOND

• Since light takes a long time to reach Earth from distant objects in space, we see them not as they are now but as they were when the light left them. We see the bright star Deneb as it was 1800 years ago, at the time of ancient Rome.

• When we look at the Andromeda Galaxy, we see it as scientists believe it was over 2 million years ago, when the first human-type creatures evolved in Africa.

The scale of the universe

What we can see of space is only a tiny fraction of what is there. With powerful telescopes, intensely bright clusters of stars or galaxies (see pg52 [j17]) called quasars can be seen 13 billion light-years away. So if there are quasars equally far away in all directions, the universe must be at least 26 billion light-years across. The light of some stars, when seen through a telescope, may be thousands or even millions of light-years away.

Read further › light pg39 (d22); pg54 (j6)

IT'S A FACT

• It takes light about eight minutes to reach us from the Sun.

• It takes light four years to reach us from Proxima Centauri, the nearest star to the Sun.

▲ Even nearby stars are over 40 trillion km away; many stars are billions of time further.

Check it out!

• http://www.kidsastronomy.com/academy

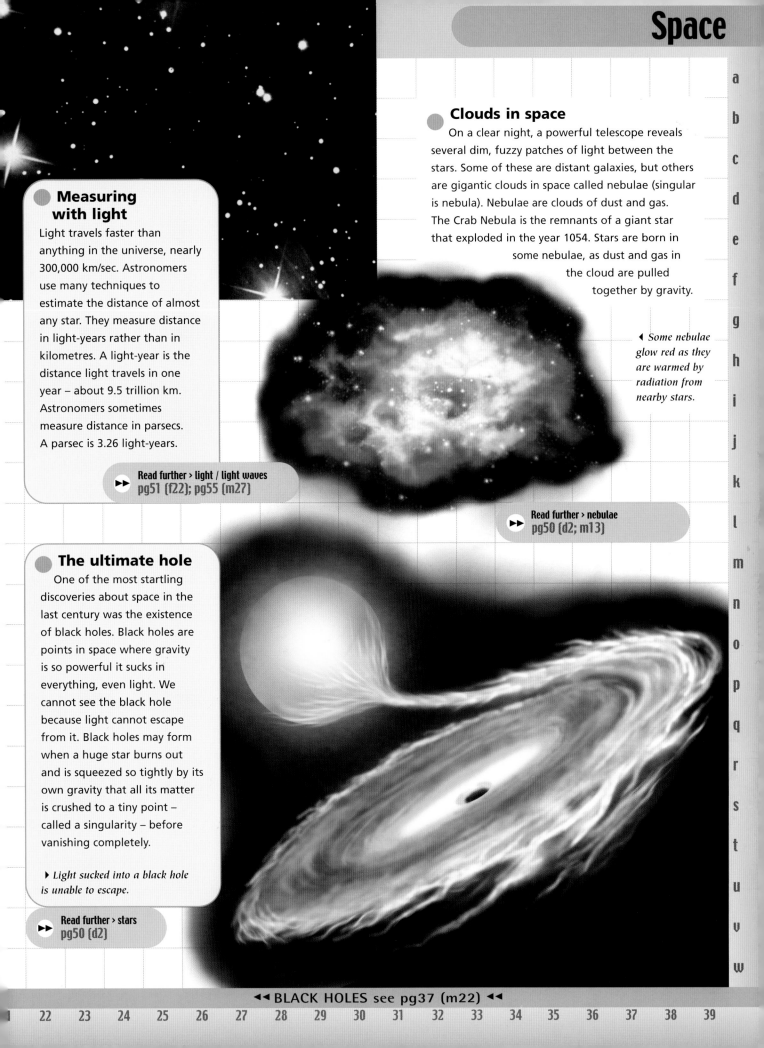

Measuring with light

Light travels faster than anything in the universe, nearly 300,000 km/sec. Astronomers use many techniques to estimate the distance of almost any star. They measure distance in light-years rather than in kilometres. A light-year is the distance light travels in one year – about 9.5 trillion km. Astronomers sometimes measure distance in parsecs. A parsec is 3.26 light-years.

Read further › light / light waves
pg51 (f22); pg55 (m27)

Clouds in space

On a clear night, a powerful telescope reveals several dim, fuzzy patches of light between the stars. Some of these are distant galaxies, but others are gigantic clouds in space called nebulae (singular is nebula). Nebulae are clouds of dust and gas. The Crab Nebula is the remnants of a giant star that exploded in the year 1054. Stars are born in some nebulae, as dust and gas in the cloud are pulled together by gravity.

◀ *Some nebulae glow red as they are warmed by radiation from nearby stars.*

Read further › nebulae
pg50 (d2; m13)

The ultimate hole

One of the most startling discoveries about space in the last century was the existence of black holes. Black holes are points in space where gravity is so powerful it sucks in everything, even light. We cannot see the black hole because light cannot escape from it. Black holes may form when a huge star burns out and is squeezed so tightly by its own gravity that all its matter is crushed to a tiny point – called a singularity – before vanishing completely.

▶ *Light sucked into a black hole is unable to escape.*

Read further › stars
pg50 (d2)

◀◀ BLACK HOLES see pg37 (m22) ◀◀

White ball of rock

THE MOON is the biggest, brightest object in the night sky, shining almost like a night-time sun. Yet it has no light of its own. It is just a big cold ball of rock, and it shines only because it reflects the light of the Sun. It is Earth's companion in space, about 384,000 km away, and circles slowly around it once a month. As the Moon moves around, it also rotates (turns) slowly on its axis, so that the same face always points towards us. The far side of the Moon can never be seen from the Earth's surface.

▼ *After each full Moon, the visible portion of the Moon shrinks again.*

Full Moon

Waning Moon

Half Moon

Old Moon

New Moon

● Walking on the Moon

When astronauts landed on the Moon in 1969, they found a landscape of cliffs and plains, completely covered in many places by a fine white dust. This lunar dust was created long ago when the Moon's surface broke up under the impact of meteoroids. Because there is no air, wind, rain or snow on the Moon, the dust never moves – and so the footprints left behind by the astronauts will be there for millions of years.

▶ *The Earth seen from the Moon.*

● Phases (changes) of the Moon

All that can be seen of the Moon from Earth is its brightly lit, sunny side *(see pg43 [c27])*. As it circles the Earth, the sunny side of the Moon is seen from different angles and so it seems to change shape. At New Moon, the Moon is positioned directly between the Earth and the Sun and all that can be seen from Earth is just a crescent-shaped glimpse of the sunny side. Over the next two weeks, more and more of the Moon is revealed until at Full Moon, when it is furthest away from the Sun, all of it becomes visible. During the next two weeks, less and less of the Moon is visible until it returns to a crescent shape, called the Old Moon.

Read further ▸ eclipse pg43 (b22)

▶▶ EARTH'S ORBIT see pg60 (m2) ▶▶

1   2   3   4   5   6   7   8   9   10   11   12   13   14   15   16   17   18   19   2

Seas and craters

All over the Moon are large, dark patches that people once thought were seas, so they are called *Mare*, from the Latin for sea. Today, scientists know they are vast, dry plains formed by ancient lava from volcanoes that erupted early in the Moon's life. Most of the craters that pit the Moon's surface also date from early in the Moon's life. They were formed by the impact of huge rocks that crashed down from space.

Read further > Moon's surface
pg40 (o2)

▶ *The Moon's surface is pitted with ancient craters that were made by the impact of meteoroids.*

THE MOST MOONS

Planet	Moons
Uranus	21
Saturn	18
Jupiter	16
Neptune	8
Mars	2

Earth and Pluto each have 1 moon

To scale
1 square = 3000 km

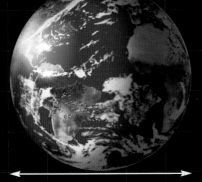

The Earth and the Moon shown to scale

Moon = 3500 km across

Earth = 12,756 km across

Moon landing

The Moon is the only other world humans have ever visited. The first men to walk on the Moon were the Americans, Neil Armstrong and Buzz Aldrin, on the *Apollo 11* space mission. They touched down on its surface on 20 July 1969. The first woman in space was the Russian, Valentina Tereshkova.

▼ *Alan Bean from* Apollo 12.

Read further > space travel
pg40 (o2); pg56 (h32)

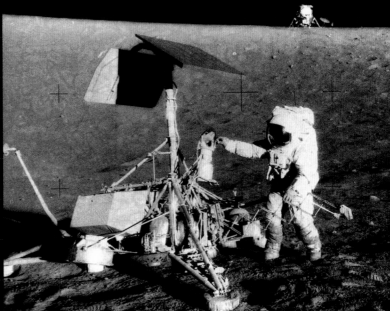

Check it out!
- http://kids.msfc.nasa.gov/Earth/Moon/
- http://www.dustbunny.com/afk/howdo/howdo.htm

▶▶ VOLCANOES see pg70 (d2) ▶▶

j
k
l
m
n
o
p
q
r
s
t
u
v
w

Great ball of fire

THE SUN is a star, just like all the stars in the night sky. In fact, it is a medium-sized star in the middle of its 10 billion-year life. Yet it is much nearer than any other star – just 150 million km away. Like all stars, it is incredibly hot (see pg51 [q23]). Huge pressure inside the Sun creates temperatures of over 15 million°C. This tremendous heat turns the Sun's surface into a raging inferno that burns so brightly that it floodlights the Earth, giving us daylight.

IT'S A FACT

• Each 6 square cm of the Sun's surface burns with the brightness of 1.5 million candles!

• The Sun is 100 times wider than the Earth.

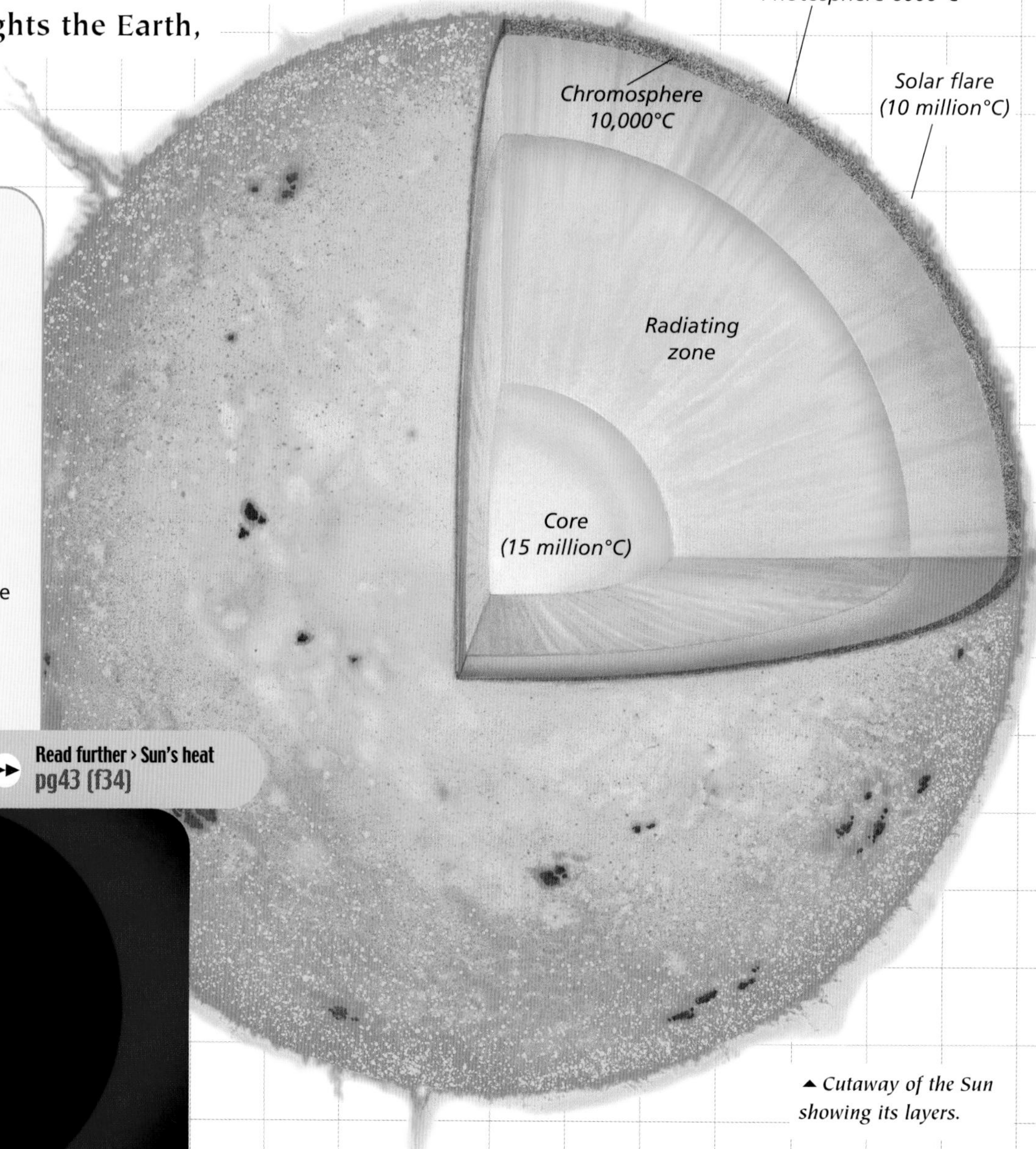

Inside the Sun

The Sun is made mostly of two gases: about three-quarters hydrogen and one-quarter helium. The energy that is generated inside its core takes 10 million years to rise to the surface, passing through several layers, including the glowing surface or photosphere, a forest of flames called the chromosphere and a crowning halo of fire called the corona.

▼ The Sun's corona flares out behind the Moon during a solar eclipse.

Read further › Sun's heat
pg43 [f34]

Photosphere 6000°C

Chromosphere 10,000°C

Solar flare (10 million°C)

Radiating zone

Core (15 million°C)

▲ Cutaway of the Sun showing its layers.

►► USE OF SUN'S ENERGY see pg205 (j22) ►►

1 2 3 4 5 6 7 8 9 10 11 12 13 14 15 16 17 18 19

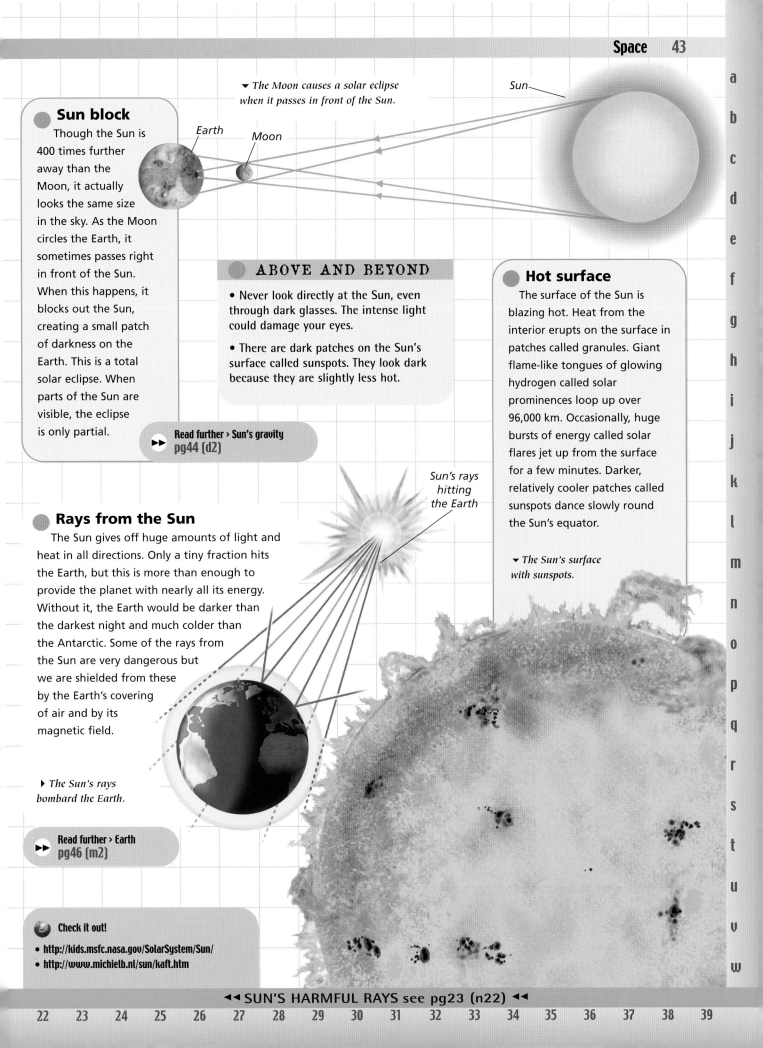

▼ *The Moon causes a solar eclipse when it passes in front of the Sun.*

Sun

Earth

Moon

Sun block

Though the Sun is 400 times further away than the Moon, it actually looks the same size in the sky. As the Moon circles the Earth, it sometimes passes right in front of the Sun. When this happens, it blocks out the Sun, creating a small patch of darkness on the Earth. This is a total solar eclipse. When parts of the Sun are visible, the eclipse is only partial.

▶▶ **Read further › Sun's gravity pg44 (d2)**

ABOVE AND BEYOND

• Never look directly at the Sun, even through dark glasses. The intense light could damage your eyes.

• There are dark patches on the Sun's surface called sunspots. They look dark because they are slightly less hot.

Hot surface

The surface of the Sun is blazing hot. Heat from the interior erupts on the surface in patches called granules. Giant flame-like tongues of glowing hydrogen called solar prominences loop up over 96,000 km. Occasionally, huge bursts of energy called solar flares jet up from the surface for a few minutes. Darker, relatively cooler patches called sunspots dance slowly round the Sun's equator.

▼ *The Sun's surface with sunspots.*

Sun's rays hitting the Earth

Rays from the Sun

The Sun gives off huge amounts of light and heat in all directions. Only a tiny fraction hits the Earth, but this is more than enough to provide the planet with nearly all its energy. Without it, the Earth would be darker than the darkest night and much colder than the Antarctic. Some of the rays from the Sun are very dangerous but we are shielded from these by the Earth's covering of air and by its magnetic field.

▶ *The Sun's rays bombard the Earth.*

▶▶ **Read further › Earth pg46 (m2)**

Check it out!

• http://kids.msfc.nasa.gov/SolarSystem/Sun/
• http://www.michielb.nl/sun/kaft.htm

◀◀ SUN'S HARMFUL RAYS see pg23 (n22) ◀◀

Circling planets

EARTH IS not alone in space. Including Earth, eight planets circle, or orbit, the Sun. They move around the Sun in the same direction, in elliptical (oval) orbits, and are held in place by the pull of the Sun's gravity. Many of the other planets have their own moons and in between the planets are tiny chunks of rock called asteroids. Together, the Sun, Earth, the other planets, their moons and the asteroids are called the Solar System.

Solar System

All the eight planets of the Solar System orbit the Sun in the same plane. Pluto, a dwarf planet, cuts across at an angle. The further a planet is from the Sun, the longer it takes to complete its orbit. Mercury, the nearest planet to the Sun, takes just 88 days, Venus 225 days and Earth 365 days, but distant Neptune takes 165 years. Dwarf planet Pluto, which is even more remote, takes almost 250 years.

▸ *How the planets circle the Sun.*

Read further › solar planets
pg47 (b22); pg48 (b22)

▾ *Galaxies such as this form from swirling gas and dust.*

How it began

By measuring the age of meteorites (rocks that fall to Earth from space), scientists have worked out that the Solar System is about 4.6 billion years old. When it began to form, it was a whirling mass of stardust and gases, but as it spun around quickly, gravity began to pull it tighter together. Eventually, the dense centre formed the Sun and dust further out gathered into lumps, which became the planets.

Read further › Big Bang theory
pg54 (j6)

▶▶ DISCOVERY OF ORBITING PLANETS see pg277 (b31) ▶▶

1　2　3　4　5　6　7　8　9　10　11　12　13　14　15　16　17　18　19

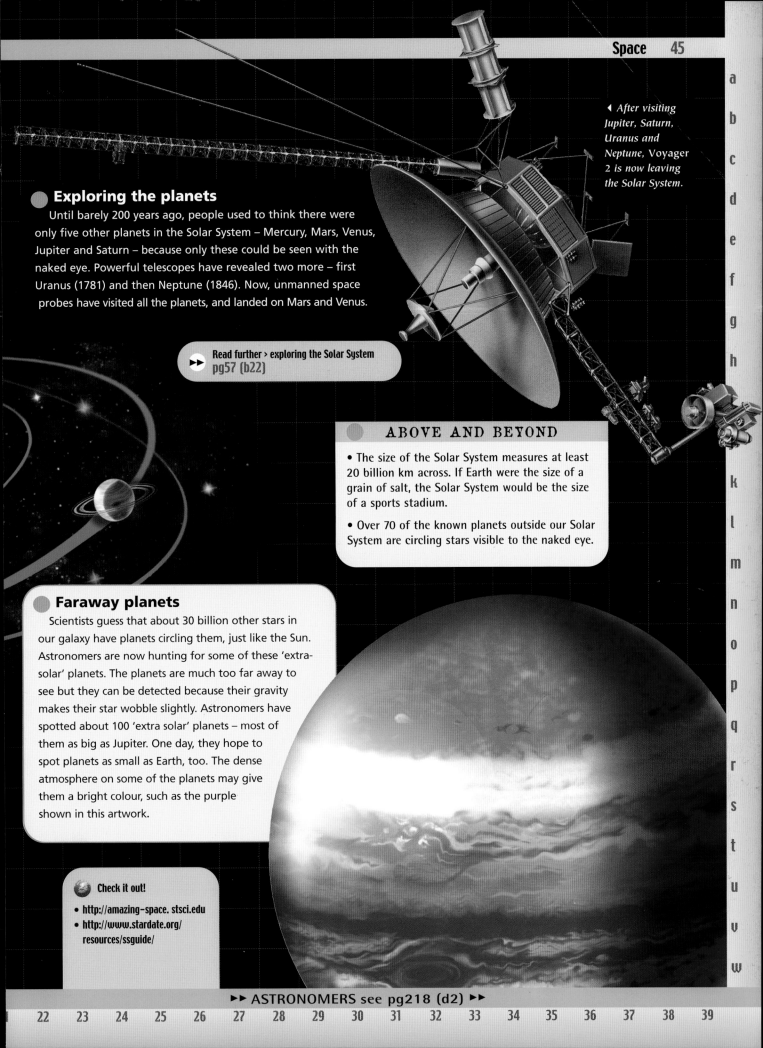

◀ *After visiting Jupiter, Saturn, Uranus and Neptune, Voyager 2 is now leaving the Solar System.*

● Exploring the planets

Until barely 200 years ago, people used to think there were only five other planets in the Solar System – Mercury, Mars, Venus, Jupiter and Saturn – because only these could be seen with the naked eye. Powerful telescopes have revealed two more – first Uranus (1781) and then Neptune (1846). Now, unmanned space probes have visited all the planets, and landed on Mars and Venus.

▶▶ Read further > exploring the Solar System
pg57 (b22)

ABOVE AND BEYOND

• The size of the Solar System measures at least 20 billion km across. If Earth were the size of a grain of salt, the Solar System would be the size of a sports stadium.

• Over 70 of the known planets outside our Solar System are circling stars visible to the naked eye.

● Faraway planets

Scientists guess that about 30 billion other stars in our galaxy have planets circling them, just like the Sun. Astronomers are now hunting for some of these 'extra-solar' planets. The planets are much too far away to see but they can be detected because their gravity makes their star wobble slightly. Astronomers have spotted about 100 'extra solar' planets – most of them as big as Jupiter. One day, they hope to spot planets as small as Earth, too. The dense atmosphere on some of the planets may give them a bright colour, such as the purple shown in this artwork.

Check it out!

• http://amazing–space. stsci.edu
• http://www.stardate.org/
resources/ssguide/

▶▶ ASTRONOMERS see pg218 (d2) ▶▶

a b c d e f g h k l m n o p q r s t u v w

22 23 24 25 26 27 28 29 30 31 32 33 34 35 36 37 38 39

Rocky planets

THE FOUR planets nearest to the Sun are, in order, Mercury, Venus, Earth and Mars. All four are small compared to most of the planets further out, such as Jupiter. These four planets are sometimes called the 'terrestrial' or Earth-like planets. Unlike the giant outer planets, they are made mostly of rock, and have hard surfaces on which a spacecraft could land. In fact, space probes have landed on both Venus and Mars, the nearest planets to Earth. All the rocky planets have an atmosphere (a layer) of gas – although Mercury's is barely existent – but otherwise they are very different. Earth, above all, has abundant water and life, but each planet has its own unique qualities.

IT'S A FACT

• Pluto was classified as a dwarf planet in 2006.

• Mars is about one-tenth of the weight of the Earth.

Earth

Earth is the third planet out from the Sun, about 150 million km away from it. Earth is sometimes called the 'Goldilocks' planet after the fairy story in which the little girl chooses porridge that is neither too hot nor too cold. Earth is not so close to the Sun that it is scorching hot, nor so far away that it is icy cold. It is also the only planet that has huge amounts of liquid water on its surface. This combination makes it uniquely able to support life.

▶ Oceans and continents are clearly visible through Earth's atmosphere.

▶▶ Read further › Earth and Sun pg43 (l22)

Pluto, dwarf planet

Besides the four inner planets, there is another rocky dwarf planet, Pluto. Pluto is tiny – smaller than our Moon – and very far away, on the outer edge of the Solar System.

◀ Like Earth, Pluto has one moon.

▶ Mars' surface is cracked by a valley called the Vallis Marineris (Mariner Valley).

▶▶ EARTH see pg58 (d2) ▶▶

Mercury

Mercury is the nearest planet of all to the Sun, often less than 58 million km away. With almost no atmosphere to protect it, temperatures on the side facing the Sun soar to 425°C while the dark side plummets to −180°C. Mercury is so close to the Sun it travels right round in just 88 days (compared to 365 days for Earth). Yet it spins very slowly, taking over 58 Earth days. So there are fewer than two days in Mercury's year.

Read further > Mercury
pg46 (d15)

The Sun scorches Mercury's surface.

▲ *Mercury has no moon.*

Venus

Venus is almost exactly the same size as the Earth. It is about 12,000 km across and weighs about one-fifth less than the Earth. Otherwise it is unlike the Earth; its atmosphere is thick with poisonous carbon dioxide and clouds of sulphuric acid. This thick atmosphere traps the Sun's heat and makes the surface a scorching desert where temperatures rise to 470°C, making it the hottest planet in the Solar System.

◀ *Venus with its thick, dense atmosphere.*

ABOVE AND BEYOND

• Like Earth, Mars has volcanoes. Olympus Mons on Mars is the biggest volcano in the Solar System, and, at 26,590 m, is three times higher than Mount Everest.

• Venus reflects sunlight so well from its atmosphere that it shines brighter in the night sky than any other star. As it appears just after sunset and just before sunrise, it is known as the evening or morning star.

Mars

Mars is the only planet with similar daytime temperatures and an atmosphere similar to Earth's, except it is mainly carbon dioxide. It is also the only other planet with water on its surface. But Mars' water is all frozen solid in ice caps, and most of the planet is a desert, with no oceans or any sign of life – just the iron-rich red rocks and dust which earn it the nickname 'red planet', as the Mars Pathfinder mission confirmed when it landed the robot exploration vehicle *Sojourner* there in 1997. Although Mars appears to be a lifeless planet, scientists hope space probes will find traces of microscopic life under the surface.

Read further > Mars
pg47 (m33); pg56 (b14)

◀ *The Sojourner robot on Mars.*

Check it out!
• http://www.spacewander.com /USA/english.html
• http://kids.msfc.nasa.gov/Solar System/Planets/

i
j
k
l
m
n
o
p
q
r
s
t
u
v
w

▶▶ ORBITING PLANETS see pg219 (b22) ▶▶

Giant balls of gas

OUT BEYOND Mars are four planets bigger than any of the others in the Solar System: Jupiter, Saturn, Uranus and Neptune. Jupiter and Saturn are especially huge. Jupiter is twice as heavy as all the other planets combined and 1300 times bigger in size than Earth! Saturn is almost as big. Despite this, all these giant planets are made mostly of gas, not rock. Only a tiny core in the centre is rock. But the gas around is squeezed by the huge pressure of gravity until it is often liquid or even solid.

IT'S A FACT

• Neptune has winds of over 2000 km/h.

• Saturn and Jupiter have cores made of rock that are twice as hot as the Sun's surface.

Jupiter

Jupiter is by far the biggest planet in the Solar System – over 140,000 km across – and it takes almost 12 years to go round the Sun. Yet despite its immense bulk, it spins round faster than any other planet. In fact, it turns right round in less than 10 hours, which means the surface is whizzing along at almost 45,000 km/h. Its surface is covered in colourful clouds of ammonia gas whipped into storm belts by violent winds, lightning flashes and thunderclaps. One storm, called the Great Red Spot, is 40,000 km across and has lasted at least 300 years. Jupiter has a faint ring system and 16 moons.

▸ Jupiter, with the Great Red Spot clearly visible, bottom left.

Check it out!

• http://www.spacewander.com/METRIC/metric.html
• http://kids.msfc.nasa.gov/Solar System/Planets/

▶▶ GALILEAN MOONS see pg221 (b22) ▶▶

1 2 3 4 5 6 7 8 9 10 11 12 13 14 15 16 17 18 19

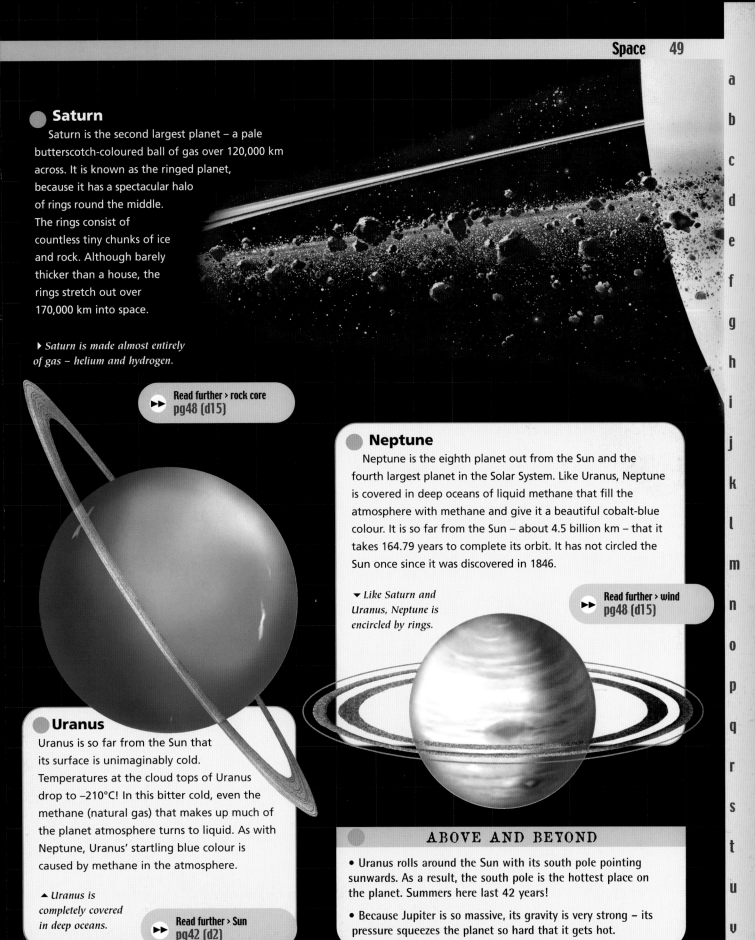

Saturn

Saturn is the second largest planet – a pale butterscotch-coloured ball of gas over 120,000 km across. It is known as the ringed planet, because it has a spectacular halo of rings round the middle. The rings consist of countless tiny chunks of ice and rock. Although barely thicker than a house, the rings stretch out over 170,000 km into space.

▸ *Saturn is made almost entirely of gas – helium and hydrogen.*

Read further › rock core
pg48 (d15)

Neptune

Neptune is the eighth planet out from the Sun and the fourth largest planet in the Solar System. Like Uranus, Neptune is covered in deep oceans of liquid methane that fill the atmosphere with methane and give it a beautiful cobalt-blue colour. It is so far from the Sun – about 4.5 billion km – that it takes 164.79 years to complete its orbit. It has not circled the Sun once since it was discovered in 1846.

▾ *Like Saturn and Uranus, Neptune is encircled by rings.*

Read further › wind
pg48 (d15)

Uranus

Uranus is so far from the Sun that its surface is unimaginably cold. Temperatures at the cloud tops of Uranus drop to –210°C! In this bitter cold, even the methane (natural gas) that makes up much of the planet atmosphere turns to liquid. As with Neptune, Uranus' startling blue colour is caused by methane in the atmosphere.

▴ *Uranus is completely covered in deep oceans.*

Read further › Sun
pg42 (d2)

ABOVE AND BEYOND

• Uranus rolls around the Sun with its south pole pointing sunwards. As a result, the south pole is the hottest place on the planet. Summers here last 42 years!

• Because Jupiter is so massive, its gravity is very strong – its pressure squeezes the planet so hard that it gets hot.

►► GRAVITY see pg220 (n13) ►►

a b c d e f g h i j k l m n o p q r s t u v w

Glowing lights

LIKE THE Sun, stars are huge, fiery balls of incredibly hot gases. They shine because they are making energy. Deep inside every shining star, huge pressure squeezes atoms of hydrogen gas together to create nuclear reactions millions of times more powerful than a nuclear bomb. These reactions boost the star's core temperature, so much that the surface glows white-hot. A star continues to glow, sending out light, heat, radio waves and other radiation until all the hydrogen is used up.

1. *Clumps of gas in this nebula start to shrink*

2. *The gas spirals around as it is pulled inwards*

3. *The new star starts making energy*

4. *The gas and dust is blown away and we can see the star shining*

▲ *The four main stages of a star's formation.*

Star quality

Stars create their energy in the same way as nuclear bombs, but they rarely explode. Medium-sized stars burn steadily for billions of years because there is a balance – between the heat energy, which pushes gases outward as they expand, and gravity, which pulls them back in. Only when the star's nuclear fuel burns out, is this balance broken, and the star shrinks or, on some occasions, explodes.

◀ *A medium-sized star.*

A star's life

Stars are starting up and dying down all over the universe. They begin in giant clouds of gas and dust, where material gathers into clumps called nebulae, each containing evaporating gas globules or EGGs, which are the beginnings of stars. Inside the dark nebulae, EGGs are squeezed by their own gravity until they become hot. When an EGG is sufficiently hot enough (at least 10 million°C), nuclear reactions begin and it becomes a star. Medium-sized stars such as our Sun burn for about 10 billion years.

◀ *Stars are born in clouds of dust and gas.*

Read further › nebulae
pg39 (b32)

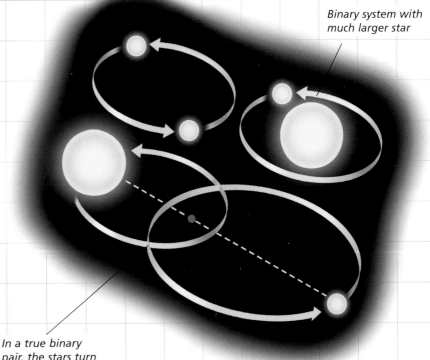

Binary system with much larger star

In a true binary pair, the stars turn together around their common centre of gravity

▲ *Binary system with similar sized stars. The stars may be close together or millions of kilometres apart.*

The brightest stars

The colour of a star's light depends on its temperature: blue stars are the hottest, red stars are the coolest. Astronomers rank the brightness of each star with a number or 'magnitude'. The brightest stars have the lowest magnitude, which may be minus numbers. Some stars look brighter than others only because they are closer to Earth, so astronomers talk of 'relative' magnitude – the brightness of a star compared to others and 'absolute' magnitudes – how bright a star really is.

Red giants

Main sequence stars

Blue stars

The Sun

Yellow stars

White dwarfs

Red stars

Increasing brightness

Increasing temperature

▲ *Graph showing how a star's brightness varies with its temperature. Medium-sized stars fall in a straight line – the main sequence – showing a simple relationship.*

Twin stars

Many stars are in companion pairs called binaries. True binaries are pairs of stars that whirl round together like a pair of dancers, held together by their mutual gravity. Sometimes, one star passes in front of the other, which then seems to grow dim. Some stars look like binaries even though they are nowhere near each other, because they are in the same line of sight from the Earth. These are called optical binaries.

HOTTEST STARS

Star	Temperature
• Blue	up to 40,000°C
• Blue-white	11,000°C
• White	7500°C
• Yellow	6000°C
• Orange	5000°C

Read further › light–years
pg39 (d22)

Check it out!

• http://www.howstuffworks.com/star.htm

►► ASTRONOMERS see pg218 (d33) ►►

Star cities

STARS ARE not scattered evenly throughout space. Instead, they cluster together in groups called galaxies, with vast stretches of completely empty space between. The three galaxies that can be seen with the naked eye look like faint blurs in the night sky, but powerful telescopes show that they contain billions of stars. Although most galaxies are too far away to be seen, astronomers estimate that there are about 100 billion in the universe. An average galaxy, such as the Milky Way, contains 100 billion stars and is about 100,000 light-years across.

IT'S A FACT

• The Milky Way Galaxy is 100,000 light-years across.

• The Sun takes 200 million years to travel once right round the middle of the Milky Way Galaxy.

▲ Our Milky Way Galaxy seen edge-on from deep space.

The Milky Way
On clear nights, far from town when there is no Moon, a faint, hazy, white band can be seen stretching right across the sky. This band is called the Milky Way. Through binoculars, it is clear that the Milky Way consists of countless stars – indeed, it is a vast cluster of over 100 billion stars. The Milky Way appears to us as a narrow band, because we are looking at it edge-on. If we could look down on it, we would see that it looks like a giant Catherine wheel, with a dense bulge at its centre containing mostly older stars.

Star cities
The biggest galaxies are egg-shaped or elliptical and may contain as many as a trillion stars. These elliptical galaxies probably formed a very long time ago, sometime over 10 billion years, not long after the dawn of the universe (see pg44 [u16]). Elliptical galaxies are rarely alone, and tend to group together into clusters.

▲ Elliptical galaxy clusters can contain thousands of galaxies of all kinds.

►► Read further › egg-shaped galaxies
pg53 (k27)

►► ASTRONOMERS see pg218 (p11) ►►

1   2   3   4   5   6   7   8   9   10   11   12   13   14   15   16   17   18   19

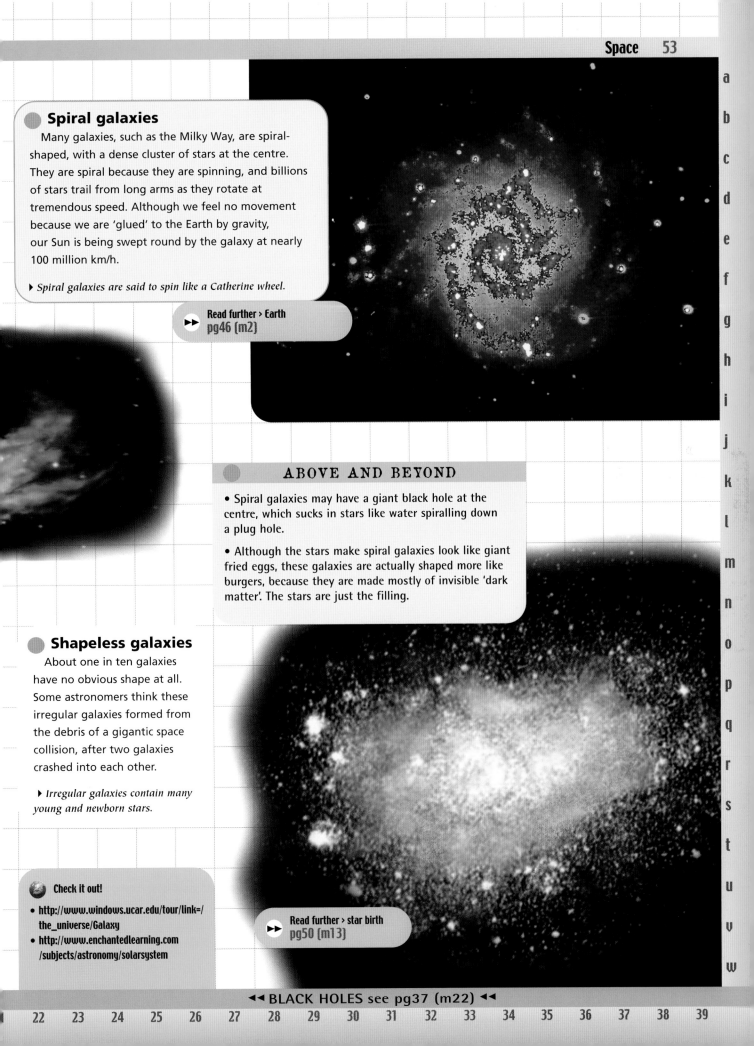

Spiral galaxies

Many galaxies, such as the Milky Way, are spiral-shaped, with a dense cluster of stars at the centre. They are spiral because they are spinning, and billions of stars trail from long arms as they rotate at tremendous speed. Although we feel no movement because we are 'glued' to the Earth by gravity, our Sun is being swept round by the galaxy at nearly 100 million km/h.

▶ *Spiral galaxies are said to spin like a Catherine wheel.*

▶▶ Read further › Earth
pg46 (m2)

ABOVE AND BEYOND

• Spiral galaxies may have a giant black hole at the centre, which sucks in stars like water spiralling down a plug hole.

• Although the stars make spiral galaxies look like giant fried eggs, these galaxies are actually shaped more like burgers, because they are made mostly of invisible 'dark matter'. The stars are just the filling.

Shapeless galaxies

About one in ten galaxies have no obvious shape at all. Some astronomers think these irregular galaxies formed from the debris of a gigantic space collision, after two galaxies crashed into each other.

▶ *Irregular galaxies contain many young and newborn stars.*

Check it out!

• http://www.windows.ucar.edu/tour/link=/
   the_universe/Galaxy
• http://www.enchantedlearning.com
   /subjects/astronomy/solarsystem

▶▶ Read further › star birth
pg50 (m13)

◄◄ BLACK HOLES see pg37 (m22) ◄◄

a b c d e f g h i j k l m n o p q r s t u v w

22 23 24 25 26 27 28 29 30 31 32 33 34 35 36 37 38 39

Big Bang

THE UNIVERSE may not always have existed. Scientists think it began about 13 to 15 billion years ago with the 'Big Bang'. It is believed that one moment there was just a tiny hot ball containing everything in the universe and then a moment later, the universe burst into existence with the biggest explosion of all time, separating into basic forces such as electricity and gravity – so big that everything is still hurtling out from it – even today.

The Big Bang theory

1. At first, the entire universe was a hot ball tinier than an atom and much hotter than any star. This swelled much, much faster than the speed of light, growing to the size of a galaxy in just a tiny fraction of a second.

2. As the universe expanded, it began to cool and tiny particles of energy and matter – each of them much smaller than atoms – began to form a thick, soup-like material.

3. After about three minutes, gravity started to pull the particles together. Atoms joined together to make gases such as hydrogen and helium, and the thick 'soup' began to clear and thin out. By the end of the third minute, the matter that surrounds us today had been created.

Check it out!
• http://curious.astro.cornell.edu/cosmology.php
• http://www.amnh.org/rose/hayden-bigbang.html
• http://cbc4kids.cbc.ca/general/the-lab/big-bang/

4. *Over time, as the young universe grew larger, the gases clumped into clouds. After several hundred million years, the clouds began to form stars and galaxies.*

● How do we know?

Astronomers developed the Big Bang theory, and worked out how long ago it occurred, by looking at how galaxies move in space. They also discovered that every galaxy in the universe is zooming away from Earth. If this is so, the universe must be expanding. If the universe is getting bigger, there must have been a time when it was much smaller – this is known as the 'Expanding Universe' theory.

▶▶ **Read further › expanding universe** pg55 (r33)

● Red shift

Astronomers are able to tell that a galaxy is moving by its colour. If a galaxy is moving away from Earth, its light waves stretch *(see pg39 [b26])*. Stretched light waves look red. The faster a galaxy is moving, the more the light waves are stretched and the redder it appears. This is called red shift.

▼ *Red shift shows distant objects are hurtling away from us.*

▶▶ **Read further › galaxies** pg52 (d2)

● ABOVE AND BEYOND

• Some astronomers think the universe will expand forever. Others think the expansion will stop then collapse back to a 'big crunch'!

• In March 2002, astronomers spotted the oldest galaxy yet seen – 13 billion light-years away and 15 billion years old. Since this is older than the estimated age of the universe, scientists may have to work out the universe's age again.

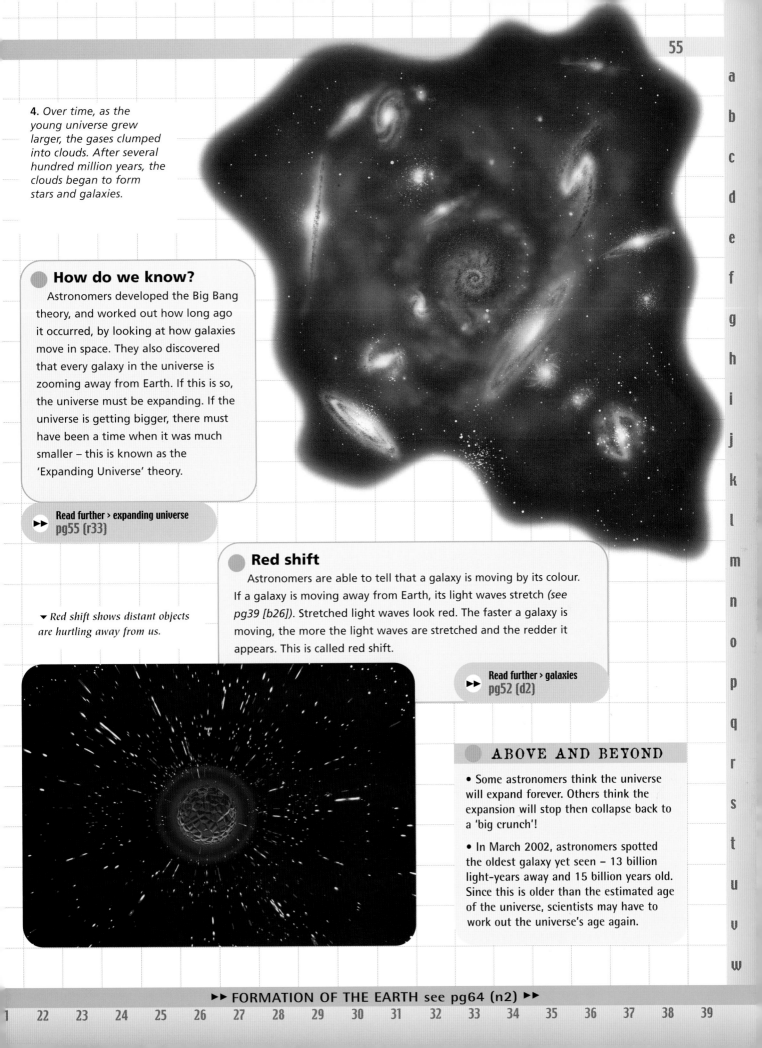

▶▶ FORMATION OF THE EARTH see pg64 (n2) ▶▶

a b c d e f g h i j k l m n o p q r s t u v w

1 22 23 24 25 26 27 28 29 30 31 32 33 34 35 36 37 38 39

Space travel

THE AGE of space travel dawned half a century ago, when the tiny Russian satellite *Sputnik 1* was blasted into space in 1957. Since then hundreds of spacecraft have been launched and the boundaries of space exploration are being pushed further and further, as spacecraft venture into the Solar System. In 1969, the astronauts of *Apollo 11* set foot on the Moon. In 1976, the *Viking 1* robot space probe landed on Mars. In 1973, *Pioneer 10* reached Jupiter. *Voyagers 1* and *2*, launched in 1977, have flown beyond Pluto, though not yet out of the Solar System altogether.

● ABOVE AND BEYOND

• Mars has already been visited by more space probes *(see pg47 [t29])* – than any other planet, though not all were successful. It may become the first planet (beyond Earth) to be visited by humans.

• The first living creature in space was a dog called Laika, which went up in the Russian *Sputnik 2* in 1957. Sadly, she could not be brought back to Earth.

Orbiter *goes into orbit around the Earth*

Orbiter *crew place satellite in space*

Orbiter *positions itself to re-enter Earth's atmosphere*

Main fuel tank falls away 130 km up

Solid fuel rocket burners fall away 45 km up

Shuttle being transported to launch pad

● Space shuttle

In the early days, manned spacecraft could only be used once, with just a tiny capsule holding astronauts as they fell back to Earth. Now astronauts are carried up into orbit above the Earth by shuttle craft, which can take off and land again and again, like an aeroplane. The Russian version was a one-off called the Buran or 'snowstorm'; the American version is known as the shuttle orbiter.

Orbiter *lands like a glider*

▶▶ **Read further > space shuttle** pg57 [h32]

● IT'S A FACT

• It will take NASA's *New Horizons* space probe ten years to reach Pluto – due to be launched in 2006.

• The first man in space was Russian cosmonaut, Yuri Gagarin, in April 1961.

🌐 Check it out!

• http://galileo.jpl.nasa.gov/
• http://www.nasa.gov/kids/kids_spacetravel.html
• http://kidsastronomy.about.com/cs/missions/index.htm

▶▶ FLIGHT see pg188 (p2) ▶▶

| 1 | 2 | 3 | 4 | 5 | 6 | 7 | 8 | 9 | 10 | 11 | 12 | 13 | 14 | 15 | 16 | 17 | 18 | 19 | 2 |

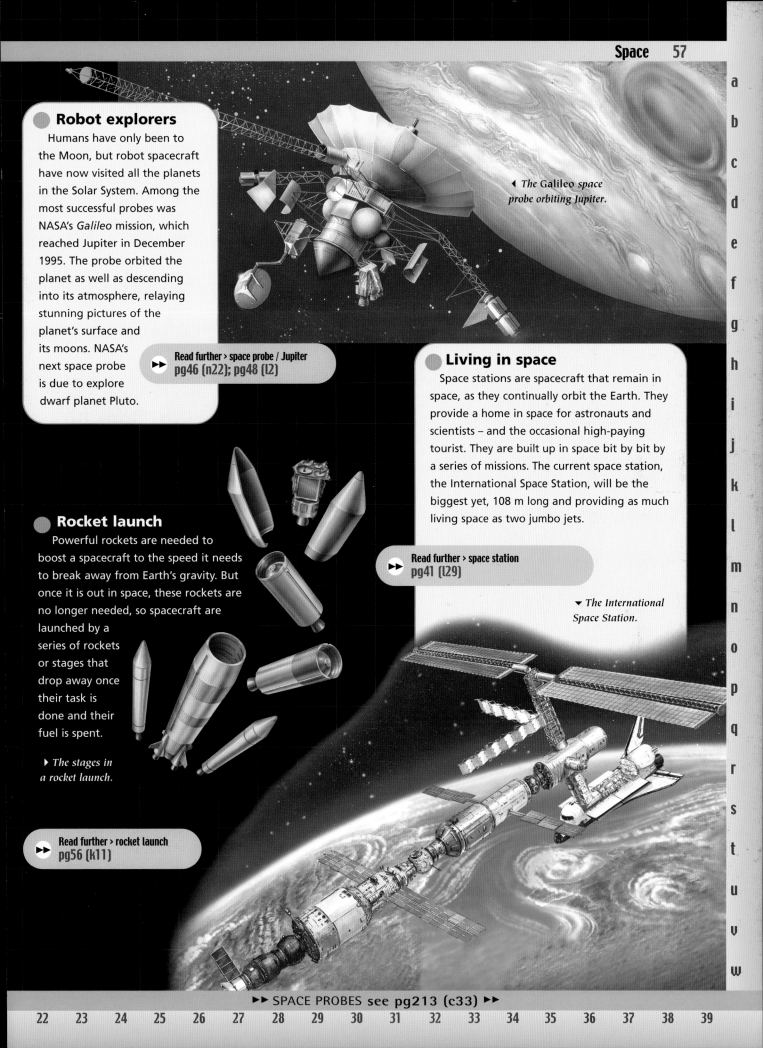

Robot explorers

Humans have only been to the Moon, but robot spacecraft have now visited all the planets in the Solar System. Among the most successful probes was NASA's *Galileo* mission, which reached Jupiter in December 1995. The probe orbited the planet as well as descending into its atmosphere, relaying stunning pictures of the planet's surface and its moons. NASA's next space probe is due to explore dwarf planet Pluto.

◀ *The* Galileo *space probe orbiting Jupiter.*

▶▶ Read further > space probe / Jupiter
pg46 (n22); pg48 (l2)

Living in space

Space stations are spacecraft that remain in space, as they continually orbit the Earth. They provide a home in space for astronauts and scientists – and the occasional high-paying tourist. They are built up in space bit by bit by a series of missions. The current space station, the International Space Station, will be the biggest yet, 108 m long and providing as much living space as two jumbo jets.

▶▶ Read further > space station
pg41 (l29)

▼ *The International Space Station.*

Rocket launch

Powerful rockets are needed to boost a spacecraft to the speed it needs to break away from Earth's gravity. But once it is out in space, these rockets are no longer needed, so spacecraft are launched by a series of rockets or stages that drop away once their task is done and their fuel is spent.

▶ *The stages in a rocket launch.*

▶▶ Read further > rocket launch
pg56 (k11)

▶▶ SPACE PROBES see pg213 (c33) ▶▶

The jewel planet

THE EARTH is one of eight planets in the Solar System that orbit (circle) the Sun. Like some of the other planets, it is a big ball of rock, wrapped around with a thin layer of gases, called the atmosphere *(see pg78 [i18])*. Yet the Earth is different from the other planets in crucial ways. From a distance, it looks like a blue-and-green jewel hanging in space. It is partly blue because, uniquely among the planets, the Earth has huge amounts of water in oceans *(see pg77 [q25])*. It is partly green because, unlike other planets, the water supports life.

Continents (see pg66 [r16])

▶▶ **Read further › tectonic plates**
    pg72 (d2); pg73 (b22)

● **Inside the Earth**

The Earth is not a solid ball. Vibrations from earthquakes *(see pg72 [k13])* and volcanic explosions *(see pg70 [o11])* have revealed a complex internal structure. Around the outside is a thin rocky shell or crust, between 6 and 40 km thick. Beneath the crust is a thick mantle of rock so hot that it flows like treacle, only very, very much slower. The mantle is about 2900 km thick. Beneath it, there is a core of metal (mostly iron and nickel). The outer core is so hot it is always molten; the inner core at the very centre of the Earth is solid because pressures are so great it cannot melt, despite top temperatures of over 7000°C.

Crust

Mantle

Outer core

Inner core

● **View from above**

From space, it is clear just how much of the Earth is covered by oceans – nearly three-quarters of its surface *(see pg77 [q25])*. Emerging above the oceans are seven masses of land *(see pg66 [s16])*. These are the continents of North and South America, Oceania, Antarctica, Africa, Asia and Europe, plus many thousands of islands, of all different sizes – some no bigger than a small rock.

IT'S A FACT

• The centre of the Earth is 6378 km below the surface.

• The Earth weighs about 6000 trillion trillion tonnes.

◀ *Viewed from space, swirls of cloud, the oceans and continents are visible on the Earth.*

Seas
(see pg77 [d29])

Atmosphere
(see pg78 [i18])

▶▶ Read further › Earth's crust
pg58 (o2)

Composition of the Earth

Most of the Earth is made from just four chemical elements: iron, oxygen, silicon and magnesium. Much of its rocky crust is made from combinations of two of these elements; oxygen and silicon, known as silicates. But there are small quantities of many other elements, such as aluminium and calcium. The various ways these elements combine mean that the Earth's crust contains many different materials.

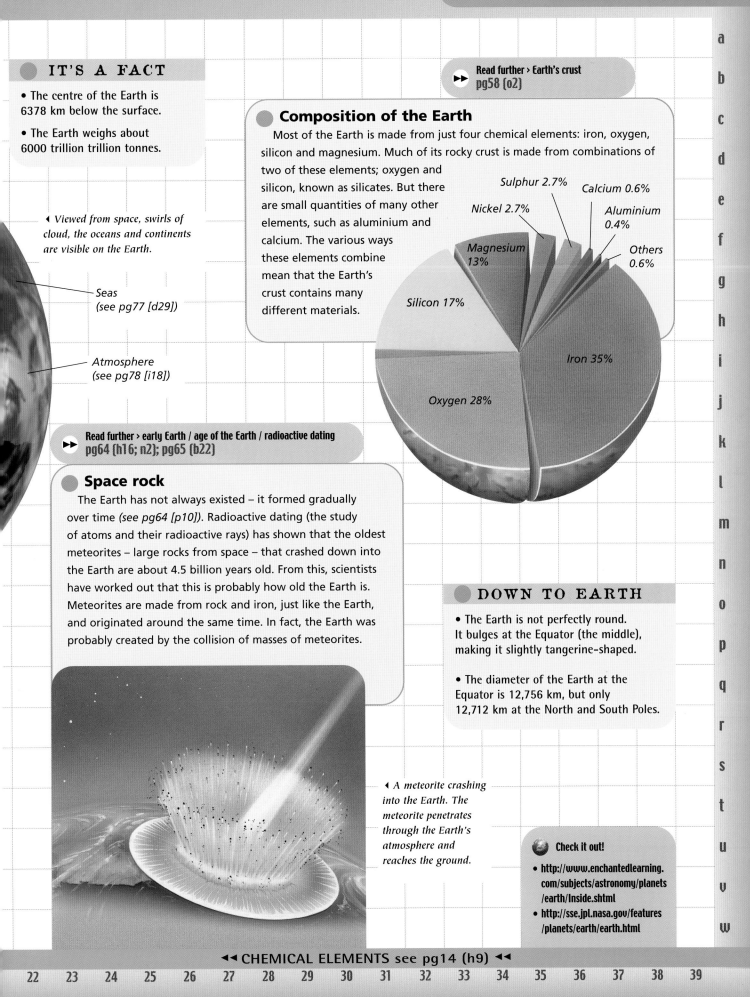

Sulphur 2.7%
Calcium 0.6%
Nickel 2.7%
Aluminium 0.4%
Magnesium 13%
Others 0.6%
Silicon 17%
Iron 35%
Oxygen 28%

▶▶ Read further › early Earth / age of the Earth / radioactive dating
pg64 (h16; n2); pg65 (b22)

Space rock

The Earth has not always existed – it formed gradually over time *(see pg64 [p10])*. Radioactive dating (the study of atoms and their radioactive rays) has shown that the oldest meteorites – large rocks from space – that crashed down into the Earth are about 4.5 billion years old. From this, scientists have worked out that this is probably how old the Earth is. Meteorites are made from rock and iron, just like the Earth, and originated around the same time. In fact, the Earth was probably created by the collision of masses of meteorites.

DOWN TO EARTH

• The Earth is not perfectly round. It bulges at the Equator (the middle), making it slightly tangerine-shaped.

• The diameter of the Earth at the Equator is 12,756 km, but only 12,712 km at the North and South Poles.

◀ *A meteorite crashing into the Earth. The meteorite penetrates through the Earth's atmosphere and reaches the ground.*

Check it out!

• http://www.enchantedlearning.com/subjects/astronomy/planets/earth/Inside.shtml

• http://sse.jpl.nasa.gov/features/planets/earth/earth.html

◀◀ CHEMICAL ELEMENTS see pg14 (h9) ◀◀

Spinning globe

THOUGH IT seems perfectly still, the Earth is actually spinning around at an average speed of over 1600 km/h. It is also hurtling through the darkness of space on its journey around the Sun at over 100,000 km/h. We are unaware of this rapid movement because we are locked firmly to the ground by gravity. But as the Earth spins and whirls through space, the view of the Sun from different places on the Earth is constantly changing, bringing not only day and night but all the seasons, too.

Earth lit having turned towards the Sun

◄ *This satellite picture shows half the Earth is exposed to the Sun at any time. Radiation from the Sun is the Earth's main source of energy. This provides huge amounts of both heat and light, without which there would be no life on Earth.*

● Day and night

At any one time, half the Earth is facing towards the Sun and is brightly lit, while the other half is facing away from the Sun and is in darkness. As the Earth turns while the Sun stays still, the dark and sunlit halves move around the world, bringing day and night to different parts. Because the Earth turns eastwards, we see the Sun rising in the east as the Earth turns our part of the world towards it, and setting in the west as it turns us away from the Sun. The Earth turns completely around once every 24 hours, which is why there are 24 hours in every day.

Earth in darkness having turned away from the Sun

 Check it out!

• http://www.enchantedlearning.com/subjects/astronomy/planets/earth/Seasons.shtml
• http://www.hexadyne.com/Educational/Science/4seasons.html

● DOWN TO EARTH

• As the Earth spins around every 24 hours, places near the poles barely move at all, while places at the Equator whizz around at over 1600 km/h.

• The Earth takes 0.242 days longer than a calendar year to complete its orbit. To make up for this, an extra day is added to the end of February every four years. This is called a leap year.

►► TIME AND SPACE see pg232 (d2) ►►

Yearly journey

▶▶ Read further > Sun's heat pg63 (c31)

The Earth's orbit around the Sun takes 365.242 days, which is why there are 365 days in a calendar year. Since the orbit is not a perfect circle but an ellipse (oval), the Earth is closer to the Sun at some points than others. Its closest point, called the perihelion, occurs on 3 January; its furthest point, called the aphelion, occurs on 4 July.

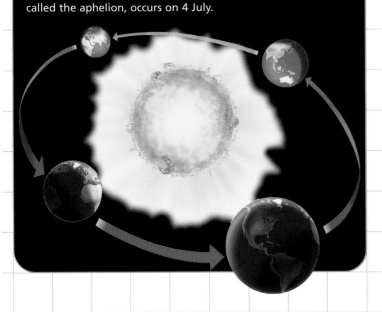

▼ The world's 24 time zones.

Time around the world

As the Earth rotates, the Sun rises in one place and sets in another. So that noon is always at the middle of the day, the world is divided into 24 time zones, one for each hour of the day. You put your clock forward 1 hour for each zone you pass through as you travel east; or behind 1 hour for each time zone as you travel west. So at noon in London, it is 7 a.m. in New York or 8 p.m. in Tokyo.

▶▶ Read further > time zones pg60 (m2)

All the seasons

The Earth does not spin upright, but is tilted at an angle, which always remains the same. When the Earth is on one side of the Sun, and the northern hemisphere (the world north of the Equator) is tilted towards it, it receives more sun, bringing summer. At the same time, the southern hemisphere is tilted away from the Sun, bringing winter. When Earth is on the other side of the Sun and the northern hemisphere is tilted away, winter occurs. In between, as the Earth moves around the Sun and neither hemisphere is tilted more towards it, we have spring and autumn.

Northern hemisphere is tilted away from the Sun – winter

Southern hemisphere is tilted towards the Sun – summer

▶▶ Read further > climate patterns pg62 (p2); pg63 (b22)

Warm and cold

THE NEARER a place is to the Equator, the warmer the weather, or climate, tends to be. At the Equator, the Sun climbs high in the sky so its rays are warm. Away from the Equator, the Sun climbs less high, so its rays give less warmth. At the North and South Poles, the Sun is so low, it gives very little warmth at all. The effect is to give the world three broad climate bands either side of the Equator: the warm tropics, the cold polar regions, and a moderate 'temperate' zone in between.

Temperate grassland (prairie and steppe)

Cool conifer forest (taiga)

North Pole

Equator

South Pole

Temperate deciduous woodland

Dry temperate

Tropical grassland

Mountainous

Tropical forest

Desert

Polar and tundra

Climate patterns

The warmth of a region's climate depends on how close it is to the Equator. But oceans and mountain ranges have a huge influence too, so the pattern of climate is complicated, with many local variations. Coastal areas tend to be damper and cooler, for instance, while continental interiors far inland tend to be drier and more extreme, with hot summers and cold winters. Antarctica has the coldest climate. It is so cold that almost nothing grows and nobody lives there.

Check it out!
• http://www.panda.org/climate
• http://www.exploratorium.edu/climate
• http://www.worldweather.org

►► GRASSLANDS AND DESERT see pg100 (d2) ►►

1 2 3 4 5 6 7 8 9 10 11 12 13 14 15 16 17 18 19

Warm tropics

The tropics are very warm, with temperatures averaging over 27°C all year round. But the tropical climate is varied. Some tropical places are warm and dry, including hot deserts such as the Sahara; some are warm and wet; and others have marked wet and dry seasons. Where it is wet in the tropics, it tends to be very wet indeed, since the warm air takes up huge amounts of moisture. Large thunderclouds often build up in the morning heat, then unleash torrents of rain in the afternoon *(see pg81 [q29])*. Steamy rainforests flourish in this hot, moist climate.

▸ *The Amazon rainforest in South America has more species of plants and animals than anywhere else on Earth.*

▶▶ **Read further › seasons**
pg61 (m22)

▶▶ **Read further › ozone layer / atmosphere / pressure**
pg63 (n22); pg78 (l2); pg79 (j22)

Global warming

When heat from the Sun reaches the Earth, some of it penetrates the atmosphere and reaches the ground. Much of this heat is then reflected back into space. Certain gases in the air trap heat reflected from the ground, rather like the glass in a greenhouse. In the past, this natural 'greenhouse effect' has kept the Earth comfortably warm. But the gases pumped into the air by the burning of coal and oil in factories and cars, for example, have trapped much more heat. Scientists believe that this is causing global (worldwide) warming of the climate, which could have devastating effects.

Heat trapped inside the atmosphere by greenhouse gases

Rays turned away by the atmosphere

Rays from the Sun

Heat reaching the Earth's surface

Trashing the Earth

In recent years, human activity has posed an increasing threat to the Earth's fragile resources, damaging everything from the atmosphere to animal life. Car exhausts and industrial plants are choking the air and turning rain acidic. Gases from supersonic jets and refrigerators are punching a hole in the world's protective ozone layer. Farming chemicals poison rivers. Unique species of animals and plants are vanishing for ever. Forests are being felled, vast areas of countryside are being buried under concrete and beautiful marine environments are being gradually destroyed.

▸ *Dangers to the world's climate caused by human activity.*

▶▶ **Read further › global warming**
pg63 (c31); pg78 (l2); pg79 (j22)

a
b
c
d
e
f
g
h
i
j
k
l
m
n
o
p
q
r
s
t
u
v
w

Earth story

DOWN TO EARTH

• Fossils only indicate to geologists whether the rock in which they are found is relatively old or young.

• Radioactive dating works because after rocks form, certain atoms break down at a steady rate, sending out rays or radioactivity. By assessing how many atoms in the rock have changed, geologists can work out its age.

THE STORY of the Earth began about 4.6 billion years ago when dust whirling around the newborn Sun started to clump into lumps of rock called planetesimals. Then, pulled together by their mutual gravity, the planetesimals clumped together to form the Earth and other planets. Soon after, a giant rock crashed into the Earth so violently that the rock melted, splashed off and cooled to become the Moon. The Earth was so shaken by the impact that all the elements in it separated. The dense metals, iron and nickel, collapsed to the centre to form its core, while lighter materials formed the Earth's rocky crust.

Early Earth

A mass of erupting volcanoes and smoke appeared when the Earth was formed. Streams of lava (molten rock) turned the Earth's surface into churning, red-hot oceans. Huge gas bubbles rose from the interior and belched out through the volcanoes to form a thick, cloudy – and highly poisonous – atmosphere. Eventually, as the Earth began to cool, a crust formed around the Earth as the lava oceans hardened.

In the beginning

When the Earth first formed, it was little more than a red-hot ball. But over half a billion years, it gradually cooled down and, slowly, a hard crust of rock began to form. An atmosphere containing poisonous gases, such as methane, hydrogen and ammonia, soon wrapped around the planet, rising from fierce volcanoes on the surface (see pg70 [p11]). After about 1 billion years, the air began to clear as water vapour that had gathered in the clouds fell as rain, to create the oceans, flooding basins in the Earth's crust to form continents.

▶▶ Read further › rocks / volcanoes

▼ The steam and gas that billowed from volcanoes formed the Earth's poisonous atmosphere.

▶▶ Read further › volcanoes / oceans
pg70 (n2); pg76 (d2)

a
b
c
d
e
f
g
h
i
j
k
l
m
n
o
p
q
r
s
t
u
v
w

Ages of the Earth

►► **Read further › Inside the Earth**
pg58 (o2)

Layers of rock tend to form one on top of another, so the oldest is usually at the bottom. The order of layers from top to bottom is known as the geological column. Even if the layers have been disturbed, it is often possible to work out the order in which they formed. Because different plants and animals lived at different times in the Earth's past, experts can date a layer of rock by the fossils it contains. Using these clues, they have built up a picture of the successive rock layers. This way, they have divided the last 590 million years of the Earth's history into 12 units of time called Periods, each lasting many millions of years.

Quaternary Period: 0–2 mya
Many mammals die out; humans evolve

Tertiary Period: 2–65 mya
First large mammals appear; birds thrive; grasslands spread

Cretaceous Period: 65–144 mya
Dinosaurs die out; first flowering plants

Jurassic Period: 144–213 mya
Age of the dinosaurs; some dinosaurs evolve into birds

Triassic Period: 213–248 mya
Mammals and seed-bearing plants appear

Permian Period: 248–286 mya
Conifers appear, but many animals die out as deserts spread

Carboniferous Period: 286–360 mya
Reptiles evolve; vast areas of swampy fern forests

Devonian Period: 360–408 mya
Insects and amphibians evolve; ferns and mosses as big as trees

Silurian Period: 408–438 mya
Plants appear on land and fish in rivers

Ordovician Period: 438–505 mya
Sahara is covered in ice; fish-like creatures evolve in the sea

Cambrian Period: 505–590 mya
No life on land but shellfish thrive in the oceans

Precambrian Time: Before 590 mya
First micro-organisms appear and give atmosphere the oxygen that larger animals need to breathe

▲ *Timeline showing the Earth's formation millions of years ago (mya) plus layers of rock built up through the ages.*

IT'S A FACT

• If all the Earth's history were crammed into the hours of one day, humans would appear less than 2 minutes before midnight!

• The oxygen most animals need to be able to breathe was put into the air by minute plants in the sea, called cyanobacteria, over billions of years.

Fossil record

The first signs of life on the Earth – probably tiny bacteria – appeared almost 4 billion years ago. But the first animals with shells and bones emerged less than 600 million years ago. Some have been preserved as fossils – over time their hard remains have turned to stone. With the help of fossils like the ammonite shellfish, geologists have built up a detailed picture of the Earth's history.

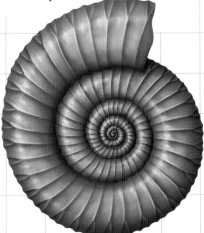

▲ *The ammonite's body was covered by a spiral shell. The body rotted while the shell became a fossil.*

Check it out!

• http://www.kidscosmos.org/kid-stuff/
kids-basalt-history.html

Moving continents

SLOWLY, SLOWLY, the Earth's surface is moving around beneath our feet all the time. Look at a map of the world and you will see, for example, that the west coast of Africa looks as if it would slot into the east coast of South America like pieces of a jigsaw. The reason is that 220 million years ago – just before the age of the dinosaurs – they were actually joined together. In fact, all the world's continents were joined together then, in one huge landmass that geologists call Pangaea. Pangaea gradually split up into today's continents as plate movements caused earthquakes. The continents drifted to where they are today (continental drift) and are still moving!

● IT'S A FACT

• New York is moving about 2.5 cm further away from London every year.

• On average, continents move at the same rate as fingernails grow – about 2 mm every month.

• Some tectonic plates have moved so far, they have travelled half way around the globe.

▶▶ **Read further › earthquakes pg73 (b22)**

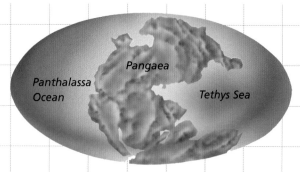

220 million years ago (mya) *there was just one giant land mass, called Pangaea (meaning 'all Earth'), and one giant ocean, known as Panthalassa. But a long arm of the ocean, the Tethys Sea, stretched into the heart of Pangaea*

200 mya *Pangaea split either side of the Tethys Sea. To the north was Laurasia, including North America, Europe and most of Asia. To the south was Gondwanaland, including South America, Africa, Australia, Antarctica and India*

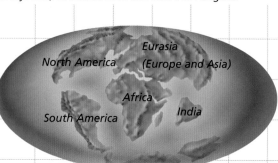

135 mya *the South Atlantic Ocean opened up between the continents of Africa and South America. India then broke off from Africa and drifted towards Asia. Europe and North America were still joined at this time*

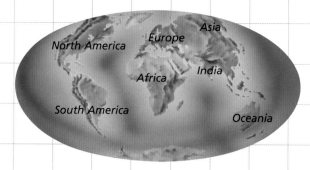

Today *North America and Europe are widely separated, having split 60 million years ago. India has crunched into Asia, Australia is moving into the tropics and Antarctica has moved to the South Pole*

▶▶ NAIL GROWTH pg155 (l22) ▶▶

The world's biggest plates

It is not just the continents that are moving – so are the ocean beds. In fact, the whole of the Earth's surface is on the move. Its rigid outer shell of rock is split into about 20 giant slabs called tectonic plates: nine huge ones and about 12 smaller ones. These plates are constantly on the move, slipping past each other, and jostling this way and that. The continents are embedded in these plates like currants in a bun, and move with them.

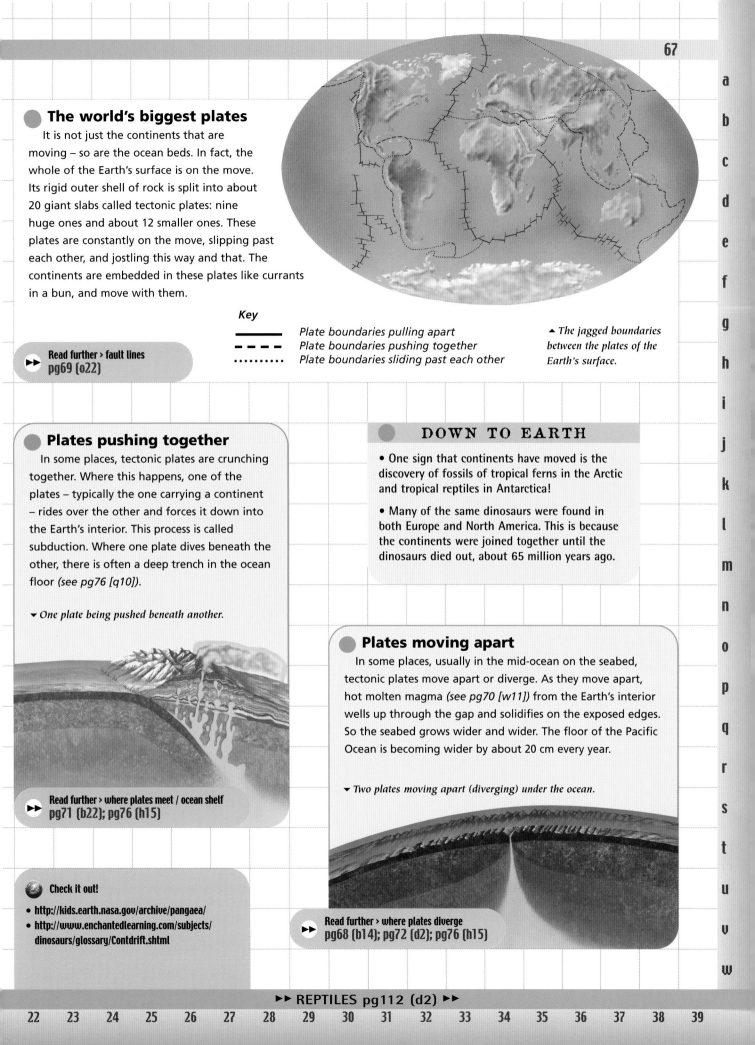

Key

———————— *Plate boundaries pulling apart*

– – – – – *Plate boundaries pushing together*

·········· *Plate boundaries sliding past each other*

▲ *The jagged boundaries between the plates of the Earth's surface.*

▶▶ Read further > fault lines
pg69 (o22)

Plates pushing together

In some places, tectonic plates are crunching together. Where this happens, one of the plates – typically the one carrying a continent – rides over the other and forces it down into the Earth's interior. This process is called subduction. Where one plate dives beneath the other, there is often a deep trench in the ocean floor *(see pg76 [q10])*.

▼ *One plate being pushed beneath another.*

▶▶ Read further > where plates meet / ocean shelf
pg71 (b22); pg76 (h15)

DOWN TO EARTH

• One sign that continents have moved is the discovery of fossils of tropical ferns in the Arctic and tropical reptiles in Antarctica!

• Many of the same dinosaurs were found in both Europe and North America. This is because the continents were joined together until the dinosaurs died out, about 65 million years ago.

Plates moving apart

In some places, usually in the mid-ocean on the seabed, tectonic plates move apart or diverge. As they move apart, hot molten magma *(see pg70 [w11])* from the Earth's interior wells up through the gap and solidifies on the exposed edges. So the seabed grows wider and wider. The floor of the Pacific Ocean is becoming wider by about 20 cm every year.

▼ *Two plates moving apart (diverging) under the ocean.*

▶▶ Read further > where plates diverge
pg68 (b14); pg72 (d2); pg76 (h15)

Check it out!

• http://kids.earth.nasa.gov/archive/pangaea/
• http://www.enchantedlearning.com/subjects/dinosaurs/glossary/Contdrift.shtml

▶▶ REPTILES pg112 (d2) ▶▶

a b c d e f g h i j k l m n o p q r s t u v w

22 23 24 25 26 27 28 29 30 31 32 33 34 35 36 37 38 39

Mountain high

Read further › formation of volcanoes
pg71 (b22)

MOUNTAINS LOOK solid and unchanging, but they are being built up, then worn away by the weather, all the time. The world's highest mountains were actually formed quite recently in the Earth's history. The Himalayas, for instance, were built up in the last 40 million years, and are still growing, even today. The most ancient mountain ranges have long been worn flat, or reduced to hills, such as New York's Adirondacks, which are now over 1 billion years old.

Neat folds

A few mountains, such as Washington's Mount St Helens, are volcanoes – tall cones built up by successive eruptions of lava and ash. Most, however, are thrown up by the immense power of the Earth's crust moving. Some are huge slabs called fault blocks, or 'horst', caused by powerful earthquakes. But all the world's great mountain ranges, such as the Andes and Rockies, were made by the crumpling of rock layers as tectonic plates pushed against each other. Such mountains are called fold mountains.

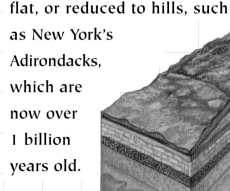

▸ *Three types of mountain range.*

Volcanic peak

Fold mountain

Fault block mountain

To scale
Each square = 1000 m

The highest mountains – measured from sea level to summit – in each continent, to scale

Jayakusuma (Oceania)	Elbrus (Europe)	Kilimanjaro (Africa)	Mt McKinley (North America)	Aconcagua (South America)	Mount Everes (Asia)
5030 m	5642 m	5895 m	6194 m	6960 m	8863 m

IT'S A FACT

• If you travelled from London to Paris and back again eight times, you would cover the same distance as the length of the Andes mountain range.

• The largest recorded volcanic eruption happened in 1550 BC in Santorini, Greece.

Folding rock

Read further › folds
pg68 (b14)

Most rocks form in flat layers called strata. Some rocks are sedimentary and form from sand and mud settling on the seabed. Others are volcanic, such as the vast basalt plateaux at the heart of many continents. Fold mountains build up where the movement of the Earth's crust tilts, crumples and squeezes, and lifts these flat layers.

Strike – the direction of the folding movement

Dip – the steepness of an individual fold

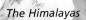
The Himalayas

Asian plate

Folded rock layers

India moving north

Himalayan mountains

The Himalayas were thrown up by the collision between India and the rest of Asia. India has been ploughing relentlessly north into Asia for the last 40 million years. As it does so, layer upon layer of rock in Asia's southern edge has crumpled, like the bow wave of a boat pushing through water or sludgy mud. While India carries on moving, the Himalayas will continue to crumple up in front of it.

Read further › faults
pg73 (b22)

Read further › Earth moving
pg67 (j22)

Round the block

As the Earth's crust moves during earthquakes *(see pg72 [m13])*, huge blocks of rock can slip or 'fault'. Sometimes, they move just a few millimetres. Occasionally, they move over many metres. But over millions of years, successive movements can move a block up or down huge distances. In California's Sierra Nevada, faulting has created a steep slope 3350 m high and hundreds of kilometres long.

▸ *Geologists describe fault movements using these terms.*

▲ *All 14 of the world's peaks over 8000 m are in the Himalayas – in Nepal, China and Kashmir.*

Throw

Heave

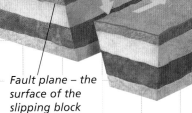

Fault plane – the surface of the slipping block

WORLD'S HIGHEST

Mountains	Height
Everest	8863 m
K2	8610 m
Kanchenjunga	8598 m
Lhotse	8511 m
Makalu	8481 m

Check it out!

• http://www.eduscapes.com/42explore/mountain.htm
• http://www.americanparknetwork.com/parkinfo/rm/geology/index.html

►► BOATS pg186 (o16) ►►

Fiery mountains

VOLCANOES ARE places where hot molten rock or magma wells up to the surface from deep within the Earth's interior. Sometimes, the magma flows out over the ground as red-hot liquid rock or lava. At other times, the volcano becomes clogged up with a thick plug of magma, then suddenly erupts in a gigantic explosion that sends up jets of steam and hurls fiery fragments of magma high into the air. Successive eruptions can build up such a huge cone of ash and lava around the volcano that it becomes a mountain *(see pg68 [i8]).*

All fired up

The biggest volcanic eruptions are powered by a combination of steam and carbon dioxide gas. They remain dissolved in the magma inside the volcano because of the extreme pressure. But as the plug of magma breaks, the pressure is suddenly released, creating an explosion big enough to send chunks of rock the size of houses many thousands of metres up into the air.

Eruptions begin with a build-up of pressure in the magma chamber beneath the volcano

As the steam and gas jet out, they carry with them clouds of ash and larger fragments of the broken plug of magma, called volcanic bombs or tephra

Bubbles of steam and gas form and swell rapidly inside the magma, and burst out like the froth from a violently shaken bottle of fizz

With the volcanic plug out of the way, magma surges up and out of the volcano, and flows down as lava

◄ *Magma chamber inside a volcano.*

◄◄ CARBON DIOXIDE see pg12 (q15) ◄◄

1 2 3 4 5 6 7 8 9 10 11 12 13 14 15 16 17 18 19 2

a
b
c
d
e
f
g
h
i
j
k
l
m
n
o
p
q
r
s
t
u
v
w

Types of volcano

Most volcanoes occur near cracks between the giant tectonic plates that make up the Earth's surface, but they come in many different shapes and sizes. Spectacular, violently erupting volcanic cones, or 'cone' volcanoes, develop where the plates are pushing together *(see pg67 [q26])*. Here, magma is trapped below ground, making it so acidic – and so thick and sticky – that it clogs up the volcano and then erupts sporadically and dramatically. Where plates are pulling apart, the magma is less acid and runnier. It reaches the surface easily and floods out steadily as lava to form a gentle slope that looks like an upturned shield, known as a 'shield' volcano.

Read further › tectonic plates
pg67 (b22); pg73 (b22)

Cone volcano

Shield volcano

▸ *Volcanoes in the Pacific spray out fiery lava fountains.*

Rock soup

The lava that gushes from the Hawaiian volcanoes in the Pacific is very runny. Because of this, the explosive gases leak out, and so the lava rarely bursts out in a huge explosion. Instead, it tends to spray out frequently in fiery fountains, or well out in slower streams of molten rock.

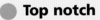
Read further › volcanic eruptions
pg70 (n2)

Boiling fountains

Even if magma does not erupt in a volcano, its tremendous heat can produce other effects. Rainwater trickling into the ground, for instance, may be heated under pressure, then burst on to the surface in a tremendous whoosh of steam called a geyser. Or a mix of hot water and mud may bubble up on the surface to create baths of boiling mud called mudpots. Sometimes, hot fumes of toxic gases escape through cracks in the rock to emerge like smoke from a chimney in 'fumaroles'.

Mudpot

Fumarole

Top notch

When a volcano erupts, it can completely empty the magma chamber as lava, ash and other debris are blown out. This leaves the top of the cone unsupported, and it collapses into the volcanic vent. This creates a huge pit or crater in the summit of the volcano. Once the volcano stops erupting, the crater may gradually fill with water to form a lake, such as Oregon's famous Crater Lake.

▾ *Geyser blowing superheated steam.*

Read further › black smokers
pg77 (l31)

Check it out!
- http://volcano.und.nodak.edu/vwdocs/kids/kids.html
- http://www.fema.gov/kids/volcano.htm

Read further › lakes
p75 (c34)

►► STEAM see pg204 (l2) ►►

Shaky ground

IT'S A FACT

• The world's most deadly earthquake occurred in Shanxi in China in 1556, killing about 830,000 people.

• In 1995, an earthquake struck Kobe in Japan, killing 5200 people, destroying more than 100,000 buildings and leaving about 250,000 people homeless.

THE GROUND sometimes trembles when a heavy truck passes by. But major earthquakes that make the ground shudder violently are set off by the movement of tectonic plates – the giant slabs of rock that make up the Earth's surface *(see pg67 [c34])*. Tectonic plates are moving all the time, radiating minor tremors as they grind past each other. But every now and then they get jammed. Then the pressure builds up until they suddenly lurch on again, sending out vibrations, called shock waves, in all directions and creating major earthquakes that can bring down mountains and destroy cities.

▾ Earthquakes start where slabs of the Earth's surface are moving in opposite directions.

Epicentre

Hypocentre (focus)

Radiating shock waves

Shock waves

In an earthquake, shock waves radiate out in circles from its origin or hypocentre (focus). Shock waves vibrate throughout the ground, but it is at the surface that they do most damage. Damage is most severe at the epicentre – the point on the surface directly above the focus – where the shock waves are strongest. But they can often be felt up to thousands of kilometres away.

▲ *Devastation to buildings caused by a Taiwanese earthquake in 1999.*

Check it out!

• http://www.fema.gov/kids/quake.htm
• http://earthquake.usgs.gov/4kids/

DOWN TO EARTH

• Most earthquakes last less than a minute. The longest recorded, in Alaska on 21 March 1964, lasted four minutes.

• Typically, tectonic plates slide only 4 or 5 cm past each other each year. In a slip that triggers a major earthquake, they can move 1 metre or more.

• In most earthquakes a few minor tremors (foreshocks) are followed by an intense burst lasting 1 or 2 minutes.

◄◄ WAVES see pg31 (o22) ◄◄

a
b
c
d
e
f
g
h
i
j
k
l
m
n
o
p
q
r
s
t
u
v
w

Earthquake zones

Places near the edges of tectonic plates, such as south-east Europe and the Pacific coast, are at a very high risk of earthquakes. In these earthquake zones, minor quakes are frequent, and a quiet period may often be the build-up to a really big one. People in California, USA, are constantly threatened by the movement of the San Andreas fault, where two great tectonic plates grind past each other *(see pg67 [c34])*. When the San Andreas fault juddered in 1906, it set off earthquakes that destroyed San Francisco.

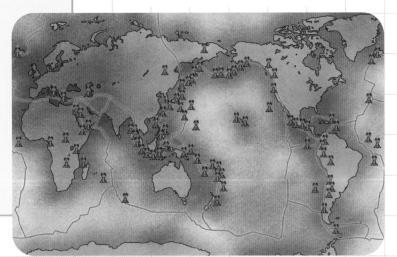

▼ *Earthquakes and volcanoes occur in the same regions, where tectonic plates meet.*

►► **Read further › earthquake devastation**
pg72 (m2)

Measuring earthquakes

Seismologists (scientists who study earthquakes) measure the strength of the shock waves with a device called a seismometer. They then grade the severity of the quake on the Richter scale, from 1 (slight tremor) to over 9 (devastating quake). The Richter scale shows the size of an earthquake – its absolute magnitude – but not its effects. So experts also rate an earthquake on the Mercalli scale, which assesses the damage on a scale of 1 (barely noticeable) to 12 (total destruction), expressed in Roman numerals, I to XII.

A seismometer records earthquake vibrations as up and down lines on paper or displays them on a computer screen

MERCALLI SCALE

III – light fittings shake

VI – windows shatter

VIII – chimneys shaken down

X – major structural damage to bridges

Tidal waves

The world's most awesome waves are called tidal waves or tsunami (pronounced 'soon-army') which are caused by earthquakes *(see pg72 [t10])*. Undersea earthquakes or a landslide into the sea can send out a giant pulse of water racing along the seabed as fast as a jet plane. When the pulse reaches shallow water, a huge wave tens of metres high rears up, swamping anything in its path.

As the pulse moves into shallow water it rears into a giant wave and swamps coastal regions

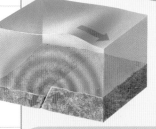

A shift in the seabed sends out a pulse of water

►► **Read further › tectonic plates**
pg69 (o22)

Water on the land

THE AMOUNT of water in the world remains constant, but is continually moving around the Earth and its atmosphere in a process called the water cycle. Rain falling from clouds gathers in rivers, lakes and oceans. Heat from the Sun causes the water to evaporate (become water vapour). As the water vapour rises into the atmosphere, it cools and condenses (changes back into water) and forms clouds. When the water in the clouds becomes too heavy, it falls back to Earth as rain and returns to the rivers. Some of the rain soaks into the ground and is used by plants. Plants return unused water as it evaporates from their leaves (transpiration).

Water, water everywhere

There is a huge amount of water in the world – over 525 million cubic km – but 97 per cent is salt water in the sea. The other 3 per cent is fresh water, but most of this is frozen in ice sheets at the poles, or deep underground. Only a very tiny portion moves round in the water cycle, but this precious water keeps rivers flowing and provides us with water to drink and plants with the water they need for growth.

1. Water evaporates from the sea and lakes and the water vapour rises into the air

2. Water is taken up from the ground by plants and transpires from their leaves

3. As the water vapour rises, it cools and condenses into droplets of water and ice crystals to form clouds

4. When the water is too heavy to be held by the clouds, they drop their moisture as rain

5. Falling rain gathers into rivers and runs directly down to the sea, or seeps into the ground, where it may be taken up by plants

To scale

Each square = 1000 km

The longest rivers in each continent. *The Amazon and the Nile can be measured from various points, thus their official lengths sometimes change*

Darling (Oceania)
2740 km

Volga (Europe)
3530 km

Mississippi-Missouri (North America)
6020 km

Yangtze (Asia)
6300 km

Nile (Africa)
6673 km

Amazon (South America)
6750 km

◄◄ ICEBERG see pg35 (b34) ◄◄

1   2   3   4   5   6   7   8   9   10   11   12   13   14   15   16   17   18   19

IT'S A FACT

• The world's shortest recorded river is the North Fork Foe River in Montana, USA, at 17.7 m long.

• Lake Superior is the largest freshwater lake in the world, bigger than Ireland. It is 560 km long, with a surface area of 82,100 sq km.

►► **Read further > lakes pg71 (k34)**

Great lakes

Many of the largest lakes in North America and Europe were created barely 10,000 years ago, during the last ice age. Lakes of water melting from the ice-filled hollows were gouged out both by the glaciers themselves and by the huge floods of water released when the glaciers melted. The Great Lakes were probably created this way, including Lake Superior.

Lake Superior, Lake Michigan, Lake Huron, Lake Ontario, Lake Erie

Rivers run down

Whenever there is enough rain or melting snow to keep them flowing, rivers run down to the sea or to lakes. In wetter parts of the world, they are kept flowing even when it is not raining or snowing, from water underground. In fact, a lot of rain does not flow straight over the land, but seeps into the ground, then bubbles out again lower down in places called springs.

▸ *Lake Miramar in Argentina.*

►► **Read further > seas and oceans pg76 (d2)**

Deltas

A river slows down as it flows into the sea, so it can no longer carry the load of silt it has collected along the way. Often, the silt is dumped in a fan-shape, or a delta, and the river splits into branches called distributaries. Where there is a strong coastal current, the head of the delta is swept into a curving or 'arcuate' form such as the Nile in Africa. Where the sea current is weak, the distributaries spread out in a ragged 'bird's foot' shape such as the Mississippi delta.

Most rivers start as tiny brooks high in the hills, tumbling over rocks and rapids

As they flow on down, brooks grow into big streams as they are joined by other streams called tributaries

Further down, streams broaden into rivers that flow through deep, meandering (winding) channels of sediment, washed down from higher up

◂ *An arcuate delta.*

DOWN TO EARTH

• Oxbow lakes form when a river meanders (changes course) cutting off patches of water before linking back up (braiding).

• Lake Baikal in Russia is the world's deepest lake. At 1743 m, it holds 20 per cent of the world's fresh water.

🌐 **Check it out!**

• http://www.geography4kids.com/files/ water_hydrosphere.html

►► ELEMENTS pg215 (j31) ►►

a b c d e f g h i j k l m n o p q r s t u v w

22 23 24 25 26 27 28 29 30 31 32 33 34 35 36 37 38 39

Ocean deep

THERE ARE five great oceans: the Pacific, the Atlantic, the Indian, the Arctic, and the Southern Ocean around Antarctica. There are also many seas, including the Mediterranean and the Red Sea. Until recently, we knew little more about the bottom of the oceans than we did about the surface of Mars. Now, surveys undertaken with sound equipment and computerized underwater craft have revealed a hugely varied landscape on the ocean bed, with high mountains, wide plains and deep valleys.

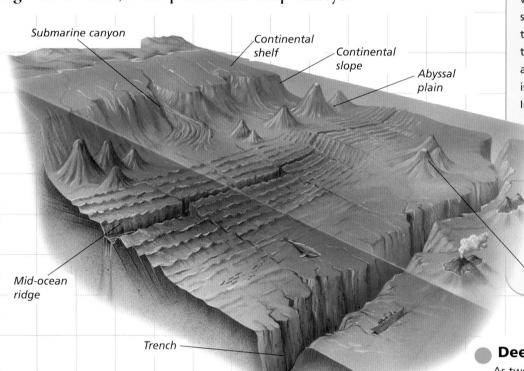

Submarine canyon

Continental shelf

Continental slope

Abyssal plain

Mid-ocean ridge

Trench

Seamount

IT'S A FACT

• The West Wind Drift (an ocean current) around Antarctica moves 2000 times as much water as the Amazon does each year.

• Oceans are, on average, about 2000 m deep.

• One of the tides in the Pacific Ocean reaches 9 m inland, along the coast of Korea.

Into the abyss

Around the edge of the ocean is a shelf of shallow water called the continental shelf. At the edge of the shelf, the ocean bed plunges steeply to the deep ocean floor, known as the 'abyssal plain'. This plain is vast, but not completely flat. In the Pacific especially, it is dotted with huge mountains, called seamounts. The world's longest mountain chain, the mid-ocean ridge, runs down through the Atlantic and into the Indian Ocean.

Deep dive

As two giant tectonic plates move apart, a deep gash opens up in the ocean floor – an ocean trench. The deepest point on the Earth's surface is the Challenger Deep in the Marianas Trench in the west Pacific, 10,920 m deep. In 1960, the *Trieste*, an underwater craft or bathyscaphe, dived almost to the bottom.

▶ *The bathyscaphe called Trieste that visited the ocean floor in 1961.*

▶▶ UNDERWATER EXPLORERS see pg187 (b25) ▶▶

1 2 3 4 5 6 7 8 9 10 11 12 13 14 15 16 17 18 19

One high tide bulge occurs at places in the ocean nearest to the Moon, as water is pulled towards the Moon

The sea moves or 'flows' upwards and inland as the tide rises

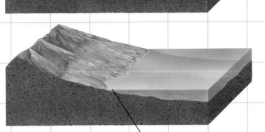

Another high tide bulge occurs in places furthest from the Moon, because the solid Earth, too, is pulled towards the Moon, leaving the ocean waters behind

The sea ebbs, sinking and retreating, as the tide drops

Rising and falling

All around the world, the sea rises and falls slightly twice every day in 'tides'. As the sea rises, it flows further up seashores. As it falls back, it slowly retreats or 'ebbs'. Tides are caused by the pull of the Moon's gravity on the oceans' waters as the Earth spins around. High tides move around the Earth in two bulges on opposite sides of the Earth. Spring tides (high tides) happen twice a month. They occur as the Moon and Sun line up with each other, combining their gravitational pull.

▶▶ Read further › spinning Earth
pg60 (d2)

DOWN TO EARTH

• The most extreme spring tides are in the Bay of Fundy in Canada, where the sea rises and falls up to 15 m.

• The Dead Sea is the lowest sea on Earth, at 400 m below sea level.

▶▶ Read further › geysers
pg71 (l22)

Undersea chimneys

In deep valleys in the mid-ocean ridges, there are amazing natural chimneys on the seabed. Called black smokers or hydrothermal vents, these chimneys are volcanic features *(see pg71 [q30])* that billow black fumes of hot gases and water. Seawater seeping into cracks in the seafloor is heated by hot volcanic magma *(see pg70 [w11])*. The heated water dissolves minerals from seabed rock and spews from the vents in scalding, mineral-rich black plumes.

▸ *Plumes from black smokers.*

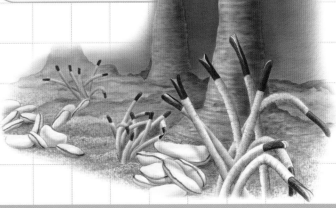

Calm waters

The Pacific is the world's largest ocean. It is twice as large as the Atlantic and covers an area of 181 million sq km – one-third of the world. The Pacific is peppered with thousands of islands – many are the peaks of undersea volcanoes and most are only about 1 m above sea level. The word 'pacific' means calm.

▾ *On average, the Pacific Ocean is 4200 m deep.*

▶▶ Read further › undersea volcanoes
pg77 (l31)

a b c d e f g h i j k l m n o p q r s t u v w

Swirling air

THE ATMOSPHERE that surrounds the Earth is barely thicker on the Earth than the peel is on an orange. Yet without it, the Earth would be as lifeless as the Moon. The atmosphere absorbs the Sun's warmth, yet shields the Earth from its most harmful rays. It gives us clean, fresh water to drink (*see pg74 [j11]*), and provides us with the air that we, and most other animals, need to breathe. Our weather is also a result of changes in the Earth's atmosphere. These changes are caused by worldwide and local variations in the heat of the Sun.

DOWN TO EARTH

• The impact of particles from the Sun on the gases of the upper atmosphere creates shimmering curtains of light called auroras in the night sky over polar regions.

• The atmosphere is a mixture of gases: 78 per cent nitrogen, 21 per cent oxygen and 1 per cent argon and carbon dioxide, plus traces of neon, krypton, zenon, helium, nitrous oxide and methane.

Atmospheric layers

The atmosphere may look invisible but it has a number of distinct layers or 'spheres'. At the bottom is the troposphere – only 10 km thick, but containing over 70 per cent of the atmosphere's gases by weight. Above that, the gases become thinner and thinner with each layer, until at about 800 km up, they are so thin or 'rarified' that it is hard to tell where the atmosphere ends and where empty space begins.

IT'S A FACT

• The world's windiest place is George V island in Antarctica, where winds often blow at 320 km/h.

• Temperatures drop to nearly –60°C at the top of the troposphere.

🌐 **Check it out!**

• http://www.enchantedlearning.com/subjects/
astronomy/planets/earth/Atmosphere.shtml
• http://www.windpower.org/en/kids/choose/wind/
tropos.htm

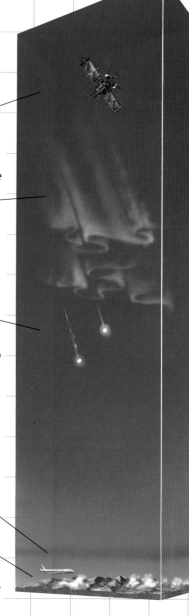

Exosphere:
500–800 km
Contains hardly any gas;
low-level satellites orbit here

Thermosphere:
80–500 km
Becomes roasted by the Sun
to up to 1800°C, but is so
thin in gases that it contains
little real heat

Mesosphere:
50–80 km
Is too thin to soak up much
heat, but is thick enough to
stop meteorites that burn up
leaving fiery trails in the sky

Stratosphere:
10–50 km
Contains the ozone layer
and becomes hotter higher
up; little water and no
weather; airliners cruise
here in the still air

Troposphere:
0–10 km
Contains three-quarters
of the atmosphere's gases
and nearly all its water;
temperatures drop by about
6.5°C every kilometre further

◄◄ ATMOSPHERE see pg35 (b22) ◄◄

Cirrus

Cumulonimbus

Cirrostratus

Nimbostratus

Stratus

Cumulus

▲ *The main classes of cloud were named in the 1800s by Luke Howard, a British weather scientist.*

Clouds

Clouds are made of tiny drops of water *(see pg74 [h13])* and ice crystals so light they float in the air. There is a large variety of clouds, but only two main shapes: fluffy, heaped 'cumulus' that form clouds when air moisture billows upwards; and flat 'stratus' clouds that form when a layer of air cools down enough for its water content to condense. Both types of cloud take different forms at different heights in the sky.

▶▶ Read further › evaporation
pg74 (d13)

▶▶ Read further › global warming / air pressure
pg63 (c31); pg81 (o22)

Hot and cold

Winds blow because the Sun warms some places more than others, creating differences in air pressure (density) that push air about. In warm places, air expands and rises, lowering the pressure. In cool spots, the air is heavy and sinks, raising the pressure. Winds blow from zones where pressure is high, called anticyclones, to zones where it is low, called cyclones or depressions. The bigger the difference in pressure, the stronger the wind.

▶▶ Read further › twisters / hurricanes
pg81 (m2); pg82 (b22)

World winds

Winds often blow from the same, or prevailing, direction in each of three belts around the world. In polar regions, cool, sinking air drives the prevailing winds away from the poles. In the tropics, warm air rising over the Equator draws winds in from either side. In the mid-latitudes in between, winds are driven away from the tropics by cool air sinking. Yet none of these winds blows directly north to south, because the world is spinning. So winds veer off to the left in the southern hemisphere and the right in the northern hemisphere.

Tropics – dry trade winds blow from the south-east or north-east towards the Equator, depending on the time of year

Mid-latitudes – warm, moist, westerly winds (winds from the west) are common

Polar regions – cold, easterly winds blow for much of the year

▼ *Northern hemisphere.*   ▼ *Southern hemisphere.*

Winds spiral clockwise from high pressure zones and anticlockwise into low pressure zones

Winds spiral in the opposite direction

a
b
c
d
e
f
g
h
i
j
k
l
m
n
o
p
q
r
s
t
u
v
w

Stormy Weather

WHEN STORMS rage, winds blow hard and rains pour down from thick grey clouds. Some storms, such as summer thunderstorms, are over in a few minutes, while tropical hurricanes can blow for over a day. But all storms share the same cause – a powerful combination of heat and lots of moisture. Summer thunderstorms happen when the hot morning sun steams water off the ground to pile up into towering thunderclouds that unleash torrents of rain. Hurricanes occur when these huge thunderclouds mushroom over warm oceans and join together into one giant, spiralling storm system.

● Twister

Tornadoes occur when a funnel of violently spinning air forms beneath a thundercloud and swoops to the ground. At the centre is an area of low pressure that sucks up everything in its path like a giant vacuum cleaner, while the terrifying winds can race around at speeds of over 400 km/h, tossing people, cars and buildings in the air like toys. From March to July every year, about 700 of these storms whirl across the Midwest of America in an area known as Tornado Alley.

▶▶ Read further > winds
pg79 (m30)

◀ Tornado Alley in the US Midwest, where tornadoes are also known as twisters.

MEXICO

● Electric sky

Thunderclouds are built up by strong updrafts on warm, humid days, or along a cold front. These clouds are so big that raindrops grow to huge sizes within them. Whirlwinds within the clouds hurl the drops together so violently that the clouds become charged with static electricity. Eventually, the charge is released in a massive flash of lightning.

▶ A thundercloud unleashes forks of lightning.

Check it out!

- http://www.fema.gov/kids/hurr.htm
- http://www.ucar.edu/ 40th/webweather/

◀◀ HEAT see pg28 (d2) ◀◀

1   2   3   4   5   6   7   8   9   10   11   12   13   14   15   16   17   18   19

Hurricane force

Hurricanes are huge tropical storms that develop over the eastern Atlantic Ocean, then wheel westwards towards the east coast of the Americas. By this time, the storm is spiralling around a tight centre or 'eye' around which rains pour and winds gust at up to 320 km/h. Each hurricane is given a name and tracked by satellite to give people plenty of warning that one is on its way – but when it arrives, dragging with it a huge surge of seawater *(see pg73 [q38])*, the impact is devastating.

Read further > sea water
pg77 (r22)

▸ *Satellite view showing the eye of a hurricane.*

WORLD'S WORST

Worst weather	Disaster
Most thunder	Tororo, Uganda, Africa averages 250 thundery days a year
Worst hailstorm	a hailstorm in 1888 battered to death 246 people in India
Worst hurricane	Hurricane Flora in 1963 killed 6000 people in the Caribbean

IT'S A FACT

• Hurricanes can be 800 km across, and take 18 hours or more to pass.

• There are about 45 hurricanes every year.

Frontal storms

Between the tropics and polar regions, in most of North America, the stormiest weather is often linked to moving depressions (low pressure zones). Depressions are mostly cold air, but a wedge of warm air intrudes into them and the worst weather occurs along the boundaries of this wedge, called fronts, where the warm air meets the cold air. As a depression moves past, these fronts bring a distinct sequence of weather.

First to arrive is the warm front, where warm air rides up gently over the cold air, bringing steady rain over long periods

After the warm front passes, there is a brief respite, then the cold front arrives. Here the cold air sharply undercuts the warm air, piling up thunderclouds and unleashing short, but heavy, rain showers and stirring up winds

Read further > air pressure
pg79 (j22)

◄◄ STORMS ON JUPITER pg48 (I2) ◄◄

22 23 24 25 26 27 28 29 30 31 32 33 34 35 36 37 38 39

The plant kingdom

THERE ARE millions of different kinds of living things on the Earth, so scientists group them to make it easier to study. One of the largest groups is the plant kingdom, with more than 400,000 different kinds of plants. Some plants are so small that you need a microscope to see them clearly, while the tallest trees can reach over 100 m in height. Plants also vary in how long they live. Some live for just a few hours, while others can live for thousands of years.

▸ *There are many different kinds, or groups, of plants and other plant-based living things. The main groups are shown here.*

Flowering plants

Broadleaved trees and bushes, flowers and herbs

Gingkos

Conifers

Cycads

Ferns

Club mosses

Horsetails

Mosses

Liverworts

Fungi

Lichens

Algae and seaweeds

Microscopic plants

● Plants with flowers

More than 250,000 types of plants grow flowers. They are known as the flowering plant group. Monocotyledons and dicotyledons are the two types of flowering plants (see pg90 [d2]). Many flowers have brightly coloured petals (see pg92 [p9]) to attract insects to pollinate them. Other types use methods such as self-pollination (see pg93 [i27]), or wind pollination (see pg93 [u34]). The flowers make seeds that grow into new plants.

Read further › monocotyledons and dicotyledons / insect pollination
pg90 [d2; j14]; pg92 (k10); pg93 (b29; d2)

►► INSECTS see pg121 (b32) ►►

1 2 3 4 5 6 7 8 9 10 11 12 13 14 15 16 17 18 19

a b c d e f g h i j k l m n o p q r s t u v w

IT'S A FACT

• The plant with the largest flower is the rafflesia, which grows up to 1 m across.

• The welwitschia plant of the southern African scrub has two leaves, each many metres long, which last for hundreds of years.

Plants with cones

Conifers are trees that have scaly or needle-like leaves that they keep all year round. They do not have flowers but grow two types of cone – one makes a yellow dust called pollen (see pg93 [u34]), the other makes seeds when it receives the pollen. The cones that contain the seeds are made from a woody material that has slits in it. When the seeds are ready to leave, the slits open and the seeds fall out.

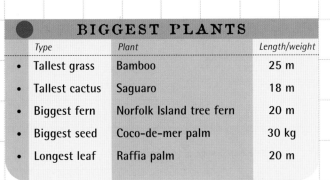
▲ Cones grow near the tips of conifer branches.

Read further > pollen
pg92 (d2)

BIGGEST PLANTS

Type	Plant	Length/weight
Tallest grass	Bamboo	25 m
Tallest cactus	Saguaro	18 m
Biggest fern	Norfolk Island tree fern	20 m
Biggest seed	Coco-de-mer palm	30 kg
Longest leaf	Raffia palm	20 m

Shady plants

Mosses, ferns and liverworts are plants that grow in damp, shady places. They do not make seeds or have vessels to carry water. Mosses grow stalks with swollen tips. The tips make spores, which float away in the air. When a spore lands in damp soil it grows into a new moss plant. Ferns' spores form in button-like swellings on the underside of their fronds (that resemble feathery leaves).

Read further > forest floor
pg99 (h22)

▲ Ferns on a forest floor grow close together, making thick vegetation.

Plants in the sea

Seaweeds grow mainly on rocky shores or underwater close to the coast. They hold on to the rocks to prevent being washed away. The part that holds the seaweed to a rock is called a holdfast, and looks like a root. It grips the rock tightly like a sucker. Seaweeds have tough, leathery fronds (leaves) to stand up to the pounding of the waves. Their bodies are flexible so that they can move with the water currents without breaking.

▸ Seaweeds such as kelp belong to the plant group called algae.

Read further > roots / underwater plants
pg85 (b22); pg89 (b34)

Plant parts

THERE ARE four major parts to a flowering plant: the roots; the stem; the leaves; and the flower. Each plays a vital role in keeping the plant alive. The roots grow into the ground, ensuring the plant does not blow away; the stem contains small tubes that carry water to all parts of the plant; the leaves use the energy from sunlight to make food (*see pg88 [j14]*) and the flower makes seeds from which new plants grow.

Stigma (female) at the top of the carpel is sticky to attract pollen

Anther   Stamen   Stigma

Anther (male) makes pollen

Stem contains many tiny tubes, running from root to stem tip. This supports leaves and flowers, and channels water and minerals up from roots

To scale
1 square = 20 cm across

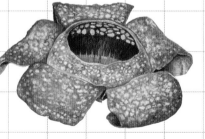

Rafflesia = 100 cm

Leaves use sunlight in a process called photosynthesis to make food – the plant's fuel

Roots grow down into soil or water. They hold the plant in place, preventing it from being blown away and allow it to draw up water and minerals

 Check it out!
• http://www.nhm.ac.uk/science/ projects/fff/

Read further › photosynthesis pg88 (d2; m2)

►► NAMING OF PLANT PARTS pg223 (m22) ►►

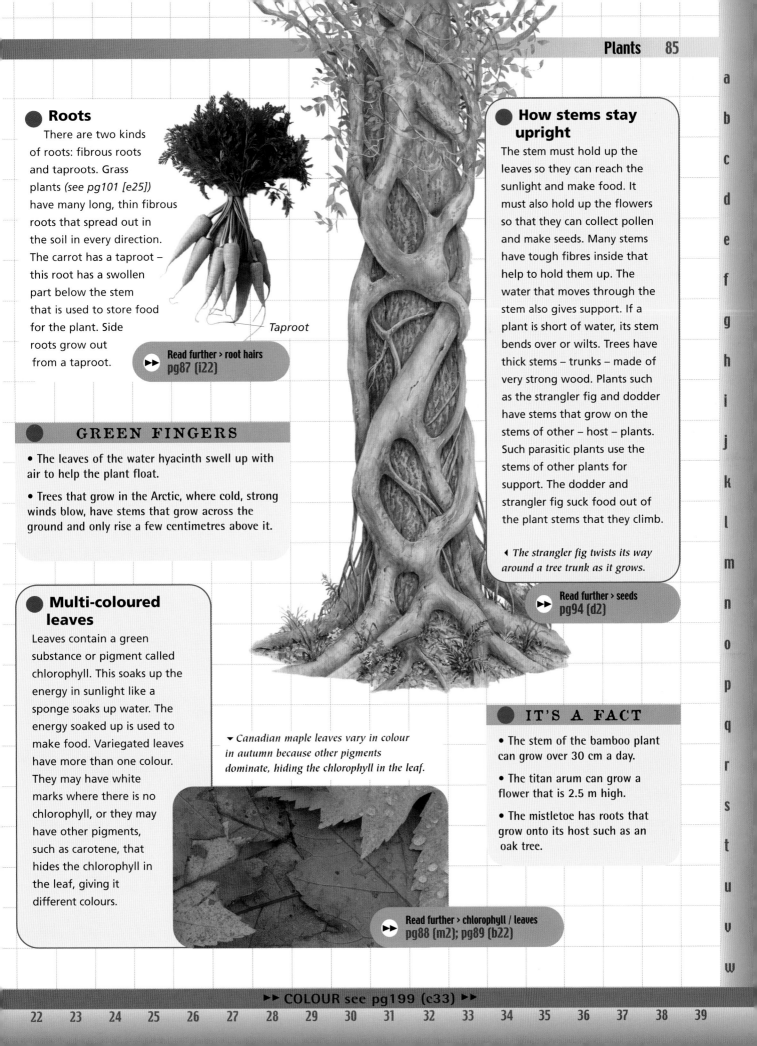

Roots

There are two kinds of roots: fibrous roots and taproots. Grass plants *(see pg101 [e25])* have many long, thin fibrous roots that spread out in the soil in every direction. The carrot has a taproot – this root has a swollen part below the stem that is used to store food for the plant. Side roots grow out from a taproot.

Taproot

Read further > root hairs pg87 (i22)

GREEN FINGERS

• The leaves of the water hyacinth swell up with air to help the plant float.

• Trees that grow in the Arctic, where cold, strong winds blow, have stems that grow across the ground and only rise a few centimetres above it.

Multi-coloured leaves

Leaves contain a green substance or pigment called chlorophyll. This soaks up the energy in sunlight like a sponge soaks up water. The energy soaked up is used to make food. Variegated leaves have more than one colour. They may have white marks where there is no chlorophyll, or they may have other pigments, such as carotene, that hides the chlorophyll in the leaf, giving it different colours.

▼ *Canadian maple leaves vary in colour in autumn because other pigments dominate, hiding the chlorophyll in the leaf.*

Read further > chlorophyll / leaves pg88 (m2); pg89 (b22)

How stems stay upright

The stem must hold up the leaves so they can reach the sunlight and make food. It must also hold up the flowers so that they can collect pollen and make seeds. Many stems have tough fibres inside that help to hold them up. The water that moves through the stem also gives support. If a plant is short of water, its stem bends over or wilts. Trees have thick stems – trunks – made of very strong wood. Plants such as the strangler fig and dodder have stems that grow on the stems of other – host – plants. Such parasitic plants use the stems of other plants for support. The dodder and strangler fig suck food out of the plant stems that they climb.

◄ *The strangler fig twists its way around a tree trunk as it grows.*

Read further > seeds pg94 (d2)

IT'S A FACT

• The stem of the bamboo plant can grow over 30 cm a day.

• The titan arum can grow a flower that is 2.5 m high.

• The mistletoe has roots that grow onto its host such as an oak tree.

Thirsty work

ALL LIVING things need water to stay alive. Nearly three-quarters of a plant is made up of water, and if it loses too much it simply dies. Plants need water to make food, too, so if a plant cannot get enough water it is also in danger of starving to death. The water inside many plants helps to hold up the stem and the leaves so they can reach the sunlight to make food. If they are short of water, the stem collapses and the leaves cannot get the sunlight the plant needs to make food.

Water escapes from leaves as water vapour

● Moving water without energy

Plants do not use any energy in sucking up water or pumping it to their leaves. Water passes into the roots of a plant from the soil. Inside the root, the water is pulled through the plant to the leaves in tiny tubes or xylem (see pg87 [n35]); dissolved food from the leaves to other parts is carried by phloem (see pg87 [o34]). Water that evaporates (transpiration) through holes in the leaves is replaced with more water as it moves up the stem.

▶▶ Read further > roots / stems pg85 (b22; b34)

Water flows up inside stem through tube-like channels called xylem

● IT'S A FACT

• The tip of a root is covered with a cap of slimy cells. The root cap protects the root tips from being worn away as they grow through the ground.

• Air holes in a leaf open during the day and close at night.

▸ The path of water in a rose plant. Water input, flow and loss in a plant is called translocation.

Roots spread out in soil to collect water

Water enters plant through its roots

◀◀ EVAPORATION see pg74 (d13) ◀◀

1   2   3   4   5   6   7   8   9   10   11   12   13   14   15   16   17   18   19

Bugs, grubs and caterpillars feed on leaves

Thicker tubes (xylem) carry water to leaf

● How water escapes

Inside the leaf are air spaces. When water reaches the air holes most of it evaporates and forms a gas called water vapour. When the water vapour evaporates it passes through holes called stomata on the underside of the leaf. More water is drawn up the plant to take its place. If the air outside the leaf is hot and dry, water vapour escapes quickly so the plant needs plenty of water to keep up the supply.

Leaf pores (stomata) where water escapes

Thinner tubes (phloem) carry sap away from leaf

Air spaces in leaf

▲ Microscopic view of holes in a leaf.

● Hairy roots

Near the tip of each root are tiny, delicate hairs. They grow out a short way into the soil and collect water. The water moves along the hair and into the root where it enters a water tube. As the tip of the root grows through the soil, the hairs further back die and new hairs grow at the root tip.

Base of stem

Main root

Secondary root

Branching root tip

◄ Roots grow thickly to take in large amounts of water.

▶▶ Read further › fibrous and taproots pg85 (b22)

GREEN FINGERS

• Leaves are covered in a layer of wax to prevent too much water from being lost or gained.

• The leaves of underwater plants take in water through their surfaces.

● Water carriers

If you break open a celery stalk, you will see fibres sticking out of the end. These fibres are made from groups of tubes *(see pg89 [f30])* that carry water through the plant. Groups of tubes like these are called vessels. Inside the vessels are coils of cellulose. These help to keep the tubes open so that water can always pass along them.

▶▶ Read further › water storage pg101 (b30)

Xylem vessels (tubes) carry water

Growing layer

Phloem vessels (tubes) carry sap

Strong fibres

▶ Stems have many tubes or vessels for carrying food and water.

● Check it out!

• http://www.ars.usda.gov/is/kids

Making food

UNLIKE ANIMALS, plants are able to make their own food. Plants get energy to make food from sunlight. Certain chemicals are needed to make food and the plants get them from the water in the ground and the air around them. When food is made, some of the energy from the sunlight is stored in it. The plants use this energy to keep them alive and growing. The whole process is called photosynthesis, which in Greek means 'building with light'.

Sun's rays carry light energy to leaf

Carbon dioxide is taken from air into leaves

Oxygen is given off from leaves

Stem

Using sunlight

Most plant leaves contain a green chemical called chlorophyll. This traps some of the energy in sunlight. During photosynthesis, plants spread out their leaves to make a large area of the chlorophyll in which the sunlight shines. Once the energy is trapped, it is used to split up water into two chemicals called hydrogen and oxygen. The plant then uses more energy to join the hydrogen with carbon dioxide in the air to make food substances called carbohydrates, mainly sugars and starches. It gives off the oxygen into the air.

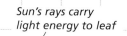

Read further › chlorophyll pg85 (n22)

▸ *Photosynthesis occuring in a tulip plant – changing simple chemicals into food using sunlight.*

GREEN FINGERS

• Huge numbers of algae in the seas make most of the oxygen we breathe, even for those people who live far from the coast.

• Carbohydrates are foods that contain the chemicals carbon, hydrogen and oxygen.

• Two important minerals that plants take from the soil are made from chemicals called nitrogen and phosphorus. Plants use them to make protein foods.

Roots

Bulb

◀◀ CHEMICALS see pg16 (d2) ◀◀

1 2 3 4 5 6 7 8 9 10 11 12 13 14 15 16 17 18 19

Cells in a leaf

Plants are made from tiny blocks of living matter called cells. There are different kinds of cell. The surface of the leaf is made from flat cells, which are transparent to let the sunlight shine through. Inside the leaf are cells that contain the chlorophyll. It is these cells that trap sunlight and make food. On the underside of the leaf are pairs of banana-shaped cells, which form the holes through which water vapour and carbon dioxide pass.

Read further > water vapour
pg87 (b34)

Waterproof wax coat

Palisade cells

Upper layer of leaf

Leaf pores (stomata)

Spongy cells

Leaf veins containing tiny tubes

Lower layer of leaf

◄ *All leaves have veins that carry water.*

Blowing bubbles

The oxygen made when sunlight breaks up water forms a gas inside the leaf. In plants that grow in the air, the oxygen simply mixes with other air gases and passes out through holes in the leaf without being seen. In water-plants, oxygen forms bubbles of gas that escape from the leaves when the plant makes food (photosynthesizes).

▸ *Canadian pondweed oxygenates in water.*

Read further > seaweed
pg83 (k30)

Finding light

Unlike other living things, plants cannot move about to find sunlight but they can grow towards it. Sometimes when plants sprout from their seeds, they are surrounded by other plants that keep them in the shade. Fortunately, the plant stems have tips that are sensitive to light, and they help the plant grow in the right direction.

▲ *While a poppy is growing towards sunlight, the plant uses food that is stored in its bulb.*

Read further > shady plants / bulbs
pg83 (b28); pg99 (i32; h22)

Deadly meat eaters

Carnivorous plants such as this pitcher plant feed on living creatures, including insects and small mammals. The plant attracts the prey with a smell of rotting meat. Once inside the plant's vase-shaped leaves, called pitchers, the victim is dissolved by chemicals known as enzymes.

▸ *The pitcher plant digests and absorbs the bodies of its prey.*

Read further > feeding
pg88 (m2)

▸▸ CARNIVORES see pg130 (d2) ▸▸

22 23 24 25 26 27 28 29 30 31 32 33 34 35 36 37 38 39

a b c d e f g h i j k l m n o p q r s t u v w

Flowering plants

THE FLOWERING plant group contains more than 250,000 different species, including flowers, herbs, grasses, vegetables and trees (but not conifers, which are gymnosperms – they make their seeds in cones). Flowering plants are divided into two main groups: monocotyledons, which have one cotyledon (food store), such as grasses, rushes, lilies and orchids and dicotyledons, which have two cotyledons – most flowers are formed like this. A plant that lives for one year *(see pg96 [m13])* produces a flower at the end of its life. Most plants that live for many years grow flowers once a year. The flower is the part in which seeds are made. Inside each seed is a new plant.

IT'S A FACT

- The Puya raimondii plant lives for 150 years, then grows its first flower and dies.
- Some flowers that grow in the Arctic turn and face the sun all day to absorb as much light as possible and also to keep warm.
- Bougainvillea (a tropical plant) does not have colourful flowers but colourful leaves.

Inside a flower

Flowers come in different shapes and sizes but most have the same parts. The young flower develops inside a bud, protected by green, leaf-like sepals. As it opens, it displays its outermost parts, the ring of petals, which are usually large and colourful to attract insects. Within the petals is a ring of male parts called stamens. Each has a long, thin stalk – the filament – topped by a brush- or bag-like anther, which contains the male reproductive cells inside their pollen grains. At the centre of the flower are the female parts, known as the carpel. This has a sticky pad, called the stigma, on top of a long stalk, called the style, which widens at its base into an ovary. Inside the ovary are the female reproductive cells in their ovules (eggs).

Read further > stamens pg93 (n30)

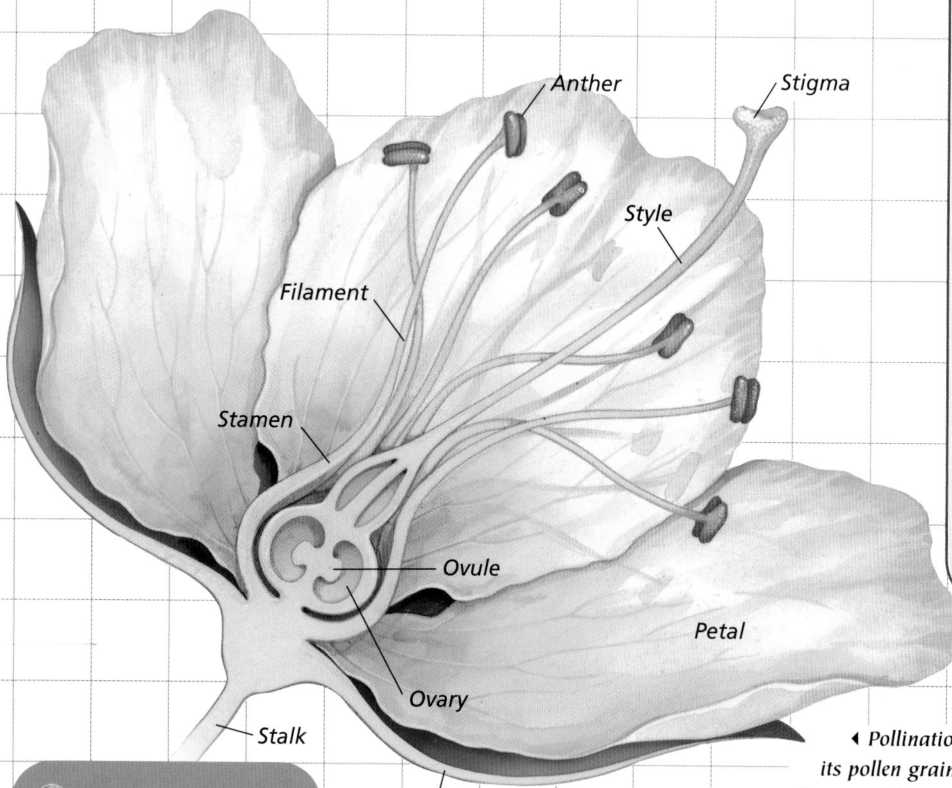

Pollination takes place when the male anther releases its pollen grains. These travel to the female stigma on flowers of the same kind. This allows the male cells in the pollen grains to reach the female cells in the ovules.

Check it out!

- http://www.ars.usda.gov/is/kids/plants/story2/flower.htm

Catkins

Some trees grow groups of flowers called catkins that hang down from a twig. Stamens hang outside the flowers in a catkin. They make pollen that is blown away by the wind. The wind rocks the catkins and stamens to make the plant release its pollen. The willow and hazel trees grow catkins early in the year before they sprout leaves. The oak grows catkins later in the spring after it has sprouted leaves.

▸ *The alder produces long, slim male catkins, and on the same tree, shorter, rounder female catkins.*

▸▸ Read further > wind pollination
pg93 (n30)

GREEN FINGERS

• Many flowers contain both the male reproductive organs (stamens) and the female reproductive organs (ovaries), but some plants have only one or the other.

• Grass flowers do not have petals. The flowers grow together at the top of a stalk.

• The name 'daisy' comes from 'day's eye' since these eye-like flowers open by day and close up at night.

Flowerheads

Some plants grow a large number of small flowers packed tightly together. The small flowers are called florets and they form a disc called a flowerhead. Many plants, such as the daisy and the dandelion, form many flowerheads that fool us into thinking that they are large flowers.

▾ *The wild daisy looks like a single bloom but it actually consists of many flowers. The flowers around the edge have a single petal.*

▸▸ Read further > petals
pg90 (j14)

Flower buds

A flower forms inside a bud *(see pg84 [e15])*. Flowers are very delicate when they are growing so the bud has a tough protective covering made from small leaves called sepals. When the flower bursts out of its bud, the sepals bend backwards and may fall off. The sepals of the tomato stay on the plant right through until the fruit is formed. They form the dark, spidery top of a tomato.

◂ *The sepals of the Iceland poppy protect the bud while it is growing.*

▴ *The sepals form the dark, spidery top of a tomato.*

Pollination

BEFORE A flower can make seeds, it must be pollinated. Pollen consists of fine yellow particles that are made by the stamens. The pollen has to be transferred to the stigma of another flower of the same type. The process by which pollen is moved from one flower to another is called pollination. There are several ways in which pollen can travel: it can be carried by insects or other animals, by wind or by water. Flowers that are pollinated by animals have bright colours to attract insects while wind-pollinated flowers are often dull.

● IT'S A FACT

• Some people are allergic to pollen. When grass plants release their pollen, these people suffer from a condition called hay fever. This can cause many different reactions such as runny eyes and sneezing.

• Bees collect pollen on their back legs to feed to their young.

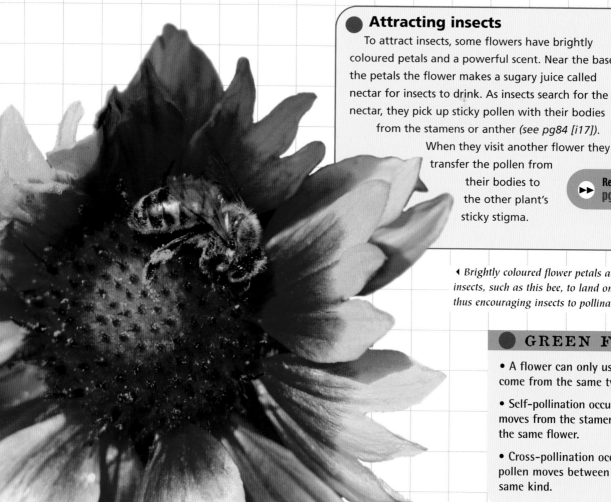

● Attracting insects

To attract insects, some flowers have brightly coloured petals and a powerful scent. Near the base of the petals the flower makes a sugary juice called nectar for insects to drink. As insects search for the nectar, they pick up sticky pollen with their bodies from the stamens or anther (see pg84 [i17]). When they visit another flower they transfer the pollen from their bodies to the other plant's sticky stigma.

► Read further > stamens pg90 (j14)

◄ Brightly coloured flower petals attract insects, such as this bee, to land on flowers, thus encouraging insects to pollinate them.

● GREEN FINGERS

• A flower can only use pollen that has come from the same type of plant.

• Self-pollination occurs when the pollen moves from the stamen to the stigma in the same flower.

• Cross-pollination occurs when the pollen moves between plants of the same kind.

►► INSECT POLLINATION see pg139 (j31) ►►

1 2 3 4 5 6 7 8 9 10 11 12 13 14 15 16 17 18 19

Bee orchids

Some plants, such as the bee orchid, can pollinate themselves if no insect visits them. The bee orchid's petals are shaped to look and smell like a female bee to attract male bees. But if no bees come along, the orchid can bend over to pollinate itself.

Spiky pollen

Flowers that are pollinated by animals make a small amount of spiky pollen. The spikes help the pollen stick to the hairs on the bodies of passing insects. The spikes hold the pollen in place as the insect flies between flowers. When the insect brushes against a sticky stigma, the pollen is pulled off.

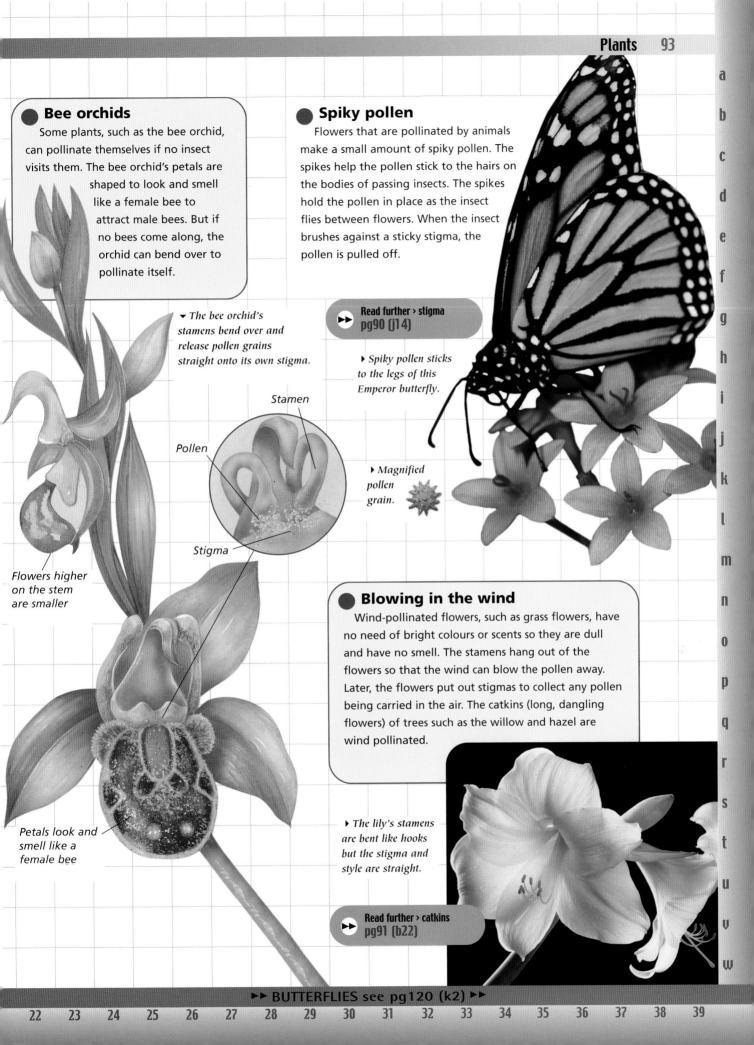

▼ The bee orchid's stamens bend over and release pollen grains straight onto its own stigma.

Read further > stigma
pg90 (j14)

▶ Spiky pollen sticks to the legs of this Emperor butterfly.

Stamen

Pollen

▶ Magnified pollen grain.

Stigma

Flowers higher on the stem are smaller

Blowing in the wind

Wind-pollinated flowers, such as grass flowers, have no need of bright colours or scents so they are dull and have no smell. The stamens hang out of the flowers so that the wind can blow the pollen away. Later, the flowers put out stigmas to collect any pollen being carried in the air. The catkins (long, dangling flowers) of trees such as the willow and hazel are wind pollinated.

Petals look and smell like a female bee

▶ The lily's stamens are bent like hooks but the stigma and style are straight.

Read further > catkins
pg91 (b22)

►► BUTTERFLIES see pg120 (k2) ►►

Germination

INSIDE A seed is a tiny plant or embryo waiting to grow. The seed also contains a store of food to help the plant grow. When the seed leaves the parent plant, it is usually dry. This protects the seed from mould and keeps it light in weight. A lightweight seed is able to travel further and land on ground where there is room for it to grow. When the seed settles in the soil, it takes in water, swells up and breaks open so that the new plant can grow out. This process of sprouting is called germination.

● Speeding up sprouting

When tiny plants start to grow, they change stored food in the seeds into substances that build their root, stem and leaves. The speed at which these changes take place is determined by heat. If the seeds are kept in warm conditions such as a greenhouse, the changes take place quickly and the seeds soon sprout. Seeds in cool conditions take longer to sprout. Some seeds, such as those of the ironbark tree, need to be scorched by wildfire before they will germinate.

▶▶ Read further › food
pg88 (m2)

‣ Gardeners try to mix seeds that flower at different times so the garden is always full of colour.

● Seed needs

Not all seeds germinate in the same way. Coconut palm trees grow on tropical beaches and the coconuts fall and germinate on the beach. They can also fall into the sea, sometimes travelling for 2000 km in different ocean currents before washing up on another warm beach, where they may sprout and grow into an coconut palm.

▶ Coconuts are the fruit of the coconut palm tree. The seed has a hollow centre that contains a sweet-tasting milk. The seed is contained in a brown, woody shell called a husk.

Check it out!

● http://www.bbc.co.uk/nature/plants/calendar/apr.shtml

▶▶ ZEBRA see pg106 (n13) ▶▶

| 1 | 2 | 3 | 4 | 5 | 6 | 7 | 8 | 9 | 10 | 11 | 12 | 13 | 14 | 15 | 16 | 17 | 18 | 19 |

a
b
c
d
e
f
g
h
i
j
k
l
m
n
o
p
q
r
s
t
u
v
w

IT'S A FACT

• A seed does not always sprout as soon as it forms. It may spend some time before germination, being inactive or dormant.

• The young plant that grows out of a seed is called a seedling.

• The first parts of a seedling that grow are the tips of the shoot and root.

Keeping growing

When a new plant has used up the food store in its seed, it must find another source of food. The root obtains water and minerals, growing strong enough to hold the plant in place. The shoot grows towards the light so that the first leaves can make food.

▶ *Plants can even get all their needs – sunlight and water – in a crack in a pavement as rainwater carrying minerals seeps in.*

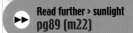
Read further > sunlight
pg89 (m22)

Stages in sprouting

An embryo inside a seed contains a food store (cotyledon), which is protected by the tough, outer casing (testa). The cotyledon then moves to the tiny plant and nourishes it, making the plant grow. As the plant increases in size, the seed case breaks open. The root is the first part to appear and it grows downwards. Later, the tiny shoots appear and grow upwards. In the bean seed shown here the food store stays underground and the shoot makes new leaves above ground.

GREEN FINGERS

• In the sunflower seed, the food store rises up through the soil on the tip of the shoot to become the first pair of leaves.

• If you plant a seed upside down, the root will still grow downwards and the shoot will still grow upwards. They always grow from the seed in the right direction.

Read further > cotyledons
pg90 (d2)

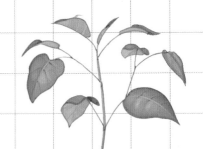

Testa (outer casing)

Cotyledon (food store)

Seed in its tough case (testa) may lie dormant until conditions for growth are right

Seed sends a root down and a shoot up

Shoot opens its first leaves

Stem and roots grow longer, and plant soon begins to grow new leaves

▶▶ GENES see pg234 (d2) ▶▶

22 23 24 25 26 27 28 29 30 31 32 33 34 35 36 37 38 39

Cycles of life

EVERY PLANT has a life cycle. It begins when the seed first germinates, then it grows and forms flowers that are pollinated, which in turn produce their own seeds. Then the cycle begins all over again. Some plants complete their life cycle in a few weeks – ephemeral plants; others repeat their cycles for hundreds of years – perennial plants. Plants that complete their cycle in one year are annuals. Those that complete their cycle in two years are biennial.

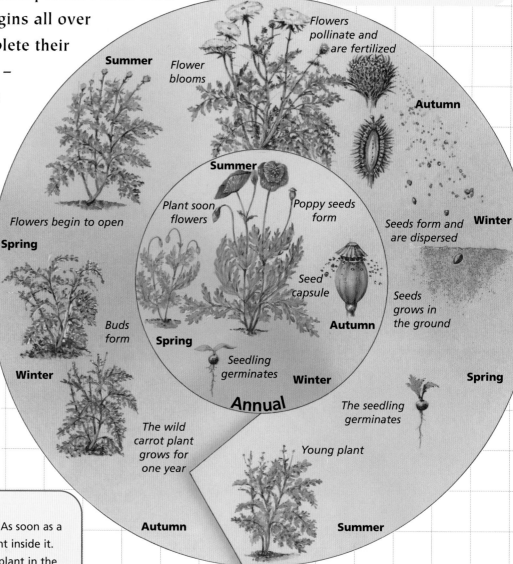

▶ *Annual plants complete their life cycles, from seed to flower to seed again, in one year. In temperate (dry) lands, most of the growth occurs during spring, with pollination in early summer and seed production and growth during spring.*

● **Annuals**

Annual plants live for one year. As soon as a seed forms, it has a tiny living plant inside it. The seed may fall from its parent plant in the autumn and lie all winter in the ground. The following spring the tiny plant bursts out of the seed and grows steadily for a few months. Finally it makes flowers, and after its seeds have formed and spread, the plant dies.

▶▶ **Read further › seeds** pg95 (b22)

▲ *Biennial plants take two years to grow from seed to a mature plant. The part-grown plant must be able to survive the harsh conditions of the cold or dry season, then continue its development the year after to flower and make seeds.*

▶▶ EARLY GROWTH IN HUMANS pg175 (b34) ▶▶

| 1 | 2 | 3 | 4 | 5 | 6 | 7 | 8 | 9 | 10 | 11 | 12 | 13 | 14 | 15 | 16 | 17 | 18 | 19 |

Ephemerals

The seed of the shepherd's purse plant sprouts soon after it lands in the soil. Such plants that grows quickly, flower, set seeds and die in a few weeks are called ephemeral plants. There are many life cycles of the shepherd's purse, one after the other throughout the year. This means that shepherd's purse seeds are being spread around at regular intervals so there is a better chance that some may find a place to grow.

▶▶ Read further › wind pollination pg93 (n30)

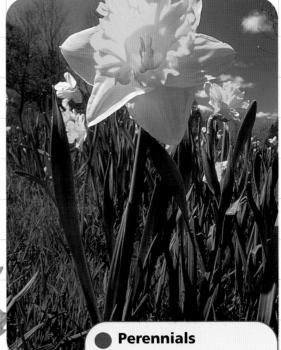

▲ Daffodils are perennials – they have bulbs and bloom every year.

Perennials

When a perennial plant has finished flowering, it may lose some of its parts that are above ground (the flower) but the roots live on underground during the winter. The new shoots sprout the following spring. Perennials, such as tulips and daffodils, have a thick underground food store, called a bulb, that stays alive during the winter when the rest of the plant has died away.

▶▶ Read further › exploding flowers pg101 (o30)

Biennials

Biennials have life cycles that take two years to complete. In the first year, or growth season, the seed sprouts and the plant grows. During this time the leaves make plenty of food, which is stored in the plant. In the second growth season biennial plants use the stored food to help them grow again, bloom with flowers and produce seeds before dying.

▶▶ Read further › biennial roots pg85 (b22)

▲ In the first year of their life, beetroots develop leaves and a fleshy, red root – they are harvested before the next year.

GREEN FINGERS

• Ephemerals (short-lived plants), such as chickweed and groundsel, can take over a bare patch of soil quickly and become weeds (plants growing in the wrong place).

• A potato plant grows underground stems, which swell up with stored food to form tubers, called potatoes. Each stem can grow into another plant the following year.

🔍 Check it out!

• http://www.bbc.co.uk/gardening/plants

▶▶ FOOD FOR GROWTH IN HUMANS pg164 (d2) ▶▶

a b c d e f g h i j k l m n o p q r s t u v w

Forest life

W HEN TREES grow together in large
groups they form forests. There
are three main types of forest: coniferous,
temperate and tropical rainforests
with broad-leaved trees. Each kind
of forest grows in different places
around the world, depending on
weather conditions. When
trees grow close together,
such as in a rainforest, the
leaves on the branches stop
most of the light reaching the forest
floor. Plants that live on the ground
have adapted to surviving in the
shade beneath the trees.

*Emergent
layer*

Canopy

● Tropical rainforests

Rainforests grow in the hot, wet
weather conditions around the
Equator – the nearest part of the Earth
to the Sun. The trees in a rainforest are
mostly broad-leaved, evergreen trees.
Most of the trees grow up to 30 m
above the ground and their branches
lock together to form a canopy. Many
small plants, called epiphytic plants,
such as orchids, ferns and bromeliads,
live on the branches of rainforest trees.
They have short roots to hold them in
place and gather the water they need
in cups made from their leaves.

►► Read further › roots
pg85 (b22)

Understorey

Undergrowth

Forest floor

◄◄ EQUATOR see pg62 (p2) ◄◄

1   2   3   4   5   6   7   8   9   10   11   12   13   14   15   16   17   18   19

Temperate forests

Temperate forests grow where summers are warm and winters are cool. They are found in parts of North America, Europe, China, Australia and Japan. Trees in temperate forests lose their leaves in winter. Therefore, in spring, before new leaves grow, light reaches the forest floor giving flowering plants a chance to flower.

Read further > sunlight
pg89 (m22)

▲ Bluebells bloom on the forest floor before the trees grow new leaves in spring.

▼ Coniferous forests grow for hundreds of kilometres in northern parts of North America, Europe and Asia, usually high up on mountainsides.

Coniferous forests

Coniferous forests grow where the summers are short and warm but the winters are long and cold. As the trees grow very close and they keep their leaves all year round, very little light reaches the forest floor so only small plants such as mosses can grow. The soil in coniferous forests usually freezes once a year, making it difficult for plants to obtain water.

Read further > mosses
pg83 (b28)

GREEN FINGERS

- One 23-hectare area of Malaysian rainforest has 375 species of tree with trunks thicker than 91 cm.
- The floor of a coniferous forest is covered in a thick layer of dead leaves because they take a long time to rot in the cold, dark conditions.
- Rainforest trees are covered with epiphytes – plants whose roots never reach the soil but take water from the air.

Can forests survive?

Forests provide people with large amounts of wood. Every second, an area of rainforest the size of a soccer pitch is cut down (logged) for timber. Within the next 100 years all the rainforests could be destroyed. Planting more trees and recycling paper materials are two ways that can help rainforests to survive.

▶ Logging can destroy whole hillsides in as little as one day.

Check it out!

- http://www.woodland-trust.org.uk/

Read further > rainforests
pg98 (o2)

►► HABITAT DESTRUCTION see pg148 (o2) ►►

Grasslands and desert

GRASSLAND FORMS where there is not enough rain for trees to grow. There is usually a long, dry season and a short season, when it rains or even snows. In the dry season, plants and seeds may lie dormant (asleep), but when rain falls the grassland briefly blooms with green leaves and brightly coloured flowers. In hot countries, during the dry season, plants face the threat of fire, but the fire does not destroy the roots so the grass can grow back again. A desert is a place where very little rain falls: there may be nine months without rain, then three months with a tiny amount. Deserts can be very hot in the daytime and very cold at night so it is difficult for plants to thrive without the mineral-rich soil and water that they need to survive.

Read further > rainforests
pg98 (o29)

IT'S A FACT

• The continent with the largest area of desert is Asia.

• The world's biggest desert is the Sahara in north Africa. It is 5000 km across at its widest point and up to 2250 km from north to south.

The savannah

The savannah is a huge area of grassland that covers most of Africa. It covers a much larger area than the rainforest or the deserts. The tallest grass on the savannah is elephant grass, which reaches 3 m in height. Some trees, such as the acacia and the baobab, which can store water and have fire-resistant trunks, grow in small numbers on the grassy plains.

▼ Acacia trees provide a small amount of protection for herds of zebra in the blazing sun and drying winds of the African savannah.

Check it out!
• http://hort.purdue.edu/ext/prairie_wildflowers.html

▾ *Prairies contain a wide variety of grass including cottonwood, switch grass, needle grass, panicgrass, asters, Idaho fescue and big bluestem grass.*

Prairies and steppes

Large areas of temperate grassland in North America are called prairies – in Russia they are called steppes. Here there is not enough rain all year round to allow trees to grow but hundreds of grasses, crops and shrubs thrive.

▶▶ Read further › forests
pg99 (h22)

GREEN FINGERS

• Joshua trees, native to North American deserts, can grow to about 9 m high.

• A large cactus can take in 1 tonne of water in a day after it has rained.

• The biggest cactus is the saguaro of southern Arizona, southeast California and northwest Mexico. It can grow up to 20 m tall and 1 m thick.

Plants like pebbles

Pebble plants grow in deserts in southern Africa. They develop thick, round leaves, coloured like stones and pebbles, that camouflage and protect them against animals that might eat them.

▶▶ Read further › desert plants
pg101 (b30)

Cacti

The largest plants in most deserts are succulents. Cacti are a particular type of succulent that grow mostly in North and South American deserts. Down the sides of the cactus are grooves that fill out when it takes in water. Cacti do not have broad leaves to make food because they would lose too much water; instead they use their thick, green, fleshy stems as leaves to store water and convert sunlight into food. A waxy layer on the stem reduces water evaporation.

▶▶ Read further › path of water
pg86 (m2)

▲ *Needle-like spikes on the cactus stem stop animals from biting their way into the plant to reach water.*

Exploding seedheads

Some plants cannot store water so they die when the desert dries up. Their seedheads, packed with seeds, stand on dry stalks until the next rain. When the water soaks into the flowerhead it makes parts twist and turn so that the flowerhead explodes and disperses its seeds. The seeds take in water and sprout quickly to make new plants.

▶▶ Read further › flowerheads
pg91 (b34)

▶ *After rain, cactus flowers bloom briefly, adding splashes of colour to the desert.*

All kinds of animals

THE WORLD is full of animals. They live on top of the highest mountains, at the bottom of the deepest seas, in tropical rainforests and in the cold, icy wastes of the polar regions. Some animals are so weird and so different from those we keep at home or see on farms or at the zoo that we might wonder whether they are animals at all. The study of animals is vitally important – to save wildlife and conserve the wonder and beauty of the natural world for the future, and to improve our farming and food supplies for an increasing world population.

► Read further > adapting
pg105 (d22)

● What is an animal?

Animals come in many different shapes and sizes, and live in a wide variety of habitats. So what defining features do they share that make them all animals? Like plants, their bodies are made of many microscopic parts called cells. However, unlike most plants, they take food into their bodies by eating it and breaking it down, rather than by building it up from simple minerals. They sense or detect features of their surroundings such as light or sound. Most animals can move about at some stage in their lives.

▼ *Different parts of the world have their own distinctive types of animal, which adapt, survive and reproduce in various habitats.*

● IT'S A FACT

• The biggest animals are 1 million million times larger than the smallest ones.

• More than 999 out of every 1000 kinds of animals that ever lived, such as dinosaurs, died out long ago.

• The total number of kinds, or species, of animals is probably more than 10 million.

►► ANIMAL SENSES see pg136 (d2) ►►

1 2 3 4 5 6 7 8 9 10 11 12 13 14 15 16 17 18 19

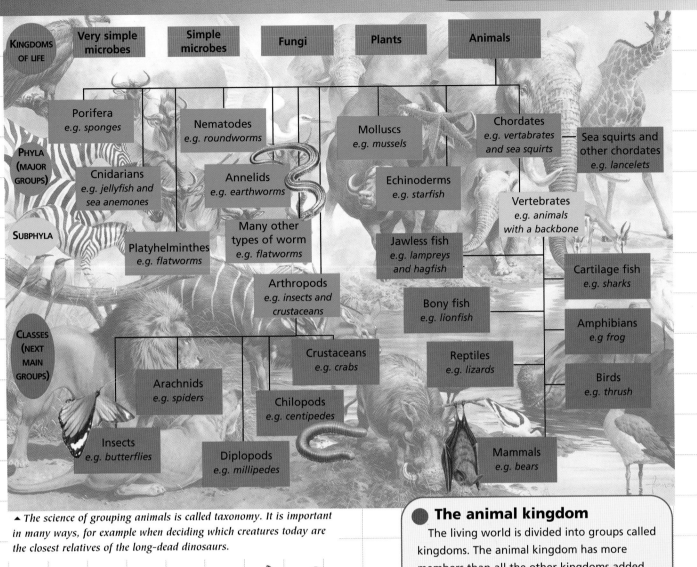

KINGDOMS OF LIFE	Very simple microbes	Simple microbes	Fungi	Plants	Animals

PHYLA (MAJOR GROUPS)

Porifera *e.g. sponges*

Nematodes *e.g. roundworms*

Molluscs *e.g. mussels*

Chordates *e.g. vertebrates and sea squirts*

Sea squirts and other chordates *e.g. lancelets*

Cnidarians *e.g. jellyfish and sea anemones*

Annelids *e.g. earthworms*

Echinoderms *e.g. starfish*

Vertebrates *e.g. animals with a backbone*

SUBPHYLA

Platyhelminthes *e.g. flatworms*

Many other types of worm *e.g. flatworms*

Jawless fish *e.g. lampreys and hagfish*

Cartilage fish *e.g. sharks*

Arthropods *e.g. insects and crustaceans*

Bony fish *e.g. lionfish*

Amphibians *e.g frog*

CLASSES (NEXT MAIN GROUPS)

Crustaceans *e.g. crabs*

Reptiles *e.g. lizards*

Birds *e.g. thrush*

Arachnids *e.g. spiders*

Chilopods *e.g. centipedes*

Insects *e.g. butterflies*

Diplopods *e.g. millipedes*

Mammals *e.g. bears*

▲ *The science of grouping animals is called taxonomy. It is important in many ways, for example when deciding which creatures today are the closest relatives of the long-dead dinosaurs.*

● Animal species

Larger groups of animals are divided into smaller groups, until a single kind or type is reached – the species. Examples of different species within larger groups are the red fox, tiger, golden eagle, housefly and giant squid *(see pg105 [f35])*. A species is not defined by its appearance, colour or size, but by breeding. If animals can breed together they are members of the same species. If they cannot breed together they are from different species.

▶▶ Read further > golden eagle
pg110 (g14)

● The animal kingdom

The living world is divided into groups called kingdoms. The animal kingdom has more members than all the other kingdoms added together. Zoologists (scientists who study animals) divide the kingdom into main groups called phyla (singular is phylum), by comparing important body features. This means the phyla are unequal in size. For example, the spoonworm phylum has 150 different kinds, which live on the seabed, while the arthropod phylum has millions of kinds including insects, crabs, spiders, centipedes and millipedes. Vertebrates are a major group, which includes mammals, fish, birds, reptiles and amphibians: all other animals are invertebrates.

▶▶ Read further > insects
pg118 (d2)

▲ *Red foxes can breed with each other, which means they are all members of the same species: Vulpes vulpes.*

Mammals 1

MAMMALS ARE the most familiar class of animals, because human beings are members. Typical mammals have a body covering of fur or hair, are warm-blooded (their body temperature stays at the same high level despite changes in the surroundings) and feed their babies on milk made by the mother in body parts called mammary glands. However, there are exceptions. The biggest mammals of all, such as whales in the sea and elephants on land, have almost no hair or fur. And some mammals go into a long winter sleep called hibernation, when their body temperatures fall to just above freezing.

Insect eaters

The insectivores (insect eaters) are mostly smallish mammals such as moles, shrews and hedgehogs. They have small, sharp teeth and eat insects, grubs, slugs, worms and similar juicy creatures. There are about 365 species, including the rat-like tenrecs from Africa, and the rare, long-nosed solenodons that live on some Caribbean islands.

▲ *There are 12 species of hedgehogs and most have sharp spines like this European hedgehog – but the desert hedgehog has coarse fur.*

▶▶ **Read further › insects / worms**
pg118 (d2); pg125 (b33)

Bears

The eight kinds of bears are members of the small mammal family, ursidae. Their foods differ greatly. Most bears eat large amounts of plant foods, such as leaves, fruits, berries and nuts, as well as meat. The giant panda eats almost nothing but bamboo. Yet the diet of the polar bear of the far north consists almost entirely of meat. It rivals the brown or grizzly bear as the biggest land predator, weighing over half a tonne and standing 3 m tall.

▸ *Polar bears are almost pure white, while their close cousins, the American black bears, are mostly black.*

▶▶ **Read further › biggest predator**
pg105 (e22)

▶▶ HUMANS see pg150 (d2) ▶▶

1 2 3 4 5 6 7 8 9 10 11 12 13 14 15 16 17 18 19

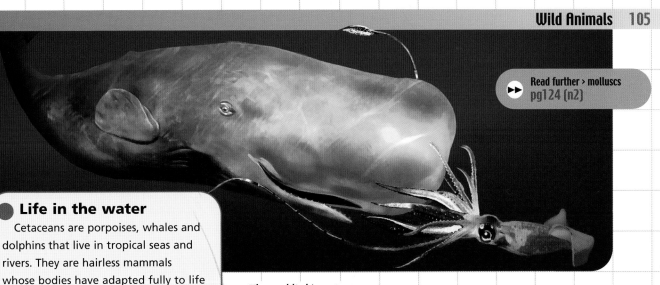

Read further › molluscs
pg124 (n2)

Life in the water

Cetaceans are porpoises, whales and dolphins that live in tropical seas and rivers. They are hairless mammals whose bodies have adapted fully to life in the water. Their front limbs are flippers, their back limbs are missing and their tails have wide flaps on either side, called flukes, for swimming. There are about 83 species of cetaceans and they are all carnivorous – they eat other animals. These great whales consume vast amounts of krill – tiny, shrimp-like creatures, while sperm whales prey on large fish and seals.

▲ *The world's biggest predator, the 50-tonne sperm whale, attacks the largest invertebrate animal, the giant squid.*

Meat-eating mammals

Any animal that eats mainly meat is known as a carnivore. Confusingly, there is also a group of mammals officially called the Carnivora. It includes dogs, foxes, jackals, bears, raccoons, weasels and stoats, civets and linsangs, hyaenas and cats.

Read further › sharp teeth
pg117 (b22)

Bats

Bats are the second-largest mammal group, with almost 1000 species. Most bats are small, live in tropical rainforests and fly at night to catch gnats, moths and similar flying insects. The flying foxes or fruit bats, with about 175 species, are bigger and eat plant foods such as fruits, seeds and sap. A bat's front limbs are actually wings that have a thin, stretchy membrane or layer, attached to very long finger bones.

Read further › flying insects
pg118 (h16)

▲ *Hyaenas have keen senses to track their victims, fierce claws and long, sharp teeth – canines – to stab and rip prey.*

ANIMAL FACTS

• The biggest mammal, and the biggest animal of all, is the blue whale. It is 30 m in length and weighs more than 100 tonnes.

• The smallest mammals are shrews on the ground and bats in the air. The pygmy shrew has a head and body smaller than the human thumb. The hog-nosed bat's wings are each about as long as a human finger.

• The longest-lived mammals include the rare, seldom-seen beaked whales – some may be more than 150 years old.

▸ *Fruit bats rest with their wings wrapped around their bodies.*

Mammals 2

IT'S A FACT

• There are more than 1650 species of rodents: this is the largest group of mammals.

• The rabbit and hare group, lagomorphs, has 80 species.

• The ungulates or hoofed mammals number about 245 species.

MOST MAMMALS are herbivores – plant eaters. The largest plant-eating group, rodents, make up 40 per cent of the mammal group. They include rats, mice, squirrels, beavers, porcupines and guinea pigs, and their cousins from South America, known as cavies. Rabbits and hares look like rodents because of their long front teeth but they belong to a different mammal order known as lagomorphs. Another large plant-eating order is the ungulates or hoofed mammals. These are divided into two types: the odd-toed ungulates – with one or three toes – such as horses, zebras, asses, tapirs and rhinos, and the even-toed ungulates – with two or four toes – such as pigs, peccaries, hippos, camels, deer, giraffes, antelopes, gazelles, cattle, sheep and goats.

Rodents

Rodents live all over the world, in almost every land habitat. One species, the beaver, can swim underwater for almost 1 km, holding its breath and keeping its nostrils and ears shut. The rodent's special feature is its front teeth, called incisors. These are very long with straight, sharp edges like chisels. They keep growing through life, so rodents can gnaw hard foods like nuts and roots, without wearing away their teeth.

▲ *Beavers gnaw through tree trunks in minutes with their long, ever-growing incisor teeth.*

▶ *Most ungulates, like zebra, are fast runners. They are able to outrun most predators from a young age.*

▶▶ **Read further › underwater**
pg109 (m31); pg111 (s31)

Odd-toed ungulates

Horses, zebras, rhinos and tapirs are called odd-toed ungulates because they have an odd number of toes per foot, each capped with a hard hoof. Horses and zebras have just one toe per foot and their legs are long and slim for running in open habitats such as grasslands. They are grazing animals, and feed mainly on grass that they chew with their powerful jaws and cheek teeth.

▶▶ **Read further › ungulates**
pg107 (b22)

Even-toed ungulates

The bison is an even-toed ungulate or 'cloven hoofed' mammal. Herds on the North American prairies were almost wiped out by European settlers in the 1500s but have since recovered some of their numbers. European bison are slightly smaller and live in thick forests, mainly in Poland and Belarussia.

▶▶ Read further › biggest mammal
pg105 (r32)

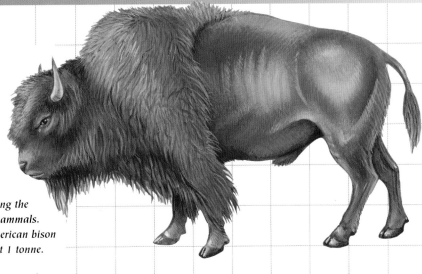

▸ *Bison are among the biggest hoofed mammals. A large male American bison can weigh almost 1 tonne.*

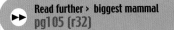

◂ *Dromedary (one-humped) camels have broad feet to keep them steady on desert sand and long eyelashes to protect them in sand storms.*

Humps store fat

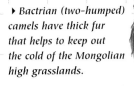

▸ *Bactrian (two-humped) camels have thick fur that helps to keep out the cold of the Mongolian high grasslands.*

Trunk and tusk

Elephants are the largest land mammals. A large, male African savannah elephant can stand 4 m tall and weigh more than 8 tonnes. All elephants are plant-eaters. They may look like hoofed mammals but they have their own order, called proboscidea.

▾ *Elephant tusks are greatly enlarged upper incisor teeth and the trunks are a very long combination of upper lip and nose.*

▶▶ Read further › herbivores
pg109 (e31)

Camel humps

Both species of camel – the one-humped dromedary of Africa, the Middle East and Australia, and the two-humped Bactrian of Central Asia – have been domesticated (bred by people) for milk, meat, hides and carrying. The camel group also includes the camel's South American relations – the guanaco and vicuna in the wild, and their domesticated descendants, the llama and alpaca.

ANIMAL FACTS

• The Sumatran rhinoceros, which has red coloured hair is a relative of the woolly rhinoceros of the last ice age.

• For many years it was believed there were only two types of elephant: African and Asian. But there are three.

• There are two species of African elephant: the African savannah elephant, large with curved tusks, prefers open country; the African forest elephant, slightly smaller with straighter tusks, likes thick woodland. Being different species, they cannot breed with each other.

◂◂ SAVANNAH see pg100 (i15) ◂◂

Mammals 3

SOME GROUPS of mammals have many members while others have very few. The marsupial group consists of about 290 species, including kangaroos and Virginia opossums, while the tubulidentata has only one living species – the aardvark from Africa. There are only four species of dugongs and manatees, also known as sirenians or 'sea cows'. These bulky plant eaters of shallow coastal waters have front limbs like paddles and flipper-shaped tails. Another group, the monotremes or egg-laying mammals, has just five species, including the duck-billed platypus and echidnas.

IT'S A FACT

• The primate group includes lemurs, monkeys, and humans, and numbers about 350 species.

• There are only two species of colugos, or flying lemurs, which live in Southeast Asian tropical forests and eat mainly plants.

▼ *The Virginia opossum may have 18 babies in one litter. After growing in her pouch for 6-8 weeks, they ride clinging to her back.*

Cows of the sea

Sirenians are the only sea mammals that eat mainly plants, although they may occasionally eat small fish for added nutrients. Their diet of seagrass, seaweeds and other aquatic vegetation is low in nourishment, so a sirenian may need to consume up to one-quarter of its body weight each day. Their closest mammal cousins are probably not seals or whales, but the elephants and hoofed mammals.

►► **Read further › hoofed mammals** pg107 (b22)

▲ *Manatees weigh more than half a tonne. They have round, spoon-like tails to help them move through the water.*

Marsupials

Marsupials live mainly in Australia, with some species found in South America and Southeast Asia. Only one kind, the Virginia opossum, has spread to North America. Many smaller marsupials resemble other types of mammals – there are marsupial mice and rats, shrews and cats, and even marsupial anteaters and moles.

►► **Read further › marsupials** pg107 (e31)

Check it out!

• http://www.enchantedlearning.com/subjects/mammals/classification/Ungulates.shtml

►► ELEPHANTS see pg146 (q2) ►►

1 2 3 4 5 6 7 8 9 10 11 12 13 14 15 16 17 18 19

Powerful digger

The aardvark emerges at night and may travel more than 20 km in search of ant nests and termite mounds. It has a variety of common names, such as earth-pig, African anteater and ant-bear. Its closest mammal relations are probably the hoofed mammal group, ungulates. The aardvark's teeth are among the most unusual of any mammal: it has no front incisors or canines but cheek teeth or molars that grow continuously. In mammals, the number and types of teeth are important in working out which of the groups are most closely related.

▶▶ Read further › ungulates
pg106 (n13)

▲ The aardvark has a long, sensitive snout to sniff out food in the dark. The nostrils are surrounded by fine hairs that keep out dust as the aardvark digs into its prey's nest.

ANIMAL FACTS

• The primate mammals include the lesser apes – nine species of gibbons – all in Southeast Asia. They swing through trees, using their very long, powerful arms and hook-like hands. The largest gibbon, the siamang, is one of the loudest of any mammals, almost equalling the South American howler monkey – the noisiest of all land animals.

• The largest meat-eating marsupial, the Tasmanian devil, has a fierce and aggressive reputation, but it rarely gets into fights with others of its kind. It eats many small animals from insects to possums. Some people keep Tasmanian devils as tame, friendly pets.

▸ A baby kangaroo is called a joey. It is as small as a grape when it is born. After six months in the pouch it is ready to leave for short periods.

Bounding along

Marsupials are pouched mammals because in most types, the female has a pocket-like pouch of skin on her front. Her baby is born at a tiny, undeveloped stage and crawls into the pouch, where it feeds on her milk and grows over many weeks. Kangaroos and wallabies are large plant eaters native to Australia. They bound along on their two enormous back legs, using their thick tail for balance.

▶▶ Read further › Australian emu
pg111 (g22)

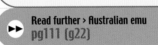

▲ Kangaroos often play fight with each other in groups.

Egg-laying mammals

One of the most extraordinary mammals is the platypus of Australia. It has a duck-like beak or bill, a flat tail and webbed feet like a beaver. It is one of the few mammals that does not give birth to babies, but lays eggs in a deep burrow. The eggs hatch after about ten days and the mother then feeds her babies on milk, as do other mammals. The four species of echidnas or 'spiny anteaters' of Australia and Southeast Asia are also egg-layers.

▶▶ Read further › beaver
pg106 (p2)

▸ The platypus feeds in streams and pools on small creatures. Its beak is very sensitive to touch and it can feed at night, just by feeling for food.

Birds

BIRDS ARE the only creatures with feathers. These protect the bird and form a large, light wing surface for flying. Feathers also help regulate a bird's body heat – like mammals, birds are warm-blooded. Some birds have feathers for camouflage (blending into the surroundings), while others have brightly coloured feathers to warn off predators or attract a mate. All birds have a beak, which is made of a strong, horn-like substance. The beak is shaped to eat certain foods. All birds also have scaly legs with clawed toes, and breed by laying eggs, usually in a nest made by the parents.

Birds of prey

Some of the largest and fiercest birds are raptors, or birds of prey. There are more than 300 species including eagles, condors, vultures, hawks, buzzards, kites, falcons, harriers and kestrels. They have powerful toes with sharp claws called talons to seize prey, and a pointed, hooked beak to tear off lumps of flesh. Most have big eyes and hunt by sight.

Read further › seizing prey pg105 (e22)

◀ *Most parent birds, such as the golden eagle, care for their chicks (babies) and bring them food. These larger birds look after their chicks for longer. A young eagle does not leave its nest for about ten weeks.*

BIRDS	
Widest wingspan	*Width*
Wandering albatross	3.6 m
Marabou stork	3.2 m
Andean condor	3 m
Swan	2.8 m

Check it out!
• http://www.enchantedlearning.com/subjects/birds/Allaboutbirds.html
• http://www.idahoptv.dialogue4kids/birdsofprey/bird.html

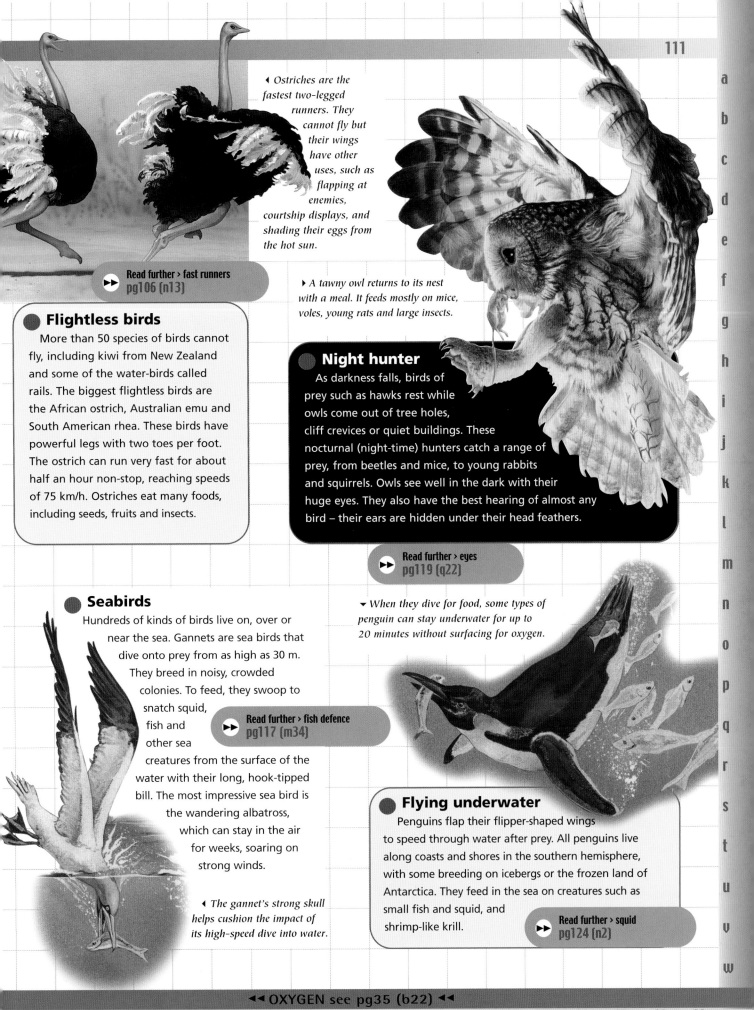

◄ *Ostriches are the fastest two-legged runners. They cannot fly but their wings have other uses, such as flapping at enemies, courtship displays, and shading their eggs from the hot sun.*

▶ *A tawny owl returns to its nest with a meal. It feeds mostly on mice, voles, young rats and large insects.*

Read further › fast runners pg106 (n13)

Flightless birds

More than 50 species of birds cannot fly, including kiwi from New Zealand and some of the water-birds called rails. The biggest flightless birds are the African ostrich, Australian emu and South American rhea. These birds have powerful legs with two toes per foot. The ostrich can run very fast for about half an hour non-stop, reaching speeds of 75 km/h. Ostriches eat many foods, including seeds, fruits and insects.

Night hunter

As darkness falls, birds of prey such as hawks rest while owls come out of tree holes, cliff crevices or quiet buildings. These nocturnal (night-time) hunters catch a range of prey, from beetles and mice, to young rabbits and squirrels. Owls see well in the dark with their huge eyes. They also have the best hearing of almost any bird – their ears are hidden under their head feathers.

Read further › eyes pg119 (q22)

Seabirds

Hundreds of kinds of birds live on, over or near the sea. Gannets are sea birds that dive onto prey from as high as 30 m. They breed in noisy, crowded colonies. To feed, they swoop to snatch squid, fish and other sea creatures from the surface of the water with their long, hook-tipped bill. The most impressive sea bird is the wandering albatross, which can stay in the air for weeks, soaring on strong winds.

Read further › fish defence pg117 (m34)

◄ *The gannet's strong skull helps cushion the impact of its high-speed dive into water.*

▼ *When they dive for food, some types of penguin can stay underwater for up to 20 minutes without surfacing for oxygen.*

Flying underwater

Penguins flap their flipper-shaped wings to speed through water after prey. All penguins live along coasts and shores in the southern hemisphere, with some breeding on icebergs or the frozen land of Antarctica. They feed in the sea on creatures such as small fish and squid, and shrimp-like krill.

Read further › squid pg124 (n2)

Reptiles

M OST OF the 8000 or so species of reptile have scaly skin, lay eggs and are 'cold-blooded'. This means, unlike mammals and birds, they cannot make heat inside their bodies. So most reptiles inhabit warm areas, basking in the sun. In scrublands and deserts reptiles sleep through long droughts. Reptiles live in all habitats except at the coldest poles – and turtles and sea-snakes are found in oceans. The major reptile groups are crocodilians, turtles and tortoises, snakes and lizards, and amphisbaenids – tropical worm-like creatures that live mostly underground.

Deadly predators

There are 23 kinds of crocodilians – crocodiles, alligators, caimans and one species of gharial. Crocodilians are powerful hunters, they lurk in swamps, lakes and rivers waiting for prey. Crocodiles are found in Asia, Africa and Australia, while alligators and caimans are usually found in North, Central and South America. They make good hunters because they can approach prey through water stealthily, with only their eyes and nostrils above the surface as they move.

▼ *The gharial has a long, thin snout and slim jaws for catching fish.*

Read further › eggs
pg115 [j22]

▼ *The alligator's snout is broad for seizing large prey.*

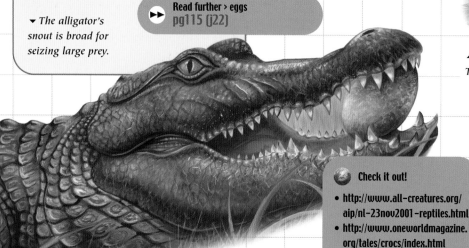

▲ *Crocodile snouts are designed to kill large prey. The alligator's snout is broad for seizing large prey.*

▼ *The black caiman's snout tapers at the end to catch small prey.*

▶▶ CROCODILE PREY see pg131 (o30) ▶▶

1 2 3 4 5 6 7 8 9 10 11 12 13 14 15 16 17 18 19

Smooth but not slippery

Snakes range from the 1-m python snake and the 200-kg anaconda, which constrict or squeeze their prey to death, to tiny thread-snakes smaller than a pencil. All hunt living prey but fewer than 50 types are deadly poisonous to humans. These include adders, vipers, mambas and cobras. The king cobra is the longest poisonous snake: it is 5 m in length. Its main prey is other snakes.

▲ *The puff adder, found in Africa, is highly venomous and is responsible for the most snake attacks on humans.*

▶▶ **Read further > rodents**
pg106 (p2)

◀ *A cobra's jaws are so loose and bendy, it can swallow prey that is bigger than its own head, such as a small rodent.*

Slow but safe

Tortoises are chelonians that live on land. Most eat plants but a few also consume small animals. Some survive in the driest deserts, where they burrow into the soil to escape heat and drought. The desert tortoise lays its eggs in a hole or under a rock or log: when these hatch some weeks later, the babies must fend for themselves.

▶▶ **Read further > eggs**
pg109 (m31)

▲ *The desert tortoise has especially large front legs, wide feet and stout claws, to burrow into the dry soil to avoid the hottest part of the day.*

Ocean wanderers

About 290 kinds of turtles and tortoises make up the reptile group called chelonians. Their main feature is the shell, made of a domed upper part, the carapace, and a flatter underside, the plastron. The carapace and plastron are formed from up to 60 curved bony plates, covered by another layer of horny plates. Some have hard, bony shells to protect against land predators; others have a streamlined carapace for swimming easily through water.

▶▶ **Read further > chelonians**
pg113 (b33)

▼ *Female sea turtles come ashore only to lay eggs in a hole on the beach. Males never touch dry land after hatching.*

▶ *The frilled lizard of Australia is up to 70 cm in length and its frill can be extended to a width of 25 cm.*

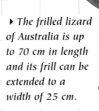

Variety of lizards

Lizards are the most wide-ranging and varied reptiles. The Galapagos iguana dives under the water to eat seaweed, the Nile monitor lizard is powerful enough to catch small antelopes, and the chameleon flicks out a sticky-tipped tongue as long as its body to grab flies. Most lizards have a long tail and four legs, but some lizards, such as slow-worms and skinks, have no limbs.

▶▶ **Read further > worms**
pg125 (b22)

▶▶ COBRA see pg138 (i12) ▶▶

a b c d e f g h i j k l m n o p q r s t u v w

22 23 24 25 26 27 28 29 30 31 32 33 34 35 36 37 38 39

Amphibians

THE NAME 'amphibian' means 'both lives', because most amphibians live on land and breed in water. Many of the 5000 species live in water when young and breathe using gills like fish. As they grow older most amphibians spend more time on land, lose their gills and breathe with their lungs. In a change in shape known as metamorphosis, amphibians develop from eggs, to larva or tadpole, to fully grown adults. The three main groups of amphibians are frogs and toads, newts and salamanders, and the smallest group, called caecilians, which are worm-like creatures.

IT'S A FACT

• The flying frog has huge feet with webbed toes that it spreads like parachutes to glide.

• The female Suriname toad carries her eggs in pouches of skin on her back.

• The biggest frog or toad is the goliath frog of West Africa. It is almost as large as a soccer ball.

Frogs and toads

Many frogs and toads have skin that makes a horrible-tasting or poisonous fluid, so predators, such as snakes and spiders, usually avoid them. Many predators build up a resistance to the milder toxins, so the frog's skin has evolved to produce a stronger poison. Toads are usually larger than frogs, have lumpier skin, and waddle rather than leap.

◀ The colours of poison-dart frogs warn predators of their poisonous skin.

▶▶ Read further › defence
pg117 (m33)

Salamanders

Giant salamanders are the largest of all the amphibians. Some species are exceptional in size: the Japanese giant salamander can grow to 1.4 m; the Chinese giant salamander can grow up to 1.5 m. Like newts, salamanders retain their tails into adulthood. Salamanders have a powerful bite and feed on shellfish, freshwater fish, worms and insects.

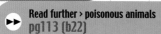

▶▶ Read further › poisonous animals
pg113 (b22)

ANIMAL FACTS

• A type of salamander, the rare axolotl, lives in a few lakes in Mexico. It keeps its larval shape and gills all through its life. However, its reproductive organs develop, so it can breed even though it looks immature.

• Amphibians are cold-blooded and in cold regions they survive long winters in a state of inactivity known as torpor. The spring peeper frog of North America can be frozen solid for weeks, then it thaws out without harm because it has a natural 'anti-freeze' substance in its blood and other body fluids.

▲ The hellbender of North America grows to 80 cm in length.

▶▶ GILLS see pg135 (j22) ▶▶

1 2 3 4 5 6 7 8 9 10 11 12 13 14 15 16 17 18 19

Newts

Newts are a type of salamander that tend to stay in water for long periods, even when air-breathing adults. Like salamanders, newts do not need to feed often as they do not use a lot of energy. However, like all amphibians, when newts do feed they flick out their long tongues to grab prey, such as worms, slugs, snails, grubs, flies and other insects and small fish.

▸ The Eastern newt is red, orange or brown with black spots. It lives on land for up to four years of its early life. After this it returns to the water to develop into an adult.

Read further › insects
pg119 (b24)

Worm-like amphibians

Caecilians, also known as gymnophiones, live mostly in the damp tropics among soil and leaves on the forest floor or in pools and swamps. They have no legs, very small eyes, and resemble large earthworms, growing up to 60 cm in length. Like other amphibians they are predators and feed on soil creatures, including earthworms.

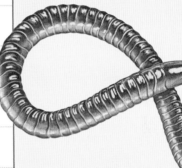

▴ Caecilians burrow powerfully, pushing soil with their broad snouts.

Read further › earthworms
pg125 (b22)

Life cycle

The life cycle of the common frog begins when the female lays a clump of jelly-covered eggs (called spawn) in fresh water. The eggs are then fertilized by the male's sperm. The eggs hatch into larvae or tadpoles. Tadpoles have gills and a long tail but no legs, and eat water plants. Gradually they metamorphose into adults. Their legs grow, their tails shrink and their lungs develop to breathe air.

Read further › eggs hatching
pg113 (b33)

Frog spawn (eggs) float on top of water

Froglet loses tail and grows into adult frog

Adult toad

Tadpoles hatch from eggs

Tadpoles grow legs and change into froglets

Adult newt

◂ The common frog's life cycle is similar to those of toads and newts. Frogs lay eggs in a clump. Toads lay eggs in long strings or 'necklaces'. Newts lay eggs singly.

▸▸ FROGS BREEDING see pg147 (l22) ▸▸

Fish

A TYPICAL FISH lives in water, has a long, slim body, large eyes, a finned tail that swishes from side to side for swimming, body fins to control its movements, a covering of scales, and feather-like gills on either side of the head that take in oxygen from the water. However, many fish lack one or more of these features. Eels are long and thin like snakes and usually scaleless, lungfish can breathe out of water, and many catfish have leathery skin or bony plates rather than scales.

ANIMAL FACTS

• The biggest hunting fish is the great white shark or white pointer. The biggest grow to about 9 m in length and weigh up to 3 tonnes.

• At 12–14 m in length and weighing more than 10 tonnes, the whale shark is the biggest fish. But it is not a fierce hunter like the great white shark. It filters small plants and animals (plankton) from seawater, using comb-like rakers on the insides of its gills.

▶▶ **Read further › predators** pg110 (g14); pg112 (o2)

IT'S A FACT

• The smallest fish, the dwarf goby, is as long as the word 'fish' and lives in streams and pools on the Philippine Islands.

• One of the longest fish is the eel-shaped oarfish of open oceans that grows to more than 8 m – one is caught about every ten years.

▼ The 6-m tiger shark prefers warm-blooded victims such as monk seals. However, it will eat almost anything, from sea turtles to rotting, leftover food thrown from ships.

Ocean killers

There are about 330 species of sharks. As well as eating plankton, which includes plant matter, all sharks eat meat, either catching victims or scavenging from dead animals. Unlike most fish, a shark's skeleton is made of cartilage (gristle) rather than bone. A shark also has unusual scales called denticles that are tiny and tooth-shaped. Much larger denticles form the shark's teeth, which are always being worn away or broken off to be replaced by new ones.

Check it out!
• http://www.kidzone.ws/sharks
• http://www.fishid.com/ facts.htm

▶▶ CATFISH see pg137 (c32) ▶▶

1   2   3   4   5   6   7   8   9   10   11   12   13   14   15   16   17   18   19

● Fish food

Different types of fish eat a huge variety of food. Piranhas have razor-sharp teeth and gather around a large animal in the water to tear off chunks of flesh. In fresh water, the pike lurks in weeds and dashes out to grab a victim in its huge mouth. Carp sift through mud for worms and other creatures. On coral reefs, butterfly fish and parrot fish eat tiny plants and animals growing on the rocks.

▼ *Piranhas live in South American rivers and swamps. They feed on other fish, insects, even fruit, but as a ferocious predatory group they can attack and kill small mammals and even humans.*

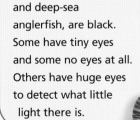

► **Read further › teeth** pg106 (p2)

● Bottom of the sea

Below about 500 m the sea is completely dark, so that colourful bodies are of no use. Most deep-sea fish, such as the gulper eel, viperfish and deep-sea anglerfish, are black. Some have tiny eyes and some no eyes at all. Others have huge eyes to detect what little light there is.

► **Read further › colour** pg121 (i32)

▶ *Deep-sea anglerfish have a blob of flesh that dangles in front of them. This attracts smaller fish that think it might be edible.*

▼ *Deep-sea lantern-fish make their own light with rows of glowing spots.*

● 'Dino'-fish

Coelacanths lived during the age of dinosaurs, about 250 million years ago, and were thought to be extinct. However, in the 1930s a coelacanth was discovered in the Indian Ocean off southern Africa. Another type was found in the 1990s in the Celebes Sea off Southeast Asia. Fish like these may have developed their fins into legs to become the first amphibian, more than 350 million years ago.

▼ *Coelacanths have fleshy, muscular bases to their fins that they use to 'walk' over rocks.*

◀ *The stonefish is the world's most poisonous fish. It produces a deadly venom from dorsal spines along its side.*

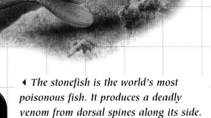

● Defence

Some fish defend themselves with poisons, which they can jab into enemies using their stiff, sharp fin spines. The lionfish or dragonfish of Southeast Asia has large, lacy-looking fins and bright colours to warn predators of its venom. In contrast, the stonefish is camouflaged as a piece of rock for protection.

► **Read further › poison** pg119 (b35); pg123 (e33)

▼ *The lionfish's organs are luminous (light reflects through).*

Insects 1

ARTHROPODS ARE invertebrate animals (lacking a backbone) with a hard outer body casing, and limbs with joints, rather than flexible tentacles. Insects are the biggest group of arthropods and the most numerous animals on Earth. More than 1 million species have been discovered. A typical adult insect has three body parts: head, thorax and abdomen. The head has the antennae or feelers, large eyes and mouthparts; the thorax bears the wings (usually four) and six legs; the abdomen contains the digestive and reproductive parts. Insects live in every land and freshwater habitat, from frozen polar regions and icy mountaintops to scrub, deserts, rivers and deep lakes. However, no insects dwell in the sea.

● ANIMAL FACTS

• Most insects have short lives of a few months, but some survive for many years. The periodic cicada is a type of bug. It dwells as a young form or nymph in the soil, eating roots and other bits of plants, for up to 17 years.

• Cicadas are also the noisiest insects, and for their size, they make the loudest sounds of any animals. Only the males 'sing'. They vibrate thin, flexible patches of body casing, like drum skins, on either side of the abdomen.

● Fast and fierce

Dragonflies are among the biggest, fastest and fiercest insects. They catch smaller insects, such as gnats, in mid-air, using their dangling legs like a scoop or basket, and then take the victim back to a favourite perch to eat. Each dragonfly has its own area or territory, which usually includes water, such as a pond or stream. It 'buzzes' rival dragonflies who come too near to chase them off their territory.

● IT'S A FACT

• Some cave crickets and cockroaches have antennae (feelers) that are ten times as long as their bodies, since they cannot see in total darkness underground and so must feel their way.

• About three in every ten species of insect are beetles.

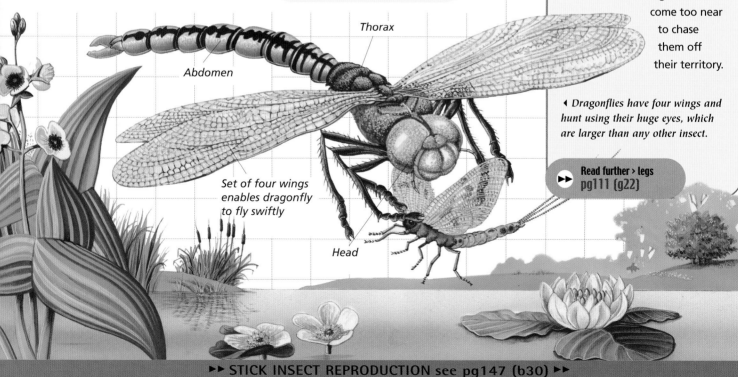

◀ Dragonflies have four wings and hunt using their huge eyes, which are larger than any other insect.

▶▶ **Read further > legs** pg111 (g22)

Thorax

Abdomen

Set of four wings enables dragonfly to fly swiftly

Head

▶▶ STICK INSECT REPRODUCTION see pg147 (b30) ▶▶

1   2   3   4   5   6   7   8   9   10   11   12   13   14   15   16   17   18   19

Insect cities

Termites are sometimes called 'white ants' but they are a separate group of insects – isopterans – with 2800 species that live mainly in the tropics. They build huge mounds of hardened mud, with a nest deep inside that may hold more than 5 million termites. They feed mainly on bits of wood, plants and decaying matter.

▲ *The female mosquito, about 2 cm in length, feeds on animal and human blood.*

◄ *A termite mound keeps its occupants cool, dark, damp and protected.*

Read further › sucking
pg121 (b22)

Read further › nests
pg110 (r11)

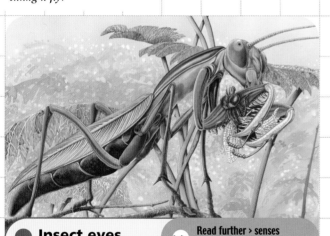

▼ *A female praying mantis eating a fly.*

Insect pests

Mosquitos, a type of fly, have needle-like mouthparts to pierce human skin and suck blood. This causes an itchy spot on the skin and sometimes spreads serious diseases such as malaria, which can be fatal. Fleas have huge rear legs for jumping, no wings and suck blood in the same way as mosquitos. Many flies, cockroaches and similar insects feed in dirt and decay and spread germs carried on their bodies, legs and mouthparts.

▼ *Great green bush crickets are also known as katydids. Most species mimic (take the appearance of) leaves or bark.*

Insect eyes

Read further › senses
pg105 (h32)

Almost all of the 2000 kinds of mantises (mantids) are fierce hunters. They grab prey with their front legs, which fold at the end like spiky scissors. An insect's eye is made of many separate parts, ommatidia, each detecting a tiny part of the scene. Mantids have huge eyes – each with more than 20,000 ommatidia. Mantids' wings are folded along their backs, ready to flash colour at their enemies.

Great leapers

Most grasshoppers and locusts, and some crickets, eat plant food. They all have two small leathery wings, like flaps, and two very large wings for flying. They can also leap great distances using their long, powerful back legs. Males 'sing' by rubbing their back legs on one of the wing veins (hard tubes that support the wings), which has a row of 'teeth' like a tiny comb.

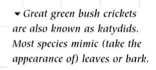
Read further › teeth / fangs
pg123 (e33)

►► HUMAN SKIN see pg154 (i11) ►►

a b c d e f g h i j k l m n o p q r s t u v w

Insects 2

NEARLY ALL insects hatch from eggs laid by the female. Only a few insect mothers, such as the earwig, care for their eggs or young. With some insects, such as grasshoppers and dragonflies, the young – nymphs – resemble their parents, although they are smaller and without wings. Nymphs gradually develop into adults by moulting (shedding their body cases) regularly. As their bodies go through little change, this type of development is incomplete metamorphosis. Other insects, such as butterflies, moths, beetles, bees, wasps and ants, have greater changes in body shape and experience a complete metamorphosis.

IT'S A FACT

• The bulkiest insect is the goliath beetle, which is 20 cm long and weighs more than 100 g.

• A caterpillar can increase its weight by more than 100 times in two weeks, which is one of the fastest growth rates of any animal.

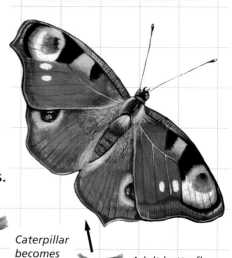

Complete metamorphosis

A butterfly's eggs hatch into small, wriggly young called larvae or caterpillars. The young eat huge amounts of food and shed their skins several times as they grow. They develop a hard body case and become inactive pupae, or chrysalises. After a time the pupa's casing splits and the adult insect emerges. Most caterpillars eat mainly leaves, while butterflies sip nectar from flowers.

Female butterfly lays tiny eggs, usually under leaves

Caterpillar becomes pupa

Adult butterfly emerges

Caterpillar hatches from eggs and eats leaves

Pupa's case splits open

▶▶ Read further › flowers pg121 (i32)

ANIMAL FACTS

• Many species of beetles have larvae (grubs) called 'worms', because they are long, legless and wriggly. They include mealworms and woodworms.

• Glow-worms are adult beetles that shine in the dark to attract a mate.

• Many types of insect live in water when young, such as the nymphs of dragonflies, damselflies, caddisflies and mayflies.

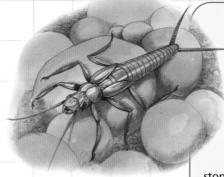

▲ *Adult stonefly nymphs rarely fly. Instead they crawl among stream-bed rocks and pebbles.*

Incomplete metamorphosis

Stonefly nymphs live in fast-flowing streams. They have wide, low bodies and strong legs with sharp claws to cling to smooth rocks in the rushing water. They grow for two or three years, then emerge and shed their skins to become adult stoneflies. Adult stoneflies look like small, short-bodied dragonflies. They fly, eat and live for only a week or two, in order to breed.

▶▶ ANIMAL REPRODUCTION see pg146 (d2) ▶▶

Hard wings

A beetle has four wings, but the front two, known as elytra, are strong and stiff. They normally lie over the beetle's back and cover and protect the larger, delicate flying wings that are folded beneath. Water beetles hunt tadpoles, worms and young fish in ponds and streams. They must rise to the surface regularly to refresh their air supplies that are in the form of tiny air bubbles stored under their elytra.

▼ *Water beetles can fly away to another pond if the one they are in dries out.*

Read further › tadpoles
pg115 (j22)

Pollination

Bees play a vital role in the reproduction of plants. As they visit colourful flowers to collect sweet nectar and tiny pollen grains for food, some pollen from the flower brushes on to the bee's feet and rubs off when it lands on the next flower. This process is called pollination and is how pollen grains are transferred from flower to flower so that flowers can develop seeds. Many other insects, such as flies and beetles, pollinate flowers in the same way.

▼ *A honeybee can make more than 500 visits to flowers in one day. The female honeybee carries pollen in a basket-shaped pouch on the hindlegs.*

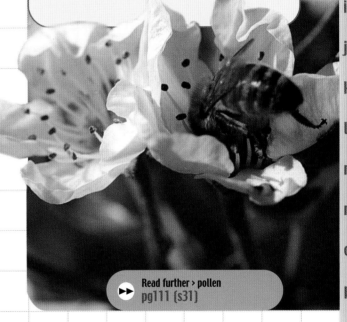

Read further › pollen
pg111 (s31)

Bugs

More than 80,000 species of insects are known as bugs. Most bugs have four wings and long, thin mouthparts that are like needles to pierce victims and suck liquid food. Pondskaters skim over water to catch and drown their prey. Aphids (greenflies and blackflies), cicadas and treehoppers suck plant sap; bedbugs feed on human blood; and shieldbugs have a shield-like body covering, which is often brightly coloured.

Read further › blood sucking
pg119 (b35)

▼ *The pondskater glides across water, ready to squeeze its prey, which are usually animals trapped at the surface in its front legs before sucking out the juices.*

 Check it out!

• http://www.enchantedlearning.com/subjects/butterflies/toc.shtml
• http://www.uky.edu/Agriculture/Entomology/ythfacts/bugfun/trivia.htm

◄◄ POLLINATION see pg92 (k10) ◄◄

22 23 24 25 26 27 28 29 30 31 32 33 34 35 36 37 38 39

More than eight legs

ARTHROPODS include insects, millipedes (four legs on each body part or segment), centipedes (two legs per segment) and another huge group – the arachnids, which have two main body segments and eight legs. Arachnids include spiders and scorpions, which live on land, and their tiny cousins, mites and ticks, known as false-scorpions, which live in water.

Centipedes and millipedes

'Centipede' means '100 feet' but most centipedes have up to 60 legs. They live mainly in tropical rainforests and are fast-moving night-time predators, using their fang-shaped, first pair of legs to jab and poison prey. The biggest species grow to 30 cm in length and their bite can cause extreme pain to humans. Some millipedes have only 24 feet, while others have more than 700 – but none can run fast. They are protected by their hard body casings and by a horrible-tasting or poisonous fluid that oozes from holes along the body.

▶ *Most millipedes feed at night on rotting leaves and old bits of plants.*

Read further > biting
pg119 (b35)

◀ *Ticks are about 1 cm in length but they grow larger when they have eaten. Mites usually grow no larger than 1 mm in length.*

Mites and ticks

Mites are tiny, eight-legged cousins of spiders. Most are smaller than this 'o' and live in the soil. A handful of earth from a forest might contain more than 1000 of them. Other types live as parasites on larger animals, sucking their blood or munching their skin, fur or feathers. Ticks are also blood-sucking parasites that live on many animals, from sheep to cats, and even occasionally on people.

Read further > blood-sucking
pg119 (b35)

BIGGEST SPIDERS

Spider	Width
South American bird-eating spider	28 cm
Central American running spider	25 cm
African hercules spider	20 cm
Cardinal spider	14 cm

◀◀ TROPICAL RAINFORESTS see pg98 (o2) ◀◀

1   2   3   4   5   6   7   8   9   10   11   12   13   14   15   16   17   18   19

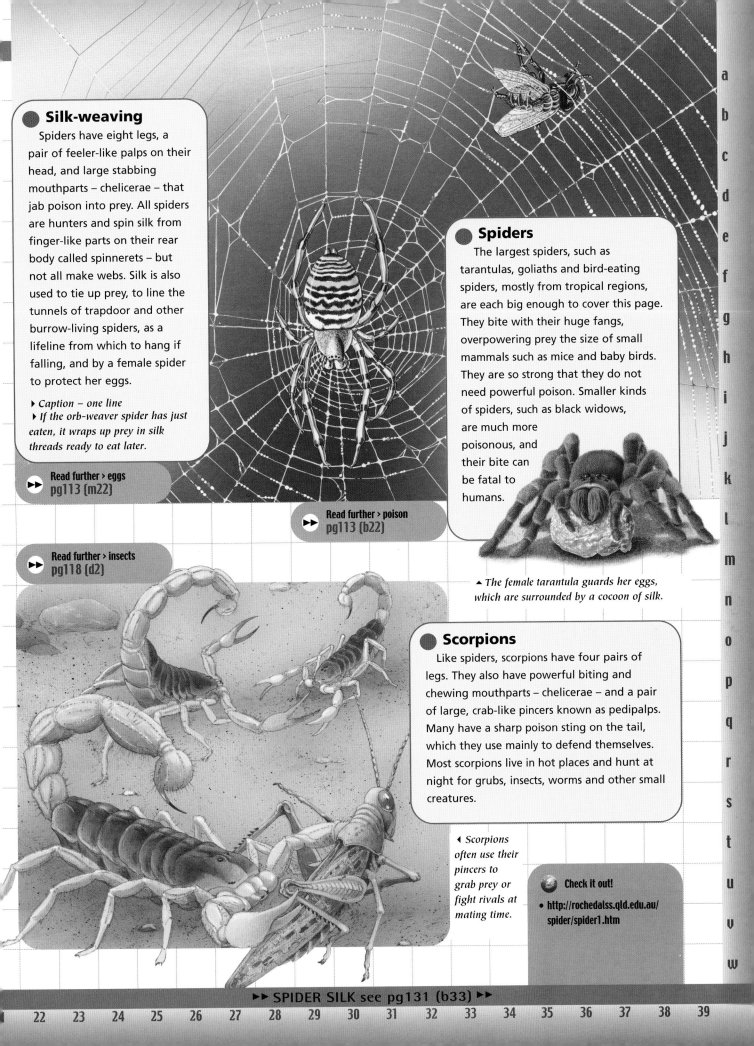

Silk-weaving

Spiders have eight legs, a pair of feeler-like palps on their head, and large stabbing mouthparts – chelicerae – that jab poison into prey. All spiders are hunters and spin silk from finger-like parts on their rear body called spinnerets – but not all make webs. Silk is also used to tie up prey, to line the tunnels of trapdoor and other burrow-living spiders, as a lifeline from which to hang if falling, and by a female spider to protect her eggs.

▸ *Caption – one line*
▸ *If the orb-weaver spider has just eaten, it wraps up prey in silk threads ready to eat later.*

▶▶ **Read further › eggs**
pg113 (m22)

▶▶ **Read further › insects**
pg118 (d2)

Spiders

The largest spiders, such as tarantulas, goliaths and bird-eating spiders, mostly from tropical regions, are each big enough to cover this page. They bite with their huge fangs, overpowering prey the size of small mammals such as mice and baby birds. They are so strong that they do not need powerful poison. Smaller kinds of spiders, such as black widows, are much more poisonous, and their bite can be fatal to humans.

▶▶ **Read further › poison**
pg113 (b22)

▲ *The female tarantula guards her eggs, which are surrounded by a cocoon of silk.*

Scorpions

Like spiders, scorpions have four pairs of legs. They also have powerful biting and chewing mouthparts – chelicerae – and a pair of large, crab-like pincers known as pedipalps. Many have a sharp poison sting on the tail, which they use mainly to defend themselves. Most scorpions live in hot places and hunt at night for grubs, insects, worms and other small creatures.

◀ *Scorpions often use their pincers to grab prey or fight rivals at mating time.*

Check it out!
• http://rochedalss.qld.edu.au/
  spider/spider1.htm

a b c d e f g h i j k l m n o p q r s t u v w

▶▶ SPIDER SILK see pg131 (b33) ▶▶

22 23 24 25 26 27 28 29 30 31 32 33 34 35 36 37 38 39

From molluscs to worms

CREATURES WITH hard shells such as snails, oysters, mussels and whelks belong to the huge animal group known as molluscs. However, some molluscs, including slugs and squid, have no outer shell at all. An unusual group of animals is the echinoderms, which includes starfish and sea urchins. They usually have a body shape that is radial, like a wheel with spokes, rather than two-sided with left and right, like other animals. There are also thousands of other types of strange-looking animals such as jellyfish and sponges.

▼ *Rock pools support a huge variety of life including crustaceans such as crabs and lobsters, molluscs such as snails and mussels, and sea anemones.*

Sea anemones (cnidarian)

● Molluscs

Molluscs range from tiny slugs as small as 2 mm, to giant squid with a body and tentacles 20 m in length. Most have a hard shell either outside or inside the body. Molluscs include many seashore 'shellfish' such as clams, limpets and cowries. Octopus and squid grab victims with their suckered tentacles and bite off pieces with the mouth at their centre, which is shaped like a parrot's beak.

▲ *Squid are fast swimmers, often reaching speeds of 50 km/h.*

►► **Read further › hard shells**
pg113 (m22)

● Echinoderms

All echinoderms live in the sea. Their name means 'spiny-skinned', and most sea urchins and a few starfish have sharp spines, sometimes poisonous. Other types of echinoderm include sea cucumbers, which are usually sausage-shaped and sort through seabed mud for food particles. Sea lilies are also echinoderms.

Starfish (echinoder

►► **Read further › sharp spines**
pg104 (i15)

►► MINUTE ANIMALS see pg223 (c22) ►►

All kinds of worms

The most familiar worms, such as earthworms, are called annelids. They have a long body made of many sections or segments. Other annelids include ragworms, fanworms and tubeworms on the seashore and in the sea, and leaf-shaped leeches that suck blood from other animals.

► Read further > blood–sucking pg119 (b35)

► Read further > blood–sucking pg119 (b35)

IT'S A FACT

• There are more than 100,000 different species of molluscs.

• The echinoderm phylum numbers over 6000 species.

• Annelids, such as earthworms, consist of 12,000 species.

Jellyfish

Jellyfish, sea anemones and coral polyps are all members of the cnidarian group, containing almost 10,000 different species. Most live in the sea and have a jelly-like body or stalk and a ring of tentacles that sting their prey. Coral polyps build cup-shaped cases of hard minerals around themselves; most corals gradually build up over time to form the unusual shapes of coral reefs.

► Read further > stinging prey pg123 (o32)

Cockle (mollusc)

Razorshell (mollusc)

Shell of whelk mollusc used by hermit crab

Periwinkle (mollusc)

Mussel (mollusc)

Sea urchin (echinoderm)

Sponges

Sponges have no eyes or ears, nerves or brain, bones or muscles. But they are still animals. Their bodies are made of many microscopic cells, and they take food into their bodies by 'eating'. A sponge sucks water into its bag- or flask-shaped body through many small holes in its wall, absorbs tiny bits of food through the inner lining and squirts the water out through the larger hole at the top.

Lobster (crustacean) see pg32 [t7]

Crab (crustacean) see pg33 [d35]

Sponges

Check it out!

• http://yucky.kids.discovery.com/ noflash/worm/pg000102 .html

• http://www.enchantedlearning. com/subjects/invertebrates/ mollusk/Printouts.shtml

► Read further > squirting water pg107 (h32)

Land movers

MOVEMENT DEFINES what an animal is. In general, animals can move from place to place but plants do not. Creatures travel about to find food and shelter, and avoid predators. Different types of animals use different parts of their bodies for movement. Most land (terrestrial) animals, from tiny bugs and spiders to large reptiles and mammals, use their legs for moving. But monkeys (see pg145 [e36]) and sloths also swing by their arms, snails slide on their undersides, and snakes use their whole bodies. Movement uses muscles. Vertebrates (animals with a backbone) have muscles attached to their bones. When the muscles pull on their bones, animals can crawl, walk, fly or swim.

Read further › predators
pg12 (d2); pg13 (e22)

IT'S A FACT

• Reptiles were the first creatures to live entirely on land, over 350 million years ago.

• Bears are one of the few animals to walk on the soles of their feet.

• The African fringe-toed lizard has to dance across the hot sand in the desert to keep its feet cool.

Speed saves

Fast movement is most important in open habitats such as grasslands, where antelopes, gazelles and zebras need to escape from predators such as cheetahs, lions and wild dogs. Long, slim legs can be used to gain great speed. The muscles that help these animals to run are mainly in the upper leg and body, leaving the lower leg and foot very light so it can be moved to and fro faster when running at great speed.

▲ The cheetah is the fastest land mammal, able to reach speeds of more than 100 km/h, but it can only maintain this speed for less than a minute.

Check it out!

• http://www.saburchill.com/chapters/chap0005.html

a
b
c
d
e
f
g
h
i
j
k
l
m
n
o
p
q
r
s
t
u
v
w

Moving through soil

Burrowing animals use various methods of movement. The mole uses its powerful front legs as shovels to clear the earth away as it moves forward. The worm is like a tube of muscle that contracts to make its body hard, rather like a water-filled balloon, as the worm pushes between soil grains. Mole rats have straight limbs with five thick toes with claws for digging the soil.

►► Read further › teeth
pg130 (n2)

◄ *Sloths in South American rainforests are so well camouflaged that they do not need to race away fast to escape from predators.*

▲ *Naked mole rats of East Africa have massive incisors (front teeth) to eat and dig with. They are not really naked but have sparse hairs covering their pink bodies.*

Moving in trees

Sloths and gibbons travel through trees in different ways. A gibbon's arms are twice as long as its legs, with hook-shaped hands to hang from branches. Its swinging motion is called brachiation. The sloth hangs with four limbs, moving one at a time, and is the slowest moving animal at just 300 m/h.

Muscle power

Muscles get shorter, or contract, pulling different body parts, allowing movement. In vertebrates – fish, amphibians, reptiles, birds and mammals – the muscles are joined to bones which form an endoskeleton inside the body. In insects and spiders (*see pg131 [j35]*) they are joined to the hard outer body casing – the exoskeleton.

►► Read further › inside the body
pg134 (f2; s2)

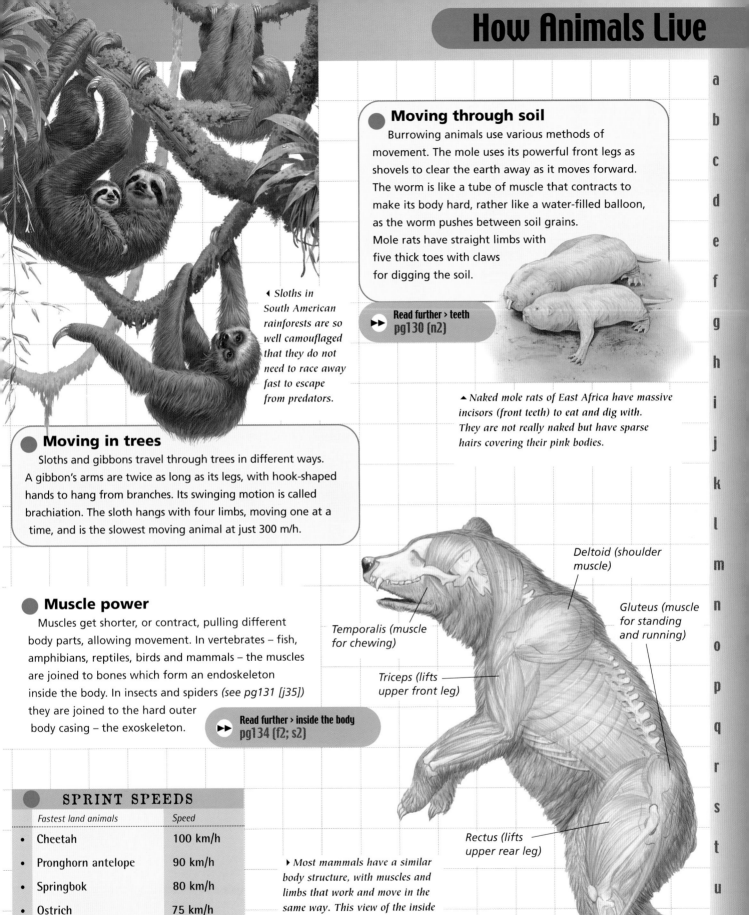

Deltoid (shoulder muscle)

Gluteus (muscle for standing and running)

Temporalis (muscle for chewing)

Triceps (lifts upper front leg)

Rectus (lifts upper rear leg)

Gastrocnemius (tilts back the rear paw)

SPRINT SPEEDS

Fastest land animals	Speed
• Cheetah	100 km/h
• Pronghorn antelope	90 km/h
• Springbok	80 km/h
• Ostrich	75 km/h
• Racehorse	70 km/h

▸ *Most mammals have a similar body structure, with muscles and limbs that work and move in the same way. This view of the inside of a bear shows some of the main muscles used for movement.*

►► HUMAN MUSCLES see pg158 (d2) ►►

Soarers and swimmers

IT'S A FACT

• Fastest of all birds is the peregrine, a type of falcon that moves at more than 250 km/h when it dives or 'stoops' to catch its prey.

• One of the fastest fish is the sailfish, moving through water at up to 100 km/h.

• The speediest mammal in water is the killer whale, moving at about 55 km/h.

B OTH AIR and water are fluid – unlike solid ground they flow when you push them. So movement in air and water requires more muscle power. More than four-fifths of the body weight in a fish is muscle, compared to two-fifths of a land mammal. Fliers and swimmers both use broad pushing surfaces – wings through air, and fins, flippers and tails through water. These surfaces produce the propulsion (forward movement), while other body parts control steering and slowing down. In a bird, the main wing areas give propulsion, while the wingtips and tail provide control. In a fish, the tail is used for propulsion, and the side fins for control.

To scale
Each square = 6 m across
Some of the largest whales in the world

Blue whale 30 m

Fin whale 22 m

Sperm whale 20 m

Sei whale 16 m

Wing shapes
Hummingbirds and nectar-sipping bats flap their short, broad wings quickly, almost 100 times per second, to push air straight down so they can hover. In contrast, a wandering albatross can soar for hours on its long, slim wings without flapping once. Its 3.5 m wingspan glides the wind from the sea provides lift (upwards force).

►► Read further › nectar eaters
pg133 (f22)

▲ *When a hummingbird hovers it tilts its head up and tail down to make its body vertical. Its wings flap in a curved figure of eight, and the whole wing twists at the joint with the body at each end of the stroke. This produces a more upward force, or lift, than simply flapping the wings to and fro.*

Check it out!
• http://www.saburchill.com/chapters/chap0012.html

◄ *One of the fastest fish, the bluefin tuna, can reach speeds of 70 km/h and migrate as far as 10,000 km across oceans.*

● Kicking to swim

Many animals live both on land and in water, so they use their legs and feet to run and swim. The hippopotamus swallows plenty of air so that it can remain underwater for some time, then it can run along the riverbed. Otters, crocodiles *(see pg131 [u34])* and frogs have toes that are joined with flaps of skin, called webbing, to make a broad surface area for kick-swimming.

● Swift swimmers

Water is very dense, so streamlining – a smooth body shape – enables fish, dolphins, seals and other sea creatures to move through it. Speedy fish such as marlin, tuna and wahoo have long, slim, tapering bodies that thin into a point. Thrust (the force to move forwards) comes from the tail, which is pulled from side to side by huge blocks of muscles along either side of the body.

Powerful rear legs kick off

Front legs cushion the landing

Webbed rear feet kick to swim and front legs steer through water

▲ *Many frogs move by leaping, which enables them to escape from predators quickly.*

►► **Read further › dolphins** pg149 [d22]

◄ *The 'flying squirrel' of North America can glide for more than 50 m, steering with its front legs, and slowing down or stopping by raising its tail.*

● Gliders

Flying squirrels, possums, lemurs, fish, lizards, even frogs, do not really fly. The only animals that truly fly with power and control are bats *(see pg136 [h13])*, birds and insects. Others are gliders, using their broad surfaces like parachutes to swoop downwards. The best mammal glider, the colugo or flying lemur, can swoop for more than 200 m.

►► **Read further › bats** pg136 [j12]

● CREATURE COMFORTS

• One of the most adaptable movers has no limbs at all. The golden tree snake can slither fast, swim well, burrow through loose soil, climb trees easily, and even launch itself from a branch and flatten its body to glide many metres.

• In habitats such as coral reefs, speed is not so important. Fish such as angelfish move their pectoral (front) fins to and fro like an oar, rather than by swishing their tails.

● Up and down

A dolphin's tail, called its flukes, looks similar to a fish's tail. A dolphin swims by arching its body up and down, not bending from side to side like a fish. Its flukes are not its 'legs' – they have no bones within them. However, its flippers, like a seal's flippers, are its 'arms', with hand and finger bones inside.

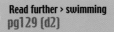►► **Read further › swimming** pg129 [d2]

▶ *Dolphins have long streamlined bodies that are propelled through water by thrusts of their tails.*

Meat eaters

ANIMALS THAT eat mainly other animals are called carnivores. Some are active predators that hunt down prey, while others use stealth or ambush methods. Meat eaters range from killer whales and sharks in the sea, big cats and wild dogs on land, and eagles and hawks in the air, to much smaller but equally deadly shrews, bats, frogs, praying mantises, dragonflies, spiders and even sea anemones. Foods such as flesh, blood and eggs contain large amounts of nourishment and energy compared to plant foods. So carnivores spend less than one-tenth of the time eating than herbivores do. Animals such as monkeys that eat both plants and meat are called omnivores.

◀ *Bears are the largest meat-eating land animals, feeding on meat such as fish and insects, as well as plants such as fruits, nuts and leaves. The sharp-ridged shape of their molar teeth has evolved to become more rounded for grinding plants and vegetation.*

▼ *This lion's skull shows a carnivore's teeth.*

● Hunting tools

Many carnivores have bodily weapons to jab into their prey, wound it and tear it apart to eat it. These include the strong, sharp, pointed teeth of sharks, alligators and mammals such as leopards, fang-like mouthparts in spiders, centipedes and predatory insects, sharp, hooked beaks of birds of prey, and the toe claws of birds and mammal hunters.

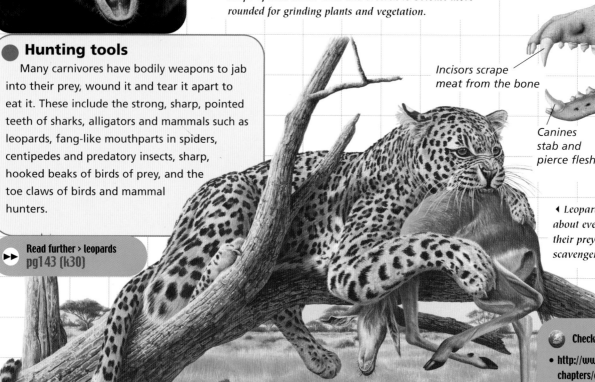

Incisors scrape meat from the bone

Canines stab and pierce flesh

Carnassials slide against each other to slice flesh

◀ *Leopards make large kills about every two days, taking their prey into trees away from scavengers such as hyaenas.*

▶▶ Read further > leopards
pg143 (k30)

◀ *With a wingspan of up to 2.3 m, the golden eagle swoops down to catch prey such as rabbits, grouse and other birds, seizing it with its sharp claws.*

Hunting methods

Read further › camouflage
pg142 (g12); pg143 (b22)

Techniques for catching prey vary greatly. Eagles and owls swoop down on to their prey silently and unnoticed from above. Wolves and wild dogs chase their prey over long distances. Cats creep near to victims and then rush or pounce on them. Some predators barely move. The shallow-water anglerfish lies camouflaged on the seabed attracting unwary victims with a fleshy blob of 'bait' on the end of its fin.

Tied in strong silk

Many spiders spin webs and wait for their prey to get stuck in them. The spitting spider is more active. It stalks prey and then squirts a glue-like chemical from its fangs, which turns into sticky threads as it flies through the air and lands on the victim. The spider even shakes its head from side to side to make the threads zig-zag and glue down the prey. Then the spider uses its fangs for their normal purpose, to jab poison into its prey.

▼ *Spitting spiders, found mostly near human habitation, can only squirt their 'glue' up to 1 cm.*

Looks can deceive

Some animals that may not seem to be carnivores actually are. A starfish preys on shellfish stuck to the rocks, and can take a whole day to lever one open and digest its flesh. Sea anemones and jellyfish may look harmless but they actually eat fish, prawns and other victims.

Read further › seabed
pg143 (b22)

Read further › crab spiders
pg142 (s11)

◀ *Sea anemones wait for victims on the seabed and coral reefs, before trapping prey with their sticky, stinging tentacles.*

Feasting

Read further › hunting
pg137 (b22)

Some hunters kill one large victim to last them a long time. A zebra or wildebeest can provide a crocodile with enough energy to last several months before its next meal. Other predators catch only tiny prey, but many of them. In one day a giant anteater consumes 20,000 ants and termites, and a blue whale can gulp in half a million child's toe-sized krill.

CREATURE COMFORTS

• Mammals and birds of prey are warm-blooded, so they need to eat more food to provide the energy needed to heat their bodies, unlike cold-blooded animals.

• For this reason, a big cat must eat about ten times more food each year than a crocodile of similar body size.

▼ *Crocodiles glide underwater unnoticed before surging out of the water to catch their prey.*

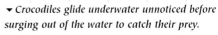

◀◀ SPIDERS see pg123 (e33) ◀◀

a
b
c
d
e
f
g
h
i
j
k
l
m
n
o
p
q
r
s
t
u
v
w

22 23 24 25 26 27 28 29 30 31 32 33 34 35 36 37 38 39

Plant eaters

MORE THAN three-quarters of all animals are herbivores – plant eaters. In any habitat, there are always more herbivores than carnivores as the carnivores must feed on the plant eaters. Plant eaters range from elephants *(see pg146 [p14])* and hippos, to bugs, beetles, moths and caterpillars. However, few animals can eat all kinds of plants. They have adapted to eat certain parts. Some eat leaves and flowers, while others chew tough roots or hard-cased nuts.

▲ *Giraffes are 'browsers', chewing on vegetation regularly throughout the day. They use their comb-like canine teeth to strip leaves from branches and have a long tongue to gather leaves and shoots from high up in the trees.*

● Living on leaves

Deer, most gazelles, giraffes and the black rhino are browsers, eating leaves from trees and shrubs. Zebras, wild cattle and the white rhino are grazers, consuming leaves or grasses from the ground. Most herbivore mammals have straight-edged front teeth for nibbling, and flat-topped cheek teeth, molars and pre-molars, for thorough chewing.

▶▶ **Read further › teeth**
pg127 (b31)

● Tough to crack

Rodents such as rats, mice, beavers and squirrels use their long, continuously-growing front teeth (incisors) to crack the hardest seeds and nuts. Parrots *(see pg149 [b36])* and macaws do this using their beaks, while tortoises use their horn-rimmed, sharp-edged jaws.

▶ *Because of their varied diet, rats spread all around the world, adapting to different conditions. A rat can cover up to 3 km in one night, foraging for food.*

● CREATURE COMFORTS

• The only place on Earth where there are no plant eaters is at the bottom of the sea where there is no light for plants to grow.

• Most deep-sea animals are detritivores, consuming the decaying and rotting remains of dead creatures.

◄ *The yellow-bellied sapsucker of North and Central America feeds on sap from broadleaved trees such as poplar, birch and maple.*

Juice suckers

Sweet, sticky sap from plants and the sugary nectar made by flowers are packed with nutrients. Many plant eaters live only on this. The yellow-bellied sapsucker bird drills tiny holes through the trunk of a tree with its long, sharp beak and extracts the sap from inside the tree. Bugs such as aphids have needle-like mouths to jab into a stem and suck up the juice.

Read further › nectar
pg128 (n14)

▼ *This horse's skull shows a herbivore's teeth.*

Incisors tear plants from the trees and ground

Row of large, broad-topped, crushing molars grind plants and vegetation

Gap (diastema) where canines used to be before herbivores adapted to plant-eating lifestyle

IT'S A FACT

• An elephant can consume up to 150 kg of food daily – the weight of two average-sized adult people.

• However, half of this food passes out the other end without being digested.

Changing diet

Some plant eaters change their foods with the seasons. Pikas, which are small-eared relatives of rabbits, nibble buds and shoots in spring and grasses and herbs in summer. In autumn they store grass and leaves in piles near their burrow to eat during winter. Storing food to eat later in the year is called caching.

▼ *The North American pika chooses its food store for the winter depending on which plants decompose (rot) the slowest. This ensures that their food is not rotten before they can eat it all.*

Read further › winter
pg141 (n27)

'Invisible' plants

Plants are the basic food for all animal life. On land, plants are easily seen. However, in the open ocean trillions of unseen microscopic plants called algae, that along with minute animals make up plankton, support animal life, too. They are eaten by whales and also tiny animals such as copepods, which become food for bigger sea creatures.

Read further › underwater food
pg137 (c32)

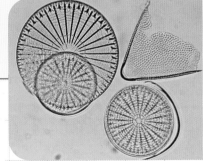

▸ *Microscopic diatoms and other algae provide food for tiny ocean plant eaters.*

Check it out!

• http://www.saburchill.com/chapters/chap0015.html
• http://www.nhm.org/mammals/page010.html

◄◄ ALGAE see pg83 (k30) ◄◄

a b c d e f g h i j k l m n o p q r s t u v w

22 23 24 25 26 27 28 29 30 31 32 33 34 35 36 37 38 39

Digestion and respiration

EVERY ANIMAL needs a vital substance to stay alive – oxygen. It combines with food to provide energy for the huge variety of life processes inside the body. Oxygen makes up one-fifth of the air, and is also dissolved in water. Animals obtain it in different ways, but the parts which do so are always known as the respiratory system. Another main body need is nourishment – nutrients for growth, energy and day-to-day maintenance. In small and simple animals, nutrients can be taken in or absorbed through the body surface, especially in water where they are all around, in dissolved form. Larger animals have a specialized digestive system to obtain food and break it down into tiny parts or molecules, which can then be absorbed into the body.

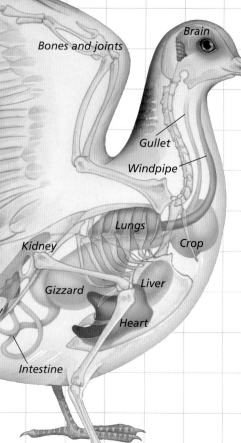

Bones and joints
Brain
Gullet
Windpipe
Lungs
Crop
Kidney
Liver
Gizzard
Ovary
Heart
Intestine
Cloaca

▲ The lungs of the respiratory system and the heart from the circulatory system take up much of the front part of the body in the pigeon's chest. The digestive, excretory and reproductive systems fill the rear part of the body.

● The digestive system

The digestive tract is a passageway through the body from the mouth to the rear end. Different parts of it are designed for certain tasks. In a pigeon, the crop is like a storage bag for recently eaten food. The muscular gizzard grinds the food into a pulp and the intestine absorbs the various nutrients into the bloodstream. The kidneys are part of the excretory system that filter wastes from the blood to form a liquid – urine – that leaves the body through the cloaca to continually clear it of waste.

▶▶ Read further › urine scent pg139 (b22)

a
b
c
d
e
f
g
h
i
j
k
l
m
n
o
p
q
r
s
t
u
v
w

Gills for water

Gills are like 'inside out' lungs. They have the same branching, frilly structure but outside the body, in contact with water. Dissolved oxygen seeps from the water to blood flowing through the gills. Most water-dwellers have some type of gills, including fish, crabs and molluscs such as octopuses and sea-slugs.

Read further › fish senses pg137 (c32)

▶ Most fish have gills. This diagram shows part of a gill. Oxygen, from the water that flows over the gills, passes into the bloodstream of the amphibian.

Primary gill filament (lamella or 'leaf')

Secondary gill filament (smaller lamella or 'leaf')

Low-oxygen water flows out through gill slit

Gill arch (stiff curve that holds out the gill filaments

Oxygen in water passes into the blood flowing through gill filaments, turning it red

High-oxygen water flows in through mouth to gill chamber

Not all the same

The axolotl, a type of salamander, keeps its tadpole gills even when adult. The lungfish has gills but also pocket-like 'pouches' with blood-rich linings that branch off the gut. If its pool dries out, a lungfish swallows air into these pouches, which absorb the oxygen.

◀ The axolotl has visible gills. If the gills become damaged, they quickly regrow.

Lungs for air

On land, vertebrates such as amphibians, reptiles, birds and mammals breathe air into lungs. Air tubes inside the lungs branch smaller and end in millions of microscopic 'bubbles', alveoli, which form a huge surface area and have plentiful blood in their linings. Oxygen from breathed-in air seeps into the blood and is spread around the body.

Read further › frogs pg129 (c28)

No special system

Small creatures such as flatworms have no special parts for respiration. Oxygen can pass straight through their thin skin. Their flattened shape means no part inside its body is more than a few millimetres away from the skin, so oxygen can easily seep this distance.

▲ Many types of flatworm are parasitic – they live inside or attached to other creatures.

Air spaces inside the lung

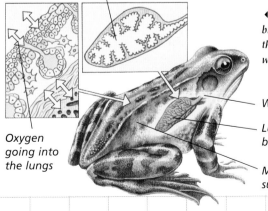

◀ Frogs actually breathe through their skin as well as lungs.

Oxygen going into the lungs

Windpipe

Lungs for breathing

Moist skin surface

CREATURE COMFORTS

• The bodies of mammals such as shrews work so fast to stay warm that they need more than 20 times more oxygen, compared to their body weight, than a large mammal such as a zebra.

• Warm-blooded animals need more oxygen than cold-blooded ones to 'burn' food to keep warm. A bird needs 15 to 20 times more oxygen than a lizard of the same size.

▶▶ RESPIRATION IN HUMANS see pg160 (m2) ▶▶

Animal senses

O VERALL, OUR own senses of sight, hearing, smell, taste and touch are good compared to many animals. But the senses of some animals are thousands of times better than ours, while others have senses that we do not have, such as being able to detect the natural magnetic force of the Earth. Each animal's senses are suited to its habitat and lifestyle, and especially the way it finds food and communicates. Night-time predators such as owls, cats and bats have big eyes to gather as much light as possible in the darkness. Creatures of the deepest seabed, where there is no light, have tiny eyes or none at all.

◀ *The bat moves its head from side to side as it flies. When it hears its high-pitched squeaks come back equally loud in both ears, it is directly facing the source of the echoes – its victim.*

▶▶ **Read further › bats**
pg129 (m22)

● **Sight and sound**

Owls are nocturnal – night-time – creatures so they need very acute hearing and large eyes to find their way at night. Bats have good sight, yet they cannot see in total darkness. They use their hearing in a system called echolocation to find their way, making high-pitched clicks and squeaks – pulses of ultrasound. When the noise hits an object, it bounces back as an echo and the bat is able to work out where the object is – even a tiny midge no larger than this full stop.

▸ *The barn owl's ear openings are hidden under head feathers, but its hearing is very sensitive. One ear slightly higher than the other hears sounds coming up from the ground earlier than the other ear. These 'offset ears' allow amazingly accurate judging of the direction of a sound.*

◀◀ MAGNETIC EARTH see pg59 (c28) ◀◀

1 2 3 4 5 6 7 8 9 10 11 12 13 14 15 16 17 18 19

Smelling the air

Most animals have a better sense of smell than humans do. All animals that are hunted, from deer to mice, continually sniff the air for the scent of predators as well as for the smell of food. Smell works in water, too. Many fish have nostrils and can detect scents from many kilometres away.

▼ The white-tailed deer is found between the regions of southern Canada and northern South America. It usually faces the wind when it rests and eats to detect any sign of danger.

Read further › scent
pg139 (j24)

Read further › camouflage
pg142 (f2)

Taste sensors

In water, taste works on contact and also at a distance, rather like smell. A catfish is a 'living tongue' with taste buds over most of its body. It can also detect tiny electrical pulses passing through water. These come from the living bodies of other creatures nearby in the water, allowing the catfish to find prey that is hidden in the mud.

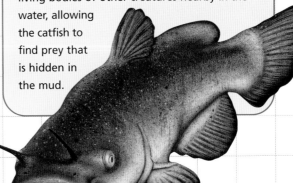

▲ The catfish's front end bristles have sensors. It has tiny pits in the skin that detect electricity, smell detectors behind the nostrils, and touch and taste sensors all over its head, especially on its barbels or whiskers.

Good vibrations

Like taste, touch works at a distance in water. Moving animals send out ripples that are detected by a fish's lateral line sense. This is a stripe along each side containing tubes or pits with very tiny hairs, which rock to and fro as ripples and water currents pass by.

Lateral line

▶ The great barracuda has a strong lateral line sense and is a fast-moving predator, relying mainly on sight in the clear tropical waters.

Read further › movement in water
pg129 (d22)

CREATURE COMFORTS

• Insects have different eyes from other animals. They are made of many tiny parts, ommatidia, like a mosaic, each one detecting just a tiny part of a scene. A dragonfly has the biggest insect eye, with more than 30,000 ommatidia.

• Most insects hear with flexible flaps of skin, 'eardrums', which are actually found on the main body rather than on the head. Some grasshoppers have 'eardrums' on their knees.

Check it out!

• http://www.earthlife.net/birds/vision.html

▶▶ HUMAN TASTE BUDS see pg171 (b22) ▶▶

a b c d e f g h i j k l m n o p q r s t u v w

Communication

COMMUNICATION MEANS passing on messages and information. People communicate by talking, making facial expressions or using body language such as waving. Animals use sound, sight and movement to communicate, as well as a range of methods including scent, taste, touch and the emitting of electrical signals. Some messages are understood only by their own kind, for example when a male frog croaks to attract a female of the same species at breeding time. Other messages can be understood by a wide variety of creatures – these are often about matters of life and death.

▼ *The cobra's extended hood reveals a pattern that is on the rear of the hood, but shows through the stretched skin and thin, see-through scales.*

▼ *While some meerkats gather food, others look out for predators, warning the group of danger by barking or shrieking loudly.*

● Warning signals

One sight-and-sound communication is widely understood in the animal world. This is rearing or puffing up to look bigger whilst making a hissing sound. This makes an animal seem bigger and fiercer, to warn off an attacker. A toad puffs up and makes a hissing sound, a cobra rears up, spreads its hood and hisses, and a cat's fur stands on end as it hisses.

▶▶ Read further › snakes and mimicry
pg143 (c30)

● Slap and thump

Sudden danger needs a short, sharp message to warn others in the group, and sound is often used. A meerkat shrieks shrilly, and many birds make a loud 'seep' or 'tic'. The first beaver to notice a predator nearby slaps its flat tail hard on the water's surface. A rabbit thumps the ground.

▶▶ Read further › defending territories
pg144 (f2)

▶▶ FACIAL EXPRESSIONS see pg159 (k33) ▶▶

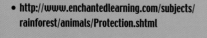

1   2   3   4   5   6   7   8   9   10   11   12   13   14   15   16   17   18   19

Leaving a message

Scent has an advantage over sights or sounds – it lasts after the sender has gone. Rhinos, hyaenas, sheep, foxes and many other animals spray strong-smelling urine or leave droppings around their territory. This shows the sex and age of the animal, and if it is ready for breeding.

◀ The male white rhinoceros marks his home range by spraying urine, leaving a scent. In order for a female to select a male rhino for breeding, the centre of his territory needs to be marked in this way to a distance of about 1 sq km.

▶▶ Read further › marking territory pg144 (f2; n32)

A series of messages

Animals often give several messages before they take severe action against attackers. A skunk's black and white stripes are easily recognized when it lifts its tail as a warning to other animals to stay away. If an enemy ignores this, the skunk jumps from side to side, turns around, raises its tail and stands on its front paws before releasing a pungent spray from under its tail to put off the enemy.

▶▶ Read further › sense of smell pg137 (b22)

▼ The striped skunk, found across central North America, can eject its foul-smelling spray to a distance of up to 3 m away.

Where's the food?

Honeybees indicate to each other the site of a rich food source, such as nectar-laden flowers, by 'dancing'. The bee flies in a figure of eight and shakes its body. The angle of the '8' and the number of waggles convey the direction and distance of food from the nest.

▶▶ Read further › nectar pg128 (n14)

▶ In the bees' honeycomb dance, the angle between the straight crossover part of the '8' and the vertical, tells other bees the angle between the Sun and the direction of the food source.

CREATURE COMFORTS

• Yellow and black is one of the commonest colour combinations used as a warning, telling predators 'I taste horrible' or 'I am dangerous'. This pattern is used by various spiders, wasps, fish, butterflies, caterpillars, frogs and snakes.

• After an animal has had an unpleasant encounter with a yellow and black creature, the animal will avoid similar colours, which helps to protect all species with these colours.

▶▶ HUMAN COMMUNICATION see pg208 (d2) ▶▶

22 23 24 25 26 27 28 29 30 31 32 33 34 35 36 37 38 39

Hibernation and migration

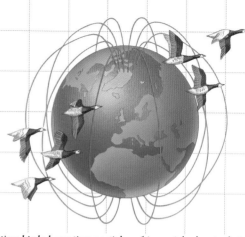

Migrating birds have tiny particles of iron-rich chemicals in their brains, which may detect the Earth's natural magnetic field.

IN THOSE regions of the world where the seasons are distinct, there are warm, bright summers when food is plentiful, followed by cold, dark winters when living conditions are very difficult. Small creatures such as insects can survive the long winter as hard-cased eggs, but mammals and birds cannot. They use two main methods or survival strategies: 'stay or go'. One is to stay in the region but go into a very deep sleep, known as hibernation, then wake up the next spring. The other is to migrate – travel away on a long journey – returning the following spring.

Flying visits

Birds are the main migrants. They can travel long distances quickly. Many types of geese and ducks live in Europe, Asia and North America during winter. Then they fly north in the spring to the Arctic, where the brief summer encourages an 'explosion' of plants, insects and other foods. The birds nest and raise their young in the Arctic, then fly back again in autumn.

▶▶ Read further › flying
pg128 (f2)

CREATURE COMFORTS

• Some animals such as lemmings and locusts migrate only occasionally. After several years of good conditions in their home region their numbers increase too much. They run out of food so set off looking for new places to live.

• Some animals actually migrate up and down mountains. Mountain sheep and cattle climb to high pastures in summer and descend to sheltered valleys in winter.

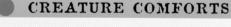

During migration, some reindeer travel up to 65 km each day. The total journey may be more than 800 km and take between two to three weeks.

Learning the way

Each spring, reindeer, known as caribou in North America, trek northwards to the treeless Arctic tundra, where mosses, grasses and other plants grow in the long hours of summer sun. Youngsters learn details of the route each year, and use their experience as they grow older to guide the next generation.

▶▶ Read further › seasonal changes
pg133 (b32)

Some salmon are born in freshwater streams, stay for a year or two, then migrate out to sea. Years later, they migrate back to the same stream they were born in, to lay their own eggs and then die.

Finding the way

Animals such as whales and birds combine methods of navigating – using the position of the Sun, Moon and stars, large landmarks such as mountains or cliffs, and even the Earth's magnetic field. In water, migrating salmon and other fish, turtles and lobsters 'smell' and 'taste' amounts of natural chemicals that change in different rivers or parts of the ocean.

Read further › birds
pg136 (j12)

Badgers live in 'setts' that have many different entrances and tunnels. During cold weather they sometimes go into a deep sleep and stay in their underground setts for long periods of time.

'Knowing' the way

Monarchs are the champion insect migrants. Each spring these butterflies leave a few over-wintering areas of southwest and North America and fly north, feeding and breeding as they go. Their offspring return in autumn. They do not live long enough to learn the route – instead it is in-built, or instinctive.

Read further › breeding
pg146 (d2)

▲ *Monarch butterflies can fly up to 80 km each day.*

IT'S A FACT

• The furthest travelling migrant is the Arctic tern that flies from the Arctic to Antarctica and back each year – covering 35,000 km.

• The birch mouse hibernates up to eight months a year, spending over two-thirds of its life asleep.

Cold and slow

Only warm-blooded animals truly hibernate. (Winter inactivity of cold-blooded animals is called torpor.) Most are rodents and bats, but bears and hedgehogs also hibernate. They feed hungrily in autumn to build up stores of fat, then fall into a deep winter sleep. Body temperature drops from about 40°C to as low as 3°C. Breathing is very slow and the heart beats once every few minutes.

Read further › storing food for winter
pg133 (b32)

Check it out!

• http://www.nk.psu.edu/nature trail/Winter/hibernation.htm

◄◄ MAGNETIC FIELDS see pg21 (b31) ◄◄

22 23 24 25 26 27 28 29 30 31 32 33 34 35 36 37 38 39

a b c d e f g h i j k l m n o p q r s t u v w

Camouflage and mimicry

▲ Chameleons change colour (camouflage) to communicate and control their temperature (going darker makes them warmer).

A RAINFOREST OR coral reef may seem empty of creatures – until a closer look reveals 'leaves' that are really butterflies *(see pg141 [d37])*, or 'seaweed' that is a fish. Blending with the background is called camouflage. It keeps animals hidden from predators – and also helps predators hide from their prey before catching it. Camouflage usually involves colours, patterns and shapes, but it can also include movements, sounds and smells. Other animals have bright colours and patterns that act as a warning that they are venomous or have poisonous flesh. When one animal copies another, but is itself harmless, it is called mimicry.

● Master of disguise

The chameleon – a type of lizard – can change its colour and pattern in minutes to blend in with its background. It uses tiny coloured particles, called pigments, in its skin that can clump together so they are not seen, or spread out to show their hue. For example, when the chameleon moves from a leafy branch to dry twigs, it changes from green to brown.

▶▶ **Read further › stick insect**
pg147 (b30)

● IT'S A FACT

• Batesian mimicry is when several harmful, poisonous or horrible-tasting animals all resemble each other.

• Mullerian mimicry is when a harmless animal avoids being eaten by copying a harmful one.

● Keeping still

▶▶ **Read further › spitting spiders**
pg13 (b33)

Movement is an important part of camouflage. A crab spider or flower mantis must keep perfectly still, hidden among the same coloured petals. The slightest movement would reveal it not only to its prey – it may itself become prey for a watching lizard or bird.

◀ Crab spiders are so-called because they can walk sideways (like crabs). Some can even change colour to match different flowers.

▶▶ COLOUR see pg199 (c33) ▶▶

1 2 3 4 5 6 7 8 9 10 11 12 13 14 15 16 17 18 19

Flat as a 'carpet'

The carpet shark – or wobbegong – spends most of its time simply lying on the seabed. Its body is flattened and has lumps and frills in shades of yellow, green and brown, which resemble the seaweed-covered rocks. As an unsuspecting fish swims up to it, the carpet shark lurches forwards and opens its huge mouth to swallow the victim in one gulp.

▼ *Wobbegongs remain close to the shore in shallow water, sometimes partly lying in the open air when the tide falls.*

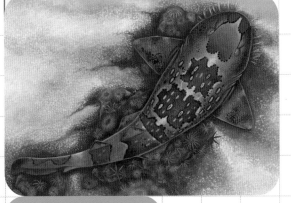

▶▶ Read further › anglerfish
pg131 (e22)

Model and mimic

The animal that a mimic copies is called the model. The venomous coral snake is a model for mimics such as the non-venomous king snake or the milksnake. Bigger predators that try to eat a coral snake get bitten, suffer pain, and learn to avoid it and any animal that looks like it. This is how mimics gain protection from predators.

▶▶ Read further › cobra
pg138 (i12)

▲ *Milksnakes are mostly nocturnal snakes that feed on amphibians and small rodents. The order of the colours in their pattern differs slightly from their model, the coral snake, but is close enough to fool any potential predators.*

Spots and stripes

▶▶ Read further › leopard
pg130 (n2)

In the forest, light shines through leaves and creates many patches of brightness and shade thus creating patchy camouflage. Most forest cats, from margays to leopards *(see pg130 [r10])* have spotted coats, as do young deer and baby wild boar, which lie silent and still in the undergrowth while their mothers feed. Animals that live in cold regions are pure or patchy white to blend in with the shade and light of the snow and ice.

◀ *The Arctic hare of Canada and Greenland has a thick, almost pure white coat to keep warm and blend in with the snow. But its coat may moult to a thinner, grey-brown one for the summer.*

CREATURE COMFORTS

• Many fish are darker on their upper side and lighter on their underside for camouflage in sunlit waters where light comes from above. This is called countershading.

• The mimic octopus can change its colours and move its tentacles to pretend to be a ray, an anglerfish or even a shark, warning off predators.

◀ *Snow leopards have thicker, lighter coats than other leopards, to blend in with their icy mountain habitat.*

◀◀ FOREST LIGHT see pg99 (h22) ◀◀

a b c d e f g h i j k l m n o p q r s t u v w

Courtship and territories

IT'S A FACT

• Some of the most complicated bird courtships are those of the male birds of paradise, which have loud songs, brightly-coloured feathers, and hang upside down from branches.

• The territorial howl of the grey wolf can reach up to 6 km away, telling rival wolf packs to stay out of its territory.

COURTSHIP IS an essential part of male and female animals getting together to mate (breed). Courtship can involve sight, sound, smell, movement or all of these. Courting partners check they are both of the same species, fully-grown and able to breed and are strong and healthy. This gives their offspring the greatest chance of being strong, fit and healthy. In some animals, breeding also depends on owning a territory. This is an area that the animal occupies and defends against others. Usually it is the male partner that performs the main courtship display and holds the territory.

● Breeding requirements

Male antelopes, such as topi, gather in a traditional area and snort, prance and clash to see who is the biggest and strongest. The winners take charge of small territories, called 'leks', at the centre of the area, where they are more attractive to females. A lek-less male cannot breed. Birds such as grouse also use the lek system.

▲ A grouse struts around with his head pointed upwards, whilst fanning his feathers and making bubbling and scraping noises to attract a female.

● Partners for life

Many animals mate with different partners each year, either one or several. However, some larger birds, such as swans, are monogamous – they mate for life. This means they only have one partner throughout their lifetime. A female swan lays up to eight eggs, which she cares for until they hatch, then both parents look after them.

▶▶ Read further > breeding
pg146 (d2)

▼ Each spring pairs of swans renew their relationship by twining their necks together and calling to each other.

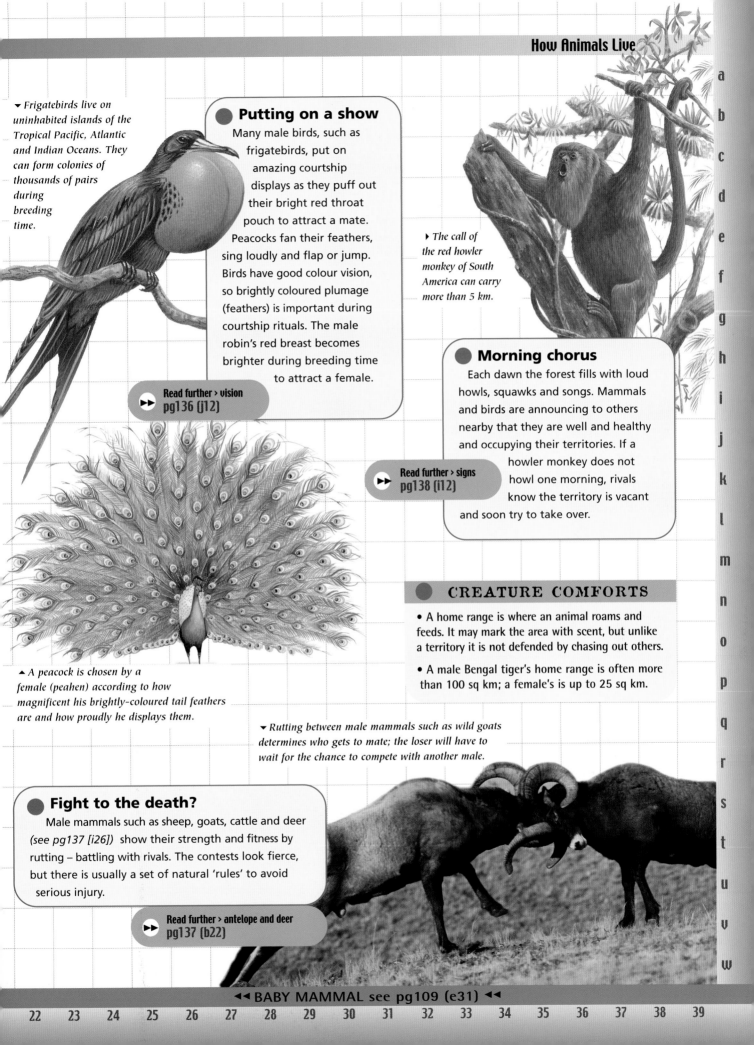

▼ *Frigatebirds live on uninhabited islands of the Tropical Pacific, Atlantic and Indian Oceans. They can form colonies of thousands of pairs during breeding time.*

Putting on a show

Many male birds, such as frigatebirds, put on amazing courtship displays as they puff out their bright red throat pouch to attract a mate. Peacocks fan their feathers, sing loudly and flap or jump. Birds have good colour vision, so brightly coloured plumage (feathers) is important during courtship rituals. The male robin's red breast becomes brighter during breeding time to attract a female.

Read further › vision
pg136 (j12)

▶ *The call of the red howler monkey of South America can carry more than 5 km.*

Morning chorus

Each dawn the forest fills with loud howls, squawks and songs. Mammals and birds are announcing to others nearby that they are well and healthy and occupying their territories. If a howler monkey does not howl one morning, rivals know the territory is vacant and soon try to take over.

Read further › signs
pg138 (i12)

▲ *A peacock is chosen by a female (peahen) according to how magnificent his brightly-coloured tail feathers are and how proudly he displays them.*

CREATURE COMFORTS

• A home range is where an animal roams and feeds. It may mark the area with scent, but unlike a territory it is not defended by chasing out others.

• A male Bengal tiger's home range is often more than 100 sq km; a female's is up to 25 sq km.

▼ *Rutting between male mammals such as wild goats determines who gets to mate; the loser will have to wait for the chance to compete with another male.*

Fight to the death?

Male mammals such as sheep, goats, cattle and deer *(see pg137 [i26])* show their strength and fitness by rutting – battling with rivals. The contests look fierce, but there is usually a set of natural 'rules' to avoid serious injury.

Read further › antelope and deer
pg137 (b22)

◀◀ BABY MAMMAL see pg109 (e31) ◀◀

22 23 24 25 26 27 28 29 30 31 32 33 34 35 36 37 38 39

a b c d e f g h i j k l m n o p q r s t u v w

Breeding

B REEDING OR reproduction – making more of the same kind – is essential for all living things. Animals use many different methods. Some small and simple creatures, such as tiny tree-shaped hydras in ponds, simply grow offspring as 'stalks' on their own bodies. This is asexual (one-parent) reproduction. But most animals reproduce sexually, when a male and female mate. The male's sperm join with – fertilize – the female's eggs. The majority of creatures, from worms to birds, lay eggs. Only mammals and a few reptiles, fish and invertebrates, give birth to babies.

Wrong offspring

The cuckoo is a 'reproductive parasite'. The female cuckoo replaces an egg in another bird's nest with her own egg, then flies away. The host bird looks after the new egg and chick, which pushes out the other chicks after it hatches.

▶▶ Read further › mating pg144 (f2)

▲ *These flycatchers are the host parents of this cuckoo chick, which may eventually grow bigger than they are.*

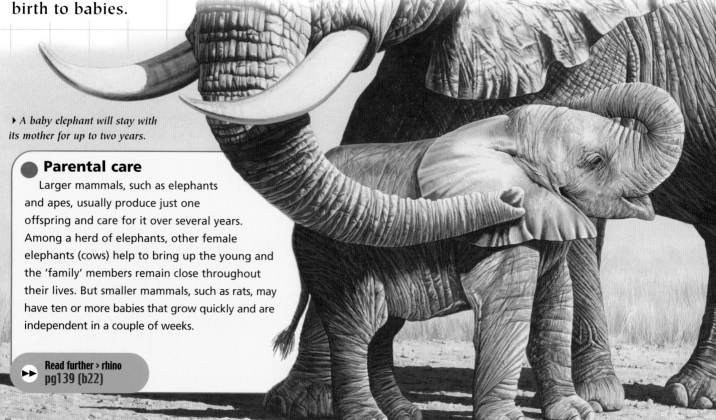

▶ *A baby elephant will stay with its mother for up to two years.*

Parental care

Larger mammals, such as elephants and apes, usually produce just one offspring and care for it over several years. Among a herd of elephants, other female elephants (cows) help to bring up the young and the 'family' members remain close throughout their lives. But smaller mammals, such as rats, may have ten or more babies that grow quickly and are independent in a couple of weeks.

▶▶ Read further › rhino pg139 (b22)

Fatherly duties

Most animals develop inside their mother, growing as eggs before being born to continue growing physically independent of the mother. However, seahorses, though they begin life in their mother, actually develop from eggs inside their father. The female seahorse lays her eggs in a pocket-like pouch on the male's front. The eggs hatch two to six weeks later into young seahorses. Then the father seems to 'give birth' as the small babies pop out of his pouch.

▸ *The seahorse anchors itself to eel grass using its tail, which is specially adapted for grasping.*

▶▶ **Read further › sea creatures** pg131 (j22)

No male needed

Some aphids (greenfly), flatworms, leeches and other smaller animals reproduce by parthenogenesis – the female can produce eggs or babies without having mated with a male. Usually the stick insect lays eggs by parthenogenesis wherby the offspring will grow into females. But if she has mated with a male, the eggs will hatch into both females and males. Parthenogenesis also occurs in some fish, stick insects and in types of whiptail and wall lizards.

▲ *Stick insects often have leaf-like bodies as a camouflage (they adopt the colour of the background) to avoid danger.*

▶▶ **Read further › camouflage** pg142 (f12)

Outside the body

On land, a female and male animal usually mate when the sperm pass into the female's body to fertilize the eggs – internal fertilization. However, in water, many kinds of frogs, fish, shellfish, worms and other animals simply release their eggs and sperm into the water, and leave fertilization to chance – external fertilization.

▾ *The chance of fertilization among frogs is increased by the male releasing his sperm straight onto the jelly-covered eggs that the female lays in the water.*

To scale

Each square = 4 cm across
Different sizes of birds' eggs

Ostrich egg
16 cm long

Hummingbird egg
1 cm long

● LONGEST GESTATION

Animal	Length of gestation
• Elephant	600–660 days
• Whale	520 days
• Rhinoceros	490 days
• Walrus	480 days
• Giraffe	460 days

● **Check it out!**
• http://www.saburchill.com/
chapters/chap0031.html

◀◀ FROG LIFE CYCLE see pg115 (j22) ◀◀

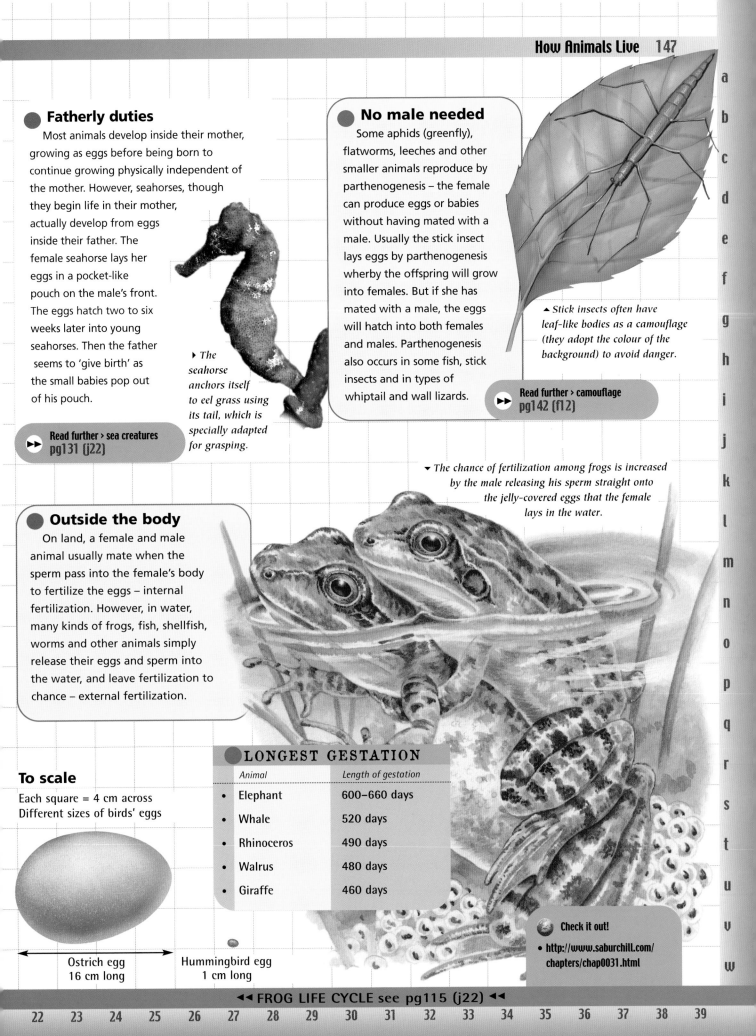

Animals in danger

IN THE next few hours, somewhere in the world, a species of animal will become extinct – completely disappear and be gone for ever. This will probably be because of human activity, such as cutting down a rainforest to turn it into farmland or polluting water with chemical pesticides. The species may be a rare kind of bird or mammal, but it is more likely to be a small insect such as a bug or beetle. Indeed, it is likely that the species is not even known to science, because only about 1.8 million animal species have been described and named by scientists. The real number of species living in the world today could be more than 20 million.

◀◀ FOREST DESTRUCTION see pg99 (o29) ◀◀

CREATURE COMFORTS

• Nearly half of the world's tropical rainforests have been destroyed over the last 50 years to clear the way for farmland or buildings.

• In some regions, powdered rhino horn or crushed tiger bones are worth more than gold for the medicinal qualities they are believed to possess.

IT'S A FACT

• It is estimated that one-quarter of all bird species are under some type of threat to their survival, mainly from habitat disturbance.

• Today's 'hot spots' of risk include the rainforests of Central and South America, West Africa and Southeast Asia, and coral reefs across the tropics.

Precious but passing away

The biggest threat to animals is the destruction of their habitat. For example, this occurs when a forest is cut down for timber and the trees are not replaced, or when houses, factories and roads are built through the countryside. When an animal such as a golden lion tamarin's natural habitat disappears, it has nowhere to breed or find food, so it may decline in numbers until it eventually dies out altogether.

▶ *Golden lion tamarins are victims of habitat destruction in coastal rainforests in Brazil. However, many have been bred in captivity, and released back into the wild.*

▶▶ Read further > breeding
pg146 (d2)

1 2 3 4 5 6 7 8 9 10 11 12 13 14 15 16 17 18 19

▶ *The pet trade is responsible for many thousands of parrot captures each year. Some species of parrot have already become extinct due to capture and habitat destruction.*

Varied threats

The rare river dolphins of the Amazon, Ganges and other great waterways face many problems. Their survival is threatened by water pollution from chemicals that are pumped into the river from factories and dams that block their way. They must compete with fishermen for food supplies and avoid boats with slashing propellers that may harm them and noisy engines that disrupt their sound-sonar communication system. Outbreaks of disease and being hunted for their meat are also great threats to their survival.

Read further > dolphins
pg129 (s22)

▲ *The number of Ganges river dolphin are now fewer than 1000.*

Rare meat

As people in poor countries struggle to feed themselves, some turn to hunting wild animals for meat or to sell as pets at large markets in towns. This fast-growing trade affects apes monkeys, wild pigs, antelopes, bats, tropical birds such as parrots, lizards and snakes, especially in poor countries such as some parts of Africa.

Read further > snakes
pg143 (c30)

Hunting and collecting

Read further > pollution
pg149 (k34)

Tigers are often killed for their luxurious fur, their teeth, which are used in unconventional medicines, and by people who enjoy the 'thrill' of hunting dangerous animals. Great white sharks are caught so often, both for 'sport' and because they may menace swimmers, that they have become a threatened species.

▼ *The biggest type of tiger, the Siberian tiger, is very rare, with fewer than 200 surviving in the wild.*

Pollution

Power stations and vehicles send fumes up into the air, factory pipes pour poisons into the rivers, lakes and seas, and pesticide and herbicide chemicals are washed down from farms. These damaging chemicals, along with disasters such as oil spills, pollute vast areas of sea and coastline and can kill fish and clog up birds' wings so that they are unable to fly and hunt.

◀ *Oil spills devastate coastal wildlife, killing fish and sea creatures that cannot breathe in the contaminated water and so suffocate.*

Read further > damage
pg149 (d22)

▶▶ OIL REFINERIES see pg205 (r26) ▶▶

a
b
c
d
e
f
g
h
i
j
k
l
m
n
o
p
q
r
s
t
u
v
w

22   23   24   25   26   27   28   29   30   31   32   33   34   35   36   37   38   39

Body basics

WE KNOW more about the human body than anything else in the universe. Yet every day we find more detailed information about how the body moves, digests food, gets rid of wastes, controls its internal conditions, fights germs and disease, and stays fit and healthy. We make amazing discoveries about how the eyes see, how the ears hear, and how the brain thinks and learns. There are exciting new facts about the body's genetic information, made of DNA, which contains all the instructions for how the body grows, develops, carries out its life processes and survives in today's hazardous world.

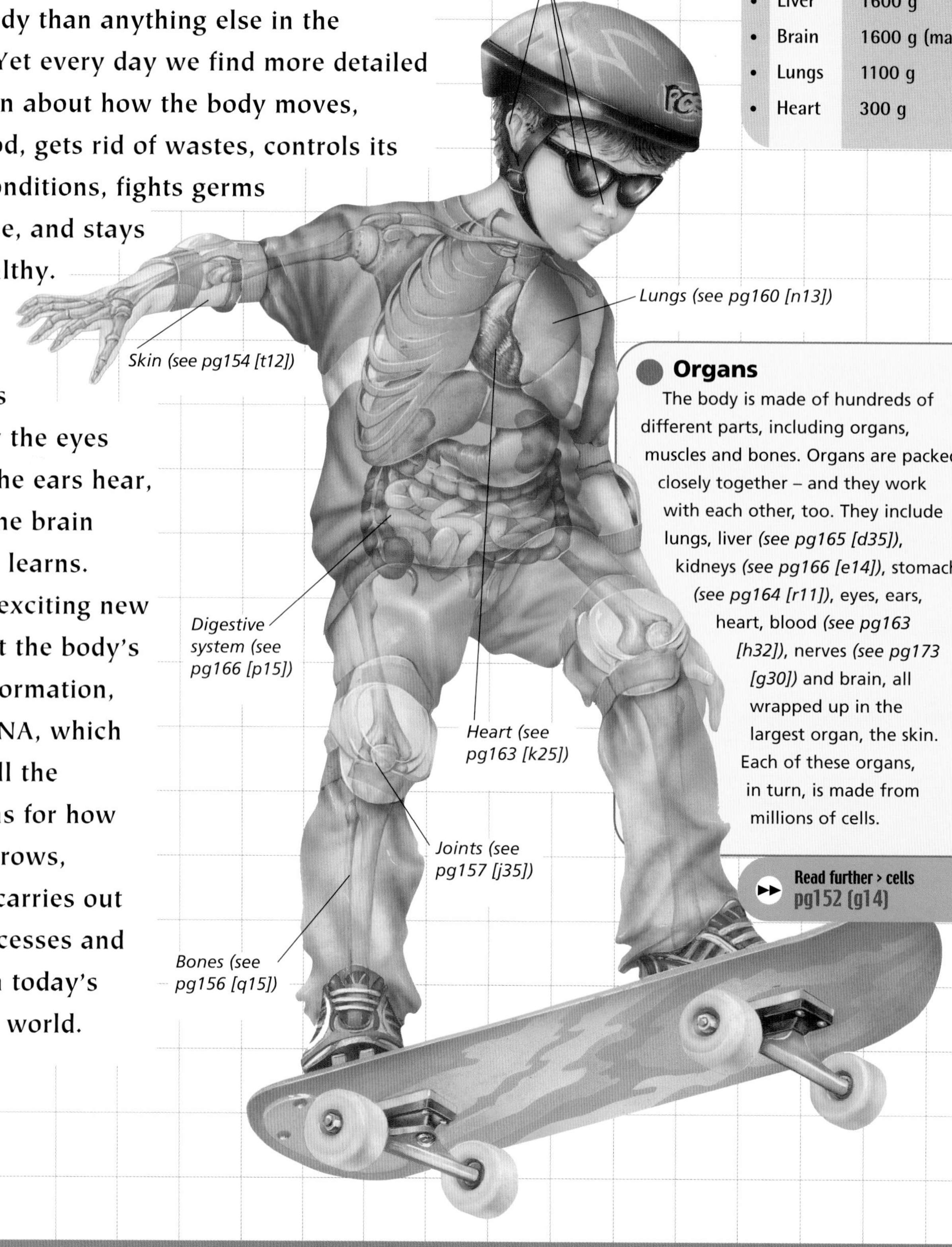

Senses (see pg168 [k10]; pg169 [e28]; pg170 [l12])

●	ORGANS	
	Organ	Weight
●	Skin	4000 g
●	Liver	1600 g
●	Brain	1600 g (males)
●	Lungs	1100 g
●	Heart	300 g

Lungs (see pg160 [n13])

Skin (see pg154 [t12])

Digestive system (see pg166 [p15])

Heart (see pg163 [k25])

Joints (see pg157 [j35])

Bones (see pg156 [q15])

● Organs

The body is made of hundreds of different parts, including organs, muscles and bones. Organs are packed closely together – and they work with each other, too. They include lungs, liver (see pg165 [d35]), kidneys (see pg166 [e14]), stomach (see pg164 [r11]), eyes, ears, heart, blood (see pg163 [h32]), nerves (see pg173 [g30]) and brain, all wrapped up in the largest organ, the skin. Each of these organs, in turn, is made from millions of cells.

▶▶ **Read further > cells** pg152 [g14]

Different outside, same inside

Human bodies have different sizes and shapes – women and men, girls and boys, old and young, wide and slim, dark and light, tall and short – with different clothes and hair styles. But inside, these bodies are almost identical. They all have the same inner parts, or organs, the same muscles and bones, and they work in the same way.

▶▶ **Read further › DNA / organs**
pg152 (b30); pg150 (j14)

Looking inside the living body

We can see inside living bodies in incredible detail, using various kinds of medical scanners. CT (computed tomography) and MRI (magnetic resonance imaging) scanners show details of the body tissues. PET (positron emission tomography) reveals how much energy is being used, especially in different parts of the brain, and can identify changes in cells that may cause disease.

▶▶ **Read further › ultrasound**
pg175 (b34)

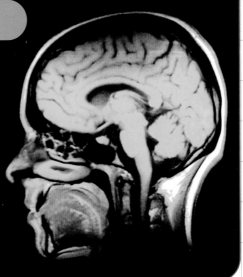

▸ *MRI scans help diagnose diseases of the brain and nervous system. A computer builds a three-dimensional image using information from the scan.*

IT'S A FACT

• Human beings are the most common large, living creatures on Earth.

• There are more than 6000 million humans in the world – far more than any kind of similar-sized animals such as lions, dolphins or even sheep.

• The world's oldest person is a Japanese woman aged about 115.

Social humans

Humans are social beings. Sometimes we want to be alone for a short time. But usually we like to be with other people, especially family and friends, as we talk, laugh and have fun together. In the fast-paced modern world, as we rush from place to place with less time to spare, the greatest fear of some people is being alone.

▶▶ **Read further › smiling**
pg159 (k33)

Check it out!

• http://www.howstuffworks.com/mri.htm
• http://www.kidinfo.com/Health/Human_Body.html

a
b
c
d
e
f
g
h
i
j
k
l
m
n
o
p
q
r
s
t
u
v
w

The micro body

THE HUMAN body is made of more than 50 million million microscopic cells. A typical cell is 0.02 mm across – about 1000 would fit on this full stop. There are at least 200 kinds of cells in the body, with different sizes and shapes, and different functions such as making products, moving substances around, delivering raw materials, collecting wastes or fighting germs. Most cells do not live for long. They wear out and die naturally at the rate of 50 million every second. However, specialized types of cells, called stem cells, are always dividing, to produce new cells that replace the old ones.

Cells and organelles

The cell's outside layer is the plasma membrane. Inside, many tiny organelles (cells with specialized functions) float in the jelly-like cytoplasm. Sausage-shaped mitochondria break down glucose sugar to release its stored chemical energy, which powers the cell's processes. Ball-shaped ribosomes are like tiny factories making new substances, especially proteins, which are the cell's main structural parts or 'building bricks'.

▶▶ **Read further › cells / glucose / nourishment** pg153 (g22); pg167 (j26); pg173 (b34)

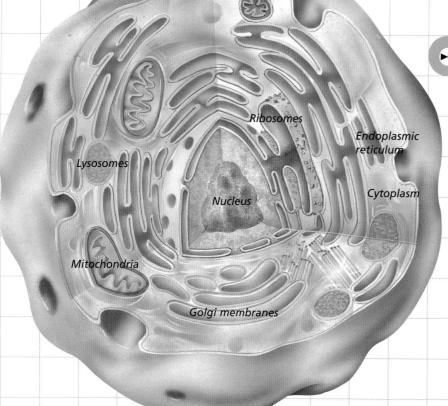

◀ *Inside a cell showing parts called organelles – cells with specialized functions.*

Plasma membrane

Ribosomes

Endoplasmic reticulum

Lysosomes

Cytoplasm

Nucleus

Mitochondria

Golgi membranes

BODY TALK

• Most cells in the body live only a short time. A cell on the inside of the cheek lasts for about 10 hours. A cell on the surface of the skin lives for about 4 weeks, and a liver cell lasts 18 months.

• The longest-lived cells are nerve cells, which last for decades.

Muscle layer

Elastic layer

Tough, outer cover

Inner lining

Plasma

Red cell

White cell

Platelets

Types of cells

Each kind of cell is shaped to carry out a particular function.

In blood, red cells are round and thin, to absorb as much oxygen as possible through their surface. Some white cells *(see pg163 [h34])* are able to alter their shape to engulf germs. The cells of the blood vessel lining are flattened and joined to make a smooth layer. Many cells of the same kind grouped together are called a body tissue.

▾ *Red blood cells (seen under a microscope) are disc-shaped. Each red blood cell contains almost 250 million haemoglobin molecules, which transport oxygen around the body.*

▶▶ **Read further › muscle / nerve cells**
pg159 (b22); pg173 (b34)

Body instructions

The instructions that tell the body how to develop its different parts and make them work together are called the human genome. They are inside each cell in the body, in the form of the chemical DNA (de-oxyribonucleic acid). The whole genome contains 46 lengths of DNA. Until it unravels to reveal its double spiral shape, each is coiled tightly to form a thicker structure – the chromosome. There are 46 chromosomes inside the nucleus of each cell.

DNA coiled into the chromosome

Single chromosome

DNA unravelling

▶▶ **Read further › egg and sperm**
pg175 (k22)

DNA's double helix shape, like a twisted rope ladder

Strands of DNA dividing to make new copies

Strands are linked by chemical subunits called bases

New strands are identical to the original ones

New strands are built upon the original ones

Each of these bases pairs up with only one other base

Check it out!
• http://www.bioanim.com
• http://www.biology.eku.edu/ RITCHISO/301notes1.htm

◀◀ MOLECULES see pg12 (j15) ◀◀

22 23 24 25 26 27 28 29 30 31 32 33 34 35 36 37 38 39

a b c d e f g h i j k l m n o p q r s t u v w

Wrapped in skin

SKIN IS often said to 'glow with health'. In fact, its surface is dead. The surface of the skin is made of hard, toughened, flattened cells that have filled with the body protein keratin, and then died. They rub away and flake off in their thousands every minute as we move about, wear clothes, wash and dry with towels. Just under the surface, more cells are always multiplying, growing, filling with keratin and dying. They gradually move up to the surface to replace the old, worn-off skin. The whole cycle of skin replacement takes about four weeks.

IT'S A FACT

• Each year the body loses about 4 kg of rubbed-off skin flakes.

• The thinnest skin, on the eyelids, is only 0.5 mm thick.

• The sole of the foot has the thickest skin, up to 5 mm thick.

Read further > nerve signals pg173 (b34)

BODY TALK

• Human skin is very tough. It can repair many minor cuts and replace itself in grazes. But certain types of damage are more serious. In particular, too much strong sunshine is bad for skin.

• The sun's invisible rays, called UV-B (ultra-violet B), can harm the fast-dividing epidermal cells just under the skin's surface. This may cause a serious form of cancer called malignant melanoma. Clothing, a hat and sunscreen cream or lotion helps to shade and protect skin from powerful sunlight.

Under the surface

The upper layer of skin is called the epidermis. At its base are fast-multiplying cells that replace the old, keratin-hardened cells that rub off the surface. Under the epidermis is the thicker dermis. It contains strong, stretchy fibres of another body protein – collagen. The dermis also contains microscopic blood vessels *(see pg163 pu32])*, the growing bases or roots of hairs, sweat glands and nerves ending in micro-sensors to detect touch.

▼ *Greatly enlarged view of skin showing its two main layers – epidermis and dermis.*

Keratin layer of epidermis

Epidermis

Hair

Basal layer, of epidermis, where new cells grow

Hair erector muscle

Gland making oily sebum to keep hair and skin waterproof

Dermis

Hair root in follicle (pit)

Sweat gland

Nerve endings

Check it out!

• http://www.skin-information.com/
• http://www.kidshealth.org/kid/body/ skin_noSW.html

▸ *Microscopic view of a hair growing from its follicle.*

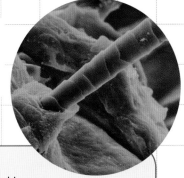

Hairs

Hairs, like skin, are dead. The only living part of a hair is at its base, where it grows in a tiny pit called a follicle *(see pg154 [u10])*. The upper part, or shaft, is made of old, dead, stuck-together hair cells. A hair on the head grows at a rate of about 3 mm each week. Body hairs grow slower; eyelash hairs grow much faster.

▶▶ **Read further › microscopic ear hairs pg169 (b22)**

Cool skin

Skin protects the softer, inner parts of the body from knocks and harm. It keeps in moist body fluids and keeps out dirt, germs and harmful substances such as strong chemicals. If the body is too hot, for example when exercising *(see pg167 [j24])*, tiny sweat glands in skin release watery sweat which oozes onto the surface of the skin. As sweat dries, it draws heat from the body and cools it.

▸ *Sweating helps keeps the body at its correct temperature.*

▶▶ **Read further › sweat pg167 (m34)**

Nails

A nail is hard, tough and dead, and made mainly of keratin. The only living part is its root, buried in the skin, which makes new nail tissue as the whole nail grows towards the fingertip or toetip. On average, fingernails lengthen about 2 mm each month. Toenails grow slightly slower. Both grow faster in summer. Nails form a stiff backing for the flexible fingertips and toetips, so we can feel, touch, sense pressure and grip.

▾ *Nails make fingertips strong enough to pluck guitar strings.*

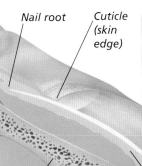

Nail root

Cuticle (skin edge)

Free edge of nail

Bone inside finger

Nail bed

▶▶ **Read further › skin and touch pg170 (r8)**

a b c d e f g h i j k l m n o p q r s t u v w

Joint effort

MORE THAN 200 bones form the body's internal supporting framework, called the skeleton. Bones are strong and stiff, giving the body its shape, protecting internal organs and holding together the soft parts such as blood vessels *(see pg163 [u30])*, nerves and guts. A single bone is rigid and tough, and can hardly bend. But the whole skeleton can move because its bones are linked at flexible joints, designed to reduce rubbing and wear. Bones are very strong, yet they are also very lightweight. They are made of active living tissue, so if they break because of too much pressure on them, they can usually repair themselves.

IT'S A FACT

- There are 206 bones in the average skeleton.
- The longest bone in the body is the thighbone or femur, about one-quarter of the body's height.
- The smallest bone is the stirrup bone in the ear – it is only slightly bigger than this U.

Skull
Collarbone (Clavicle)
Breastbone (Sternum)
Upper arm bone (Humerus)
Rib
Backbone (Vertebrae)
Forearm (Ulna)
Radius
Sacrum
Hip bone (Pelvis)
Thighbone (Femur)
Hand bones (Metacarpals)
Wrist bones (Carpals)
Kneecap (Patella)
Shinbone (Tibia)
Fibula
Ankle bones (Tarsals)
Foot bones (Metatarsals)

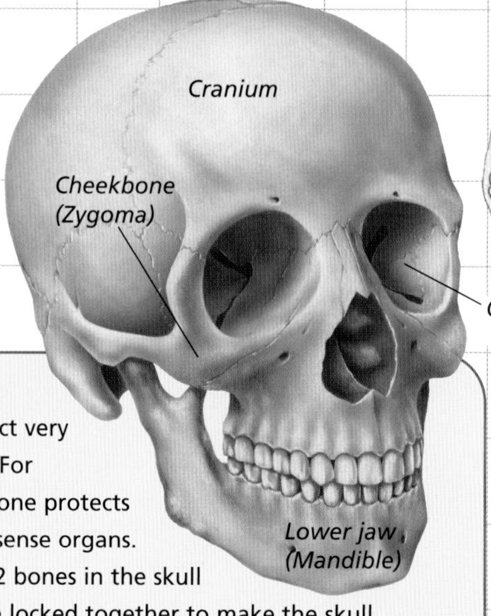

Cranium
Cheekbone (Zygoma)
Orbit
Lower jaw (Mandible)

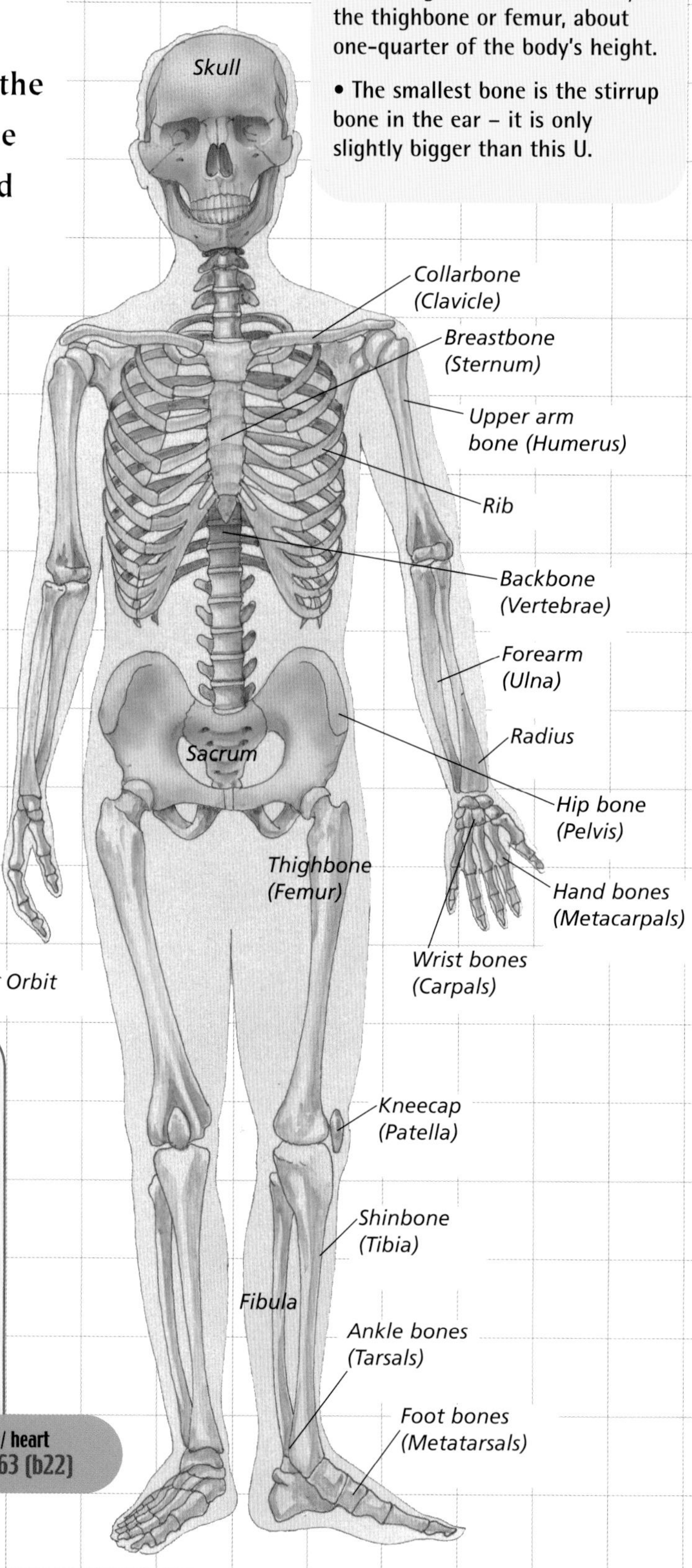

Protection

Some bones protect very delicate body parts. For example, the skull bone protects the brain and main sense organs. All but one of the 22 bones in the skull – the mandible – are locked together to make the skull incredibly strong. Two deep bowl-like sockets called orbits, in the face, protect much of the eyeballs *(see pg168 [l9])*. The backbone, ribs and breastbone form a strong cage around the heart *(see pg163 [k26])* and lungs *(see pg160 [o11])*.

Read further › lungs / heart
pg160 (m2); pg163 (b22)

Three layers

Most bones are not solid bone throughout. They have three layers. Outside is a 'shell' of hard or compact bone, which is very strong and stiff. Inside this is a layer of spongy or cancellous bone, with tiny holes for lightness. In the middle is marrow, a soft and jelly-like substance that makes new red and white cells for the blood. The whole bone is covered by a tough skin-like layer, the periosteum.

Compact bone

Marrow

Spongy bone

Osteon (rod-like subunit bone)

Periosteum

▸ *Bones grow and harden from birth to about the age of 20.*

▶▶ Read further › bone marrow
pg157 (q34)

▸ *The different parts of the knee joint work together to allow freedom of movement.*

Joints

Where bones meet in a joint, they are covered with a shiny, slightly softer substance known as cartilage, which is moistened by a slippery fluid (synovial fluid) that allows the joints to move smoothly. Ligaments are strips of strong tissue that hold bones together at the joints. Tendons are tough connective tissues that link bones to muscles (see pg158 [l6]).

Muscle

Kneecap (Patella)

Thighbone (Femur)

Ligament

Cartilage covers bone end

Tendon

Ligament

Cartilage pad

Shinbone (Tibia)

▶▶ Read further › ball and socket
pg157 (m22)

Joint designs

The body has several different types of joints, which allow different kinds of movements. The hip is a ball-and-socket joint. The rounded end of the femur fits into a cup-shaped socket in the pelvis. This design allows lots of movements – up and down, side to side, and twisting. A hinge joint, such as the knee (see pg157 [j35]), can only move up and down. The elbow is also a hinge joint, which, along with the wrist joint, allows the hand to be turned with the palm facing up or down.

▸ *Gymnasts need supple, flexible joints to achieve extreme positions like this.*

▶▶ Read further › muscles
pg158 (d2); pg159 (b22)

BODY TALK

• An adult's skeleton has 206 bones – but a baby's skeleton has over 340. This is because as the body grows, some separate bones join together to form one bone.

• Marrow is not found in all bones, and not all marrow is the same. In babies, nearly all bones contain red marrow (which makes new blood cells), but as the body grows some changes to yellow marrow (which stores fat).

a b c d e f g h i j k l m n o p q r s t u v w

Muscle power

THE BODY'S 650 muscles make up almost half of its total weight. A typical muscle is striped, long and slim, bulging in the middle, and joined to a bone at each end. However, some muscles are shaped like triangles or sheets and may be joined to several bones, to each other, or not attached to bone, such as the layer of muscle in arteries. Muscles are designed to get shorter, or contract. As they contract, they pull on the bones they are attached to, and so move the body. The contraction of the muscles is controlled by nerve signals sent out from parts of the brain called the motor centres and cerebellum (see pg173 [t27]).

Trapezius turns head

Deltoid lifts arm

Biceps bends elbow

Latissimus dorsi pulls arm back and down (muscle at the back)

Rectus femoris (in front of thigh) straightens the knee

Extensor digitorum straightens fingers

IT'S A FACT

• Muscles make up about 45 per cent of male body weight; 40 per cent in a female.

• The biggest muscle is the gluteus maximus, in the buttocks.

• The smallest muscle is the stapedius, attached to the stirrup bone in the ear, which is the size of this dash —.

▼ A muscle is a bundle of thousands of myofibres that are grouped into bundles called fascicles.

Epimysium (outer covering)

Tapering end or head of muscle

Body or belly of muscle

Tendon

Actin (thin myofilament)

Myosin (thick myofilament)

Layers of muscles

Just under the skin are dozens of muscles called the outer or superficial layer. Under these is usually another, intermediate layer, and there is also a third or deep muscle layer. Not all muscle actions cause movement. Several muscles may tense to hold a part steady and still (see pg157 [s30]). For example, when the body is standing, the neck and back muscles tense to keep it upright and balanced.

◀ Front superficial muscles.

Read further › joints
pg157 (m22)

Check it out!
• http://www.bioanim.com

To and fro
A muscle can forcefully pull or contract, but it cannot forcefully push or extend. So most muscles occur in pairs called antagonistic partners. One pulls the bone one way, and the other, on the opposite side of the bone, pulls the other way. Muscle pairs work together with other pairs as large muscle teams to move bones in many directions. When playing sport, our muscles are working in groups of pairs to respond to the moves we require.

▶▶ Read further > face muscles
pg159 [k33]

◀ *More than 50 muscles work in each arm when playing sports such as volleyball.*

BODY TALK
• Muscles need energy to work. The energy needed comes from glucose, or blood sugar, which is carried by the blood.

• When a muscle is very active it needs much greater supplies of glucose. So the heart beats faster than normal and the blood vessels to the muscles widen, supplying the muscle with three times more blood than it has when it is at rest.

Fasciae enclose large groups of muscle fibres

Muscle fibres
A muscle contains bundles of long, thin muscle fibres (myofibres), about the width of human hairs *(see pg155 [b24])*. Each fibre is made of even thinner parts called muscle fibrils (myofibrils). And each fibril contains even narrower parts, myofilaments. There are two kinds of filaments, made of different types of protein: actin, which is thin, and myosin, which is thick. These slide past each other to shorten the fibrils, causing the whole muscle to contract.

▶▶ Read further > muscle layers
pg158 (m9)

Nerve branches

Muscle fibres (myofibres)

Muscle fibril (myofibrils)

Face muscles
Most muscles pull on bones, and the bones work as long levers to move the skeleton *(see pg156 [l14])*. But in the face, several sets of muscles are joined to each other as well as to bones. There are seven muscles on each side of the mouth, which can pull it wider, up or down. More than 50 muscles are needed to make the facial expressions that show other people our thoughts and feelings.

▶▶ Read further > bones and joints
pg156 (d2)

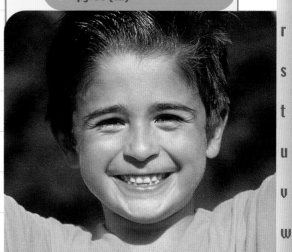

▶ *The muscles used to smile are called voluntary muscles because we can control how and when we use them, to express how we are feeling.*

Take a breath

IN AN EMERGENCY, the human body can survive without food for several days, and even without water for a day or two. But it cannot survive without air for more than a few minutes. The air around us contains the gas oxygen. We cannot see, smell or taste oxygen. But it is needed for chemical changes inside the body, which break apart the high-energy substance glucose (blood sugar) obtained from food. The energy released from glucose powers almost all of the body's life processes. The parts specialized to take in air and pass oxygen from it into the blood, for spreading around the body, are known as the respiratory system.

IT'S A FACT

• A pair of adult lungs holds about 3 litres of air.

• Opened out and laid out flat, the alveoli would cover an area about the size of half a soccer pitch.

▾ Inside the lungs, the bronchus divides into narrower bronchioles and again into even narrower alveoli.

Trachea

Muscles in wall of bronchus

Right bronchus

Air space inside bronchus

View along inside of bronchus

Right lung

Blood vessel

Alveoli

Capillaries

Bronchiole

Air spaces in alveoli

Respiratory system

The respiratory system consists of the nose, throat, larynx (voice box), trachea (windpipe), bronchi (main airways in the chest) and the lungs. Breathing in, or inspiring, draws fresh air into the lungs, where oxygen is taken in or absorbed into the blood (see pg162 [h17]). Breathing out, or expiring, causes the low-oxygen 'used air' to be pushed up along the airways and out of the body. The lungs' airways branch many times, becoming too thin to see. At the end of each branch is a group of microscopic air bubbles, called alveoli, surrounded by a network of equally tiny blood vessels, called capillaries. Oxygen seeps or diffuses from the air inside the alveoli, into blood in the capillaries, and is carried around the body.

Read further > blood vessels pg163 (p28)

Check it out!
• http://www.kidinfo.com/Health/Human_Body.html

◄◄ OXYGEN see pg35 (b22) ◄◄

1 2 3 4 5 6 7 8 9 10 11 12 13 14 15 16 17 18 19

a
b
c
d
e
f
g
h
i
j
k
l
m
n
o
p
q
r
s
t
u
v
w

● Absorbing oxygen

The main breathing muscle is the diaphragm, which is dome-shaped and sits under the lungs. When it tenses or contracts, it becomes flatter, expanding the lungs to suck in air. As the diaphragm relaxes again, the stretched lungs shrink back to their smaller size, pushing out air. Muscles between the ribs also contract when breathing in, to lift the front of the chest and help expand the lungs.

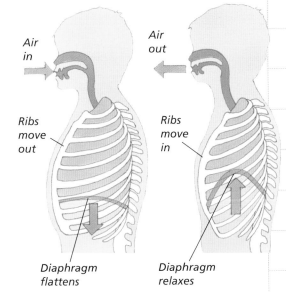

Air in

Ribs move out

Diaphragm flattens

Air out

Ribs move in

Diaphragm relaxes

> **Read further › muscle contraction**
> **pg159 (b22)**

● Carrying air

There is no air in space, so astronauts must take their own supply of it. The air is contained in a special kind of backpack, which holds a main air tank and a reserve air tank. The main tank is connected to the astronaut's helmet. Whilst wearing the helmet, the astronaut is able to breathe in oxygen that is pumped into it from the tank. Chemicals inside the tank remove the carbon dioxide that is breathed out, to keep the air in the tank fresh.

> **Read further › waste disposal**
> **pg167 (m34)**

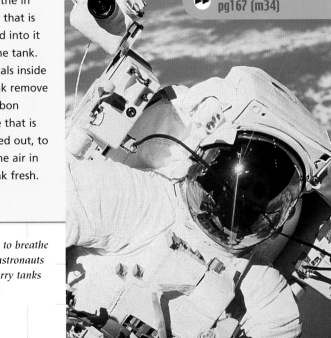

▸ *In order to breathe in space, astronauts have to carry tanks of oxygen.*

● Vocal cords

Inside the larynx (voice box), in the front of the neck, two stiff ridges called vocal cords stick out from the sides. During normal breathing there is a triangle-shaped gap for air. To speak, muscles pull the ridges almost together. Air passing through the narrow gap makes them vibrate (shake to and fro rapidly), which produces sound.

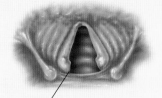

When the cords are apart, no sound is made as air can move freely past them

When the cords are pulled together by the laryngeal muscles, air is forced through a small gap and the cords vibrate to create a sound

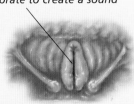

> **Read further › baby lungs**
> **pg175 (r26)**

● BODY TALK

• The bulk of air, almost 79 per cent, is the gas nitrogen, which the body does not use. Fresh air when breathed into the body contains about 21 per cent oxygen and almost no carbon dioxide.

• After air has been in the lungs and breathed out, the proportion of carbon dioxide rises to 4 per cent. The proportion of oxygen falls to 15 per cent.

◄◄ ASTRONAUTS see pg57 (h32) ◄◄

Heartbeat

BLOOD FLOWS round and round the body in a system of tubes called blood vessels. It is pumped by the heart, which has hollow chambers with strong muscular walls that contract to push the blood through the vessels. Blood carries many substances that are vital for life. These include oxygen and glucose (blood sugar) for energy, nutrients and raw materials for growth and repair, and natural body chemicals, called hormones, that control internal processes. At the same time, blood also takes away wastes and unwanted materials, including carbon dioxide, which is breathed out in the lungs.

The brain receives more blood for its size than any other part of the body

The pulmonary circulation takes blood to and from the lungs

Blood leaves the heart through a giant artery called the aorta

Blood returns to the heart through large veins called venae cavae

Radial artery

Iliac vein

Femoral artery

Saphenous vein

Peroneal artery

IT'S A FACT

• In most people, blood forms about one-twelfth (about 8 per cent) of the total body weight.

• An average adult man has a blood volume of 5 to 6 litres.

• An average adult woman has a blood volume of 4 to 5 litres.

• Compared to an adult, a baby has slightly less blood for its body size.

● Circulatory system

The heart sends blood out into thick-walled vessels, called arteries. These branch and divide as they spread around the body, becoming thinner until they are microscopic blood vessels only one-hundredth of a millimetre across, called capillaries. Capillary walls are so thin that oxygen and other substances can easily diffuse (seep) out to the parts around. Capillaries join to make wider vessels, veins, that take blood back to the heart. On average, a drop of blood takes one minute to travel from the heart, through these vessels and back again. This movement is called the circulatory system.

● Check it out!

• http://sln.fi.edu/biosci/heart.html

▶▶ Read further > blood vessels
pg163 (p28)

◄◄ ANIMAL RESPIRATION see pg134 (f2) ◄◄

1   2   3   4   5   6   7   8   9   10   11   12   13   14   15   16   17   18   19

Two pumps in one

The heart is not a single pump, but two, because the body has two circulations. The right side of the heart sends blood through the pulmonary circulation to the lungs *(see pg160 [m14])*, to pick up supplies of oxygen. This blood returns to the left side of the heart, which pumps it all around the body in the systemic circulation, to deliver the oxygen. The blood comes back to the heart again to continue its endless journey.

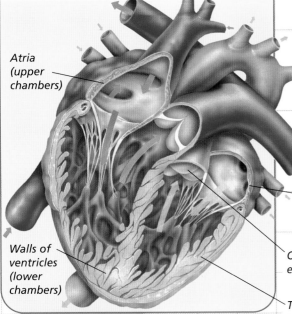

Atria (upper chambers)

Walls of ventricles (lower chambers)

Thin walls of atria stretch as blood enters from the veins

One-way valves inside the heart ensure blood flows the correct way

Thick muscular ventricle walls contract to push blood into the arteries

Read further > lungs
pg161 (b22)

A complex liquid

About half of blood is a watery fluid, plasma, with glucose, hormones and many other substances dissolved in it. The other half is composed of cells. There are three main types: red cells carrying oxygen, white cells to fight disease, and platelets to help blood to clot and seal a wound. One cubic mm of blood (the size of a pinhead) contains 5 million red cells, 8000 white cells and 350,000 platelets.

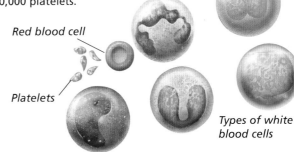

Red blood cell

Platelets

Types of white blood cells

▲ There are two main types of white blood cell: monocytes that surround and digest germs, and lymphocytes that use antibodies to destroy germs.

Read further > cells / lymph nodes
pg152 (d2); pg153 (g22); pg167 (b34)

▼ Veins are wide and their walls are thin and floppy.

Inner lining (endothelium)

Valve in vein

Elastic layer

BODY TALK

• The heartbeat rate is measured in the wrist as the pulse rate, and it varies with age and activity. A new baby's average rate is 120 to 130 per minute, even when asleep. By about the age of seven years old, this average resting rate has fallen to 80 to 90. In the adult body, the rate is around 70.

• During hard exercise, such as running a race, the adult pulse rate can double, up to about 140.

Blood vessels

Arteries have thick, stretchy walls to cope with pressure as blood surges out of the heart at high speed. Each heartbeat makes the arteries bulge all through the body. The bulge or pulsation is felt easily in the wrist as the pulse. Capillary walls are only one cell thick. Veins carry slow-moving, low-pressure blood. Because blood moves so slowly, many veins, particularly in the legs, have valves to stop blood from flowing the wrong way.

Thin muscle layer

Capillaries

Vein

Artery

Thick muscle layer

Read further > blood
pg163 (b30)

Eating for life

THE BODY takes in a huge range of foods including meat and fish, bread, rice and pasta, and fresh fruits and vegetables. But the journey for all these foods is the same. They pass into the digestive tract, which is a passageway looped and coiled within the body. As foods pass along the tract they are broken down or digested into smaller, simpler substances, called nutrients, which can be absorbed into the blood stream. The whole journey for food, from one end of the tract to the other, lasts up to 48 hours.

▲ A balanced diet including fresh vegetables, for essential minerals, and carbohydrate, for energy, is vital for a healthy digestive system.

Check it out!
- http://www.geocities.com/Area 51/Dunes/9641/digestive.htm
- http://www.borg.com/~lube hawk/hdigsys.htm

Three pairs of salivary glands make saliva

Swallowed food goes down the oesophagus (gullet)

Liver (plays an important role in processing digested food)

Stomach

Pancreas (secretes pancreatic juices)

Large intestine

Small intestine

Appendix

Rectum

Anus

IT'S A FACT
- In an adult the whole digestive tract is about 9 m long.
- The longest part of the digestive system is the small intestine, measuring 6 m.
- The large intestine is about 1.5 m long.

Digestive system
In the mouth, foods are chewed and moistened by saliva (spit). They are swallowed down the oesophagus (gullet) into the stomach, and are churned around with gastric juices that contain chemicals called acids and enzymes. These enzymes turn food into a thick soup-like substance, called chyme, which oozes into the small intestine. Here nutrients are absorbed into the blood. Waste products are stored in the rectum and leave the body through the anus.

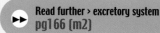
Read further › excretory system pg166 (m2)

BODY TALK
- During a large meal the stomach stretches to hold about 1.5 litres of chewed food. Its lining makes a powerful acid – hydrochloric acid – to attack and digest food. This acid also helps to kill germs (harmful microbes) in the food.
- The stomach does not digest its own lining because it is coated with a layer of slimy mucus, which resists the acid attack.

● Liver

The liver is not part of the digestive tract, but it is part of the digestive system. It receives nutrient-rich blood from the small intestine. The liver makes a green liquid called bile, which breaks down fatty foods. Bile is stored in the gall bladder. To the left of the liver and behind the stomach is another digestive organ, the pancreas. It produces powerful enzymes to aid food breakdown in the small intestine.

▶▶ **Read further › digestion / waste**
pg164 (i13); pg166 (m2)

Right lobe

Left lobe

Dividing ligament

Hepatic artery (brings oxygen-rich blood from the heart)

Bile duct

Gall bladder

Hepatic portal vein (carries food-rich blood from the small intestine)

▼ *Inside a tooth, many blood vessels and nerves pass through the pulp into the jaw bone.*

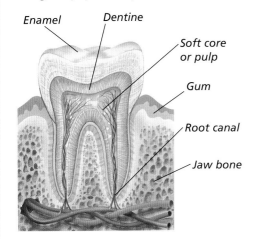

Enamel
Dentine
Soft core or pulp
Gum
Root canal
Jaw bone

● Small intestine

Most nutrients are absorbed through the small intestine lining into the blood flowing through its walls. The lining is folded into ridges called plicae, and the surfaces of the plicae are also folded, into tiny finger-like structures about 1 mm tall, called villi. Similarly, the surface of each villus is covered with thousands of microvilli. The plicae, villi and microvilli give a huge surface area for absorbing nutrients – more than 20 times the body's whole skin area.

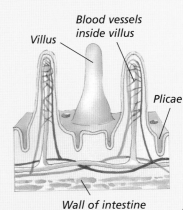

Blood vessels inside villus
Villus
Plicae
Wall of intestine

▸ *Villi line the intestine.*

▶▶ **Read further › digestive system**
pg164 (i13)

● Teeth

A person has 52 teeth, but not at the same time. The first (baby) set appear soon after birth and number 20. These deciduous teeth begin to fall out when children are about six years old, and are replaced by the second (adult) or permanent set of 32 teeth. Each tooth is covered by enamel (*see pg165 [i23]*), the hardest substance in the body. Under the enamel is slightly softer dentine. The centre of the tooth has a living pulp of blood vessels and nerves.

First incisor
Second incisor
Canine
First and second premolars
First and second molars
Third molar (wisdom tooth)

▶▶ **Read further › blood vessels**
pg163 (p28)

▲ *The adult teeth in one half of the lower jaw.*

To scale
Each square of the grid = 1 cm

Average baby molar tooth is 0.5 cm

Average adult molar tooth is 1.5 cm

◀◀ ANIMAL TEETH see pg133 (q22) ◀◀

Water and waste

THE BODY'S thousands of internal chemical processes, which work together, are known as its metabolism. This produces wastes of many kinds. Two main systems get rid of such body wastes. The digestive system removes not only bits of leftover and undigested food, but also some wastes of metabolism. The other waste disposal system is the urinary system whose main organs are the kidneys. They filter waste products, unwanted salts and water from the blood, and dispose of them in a watery fluid called urine. The amount of urine that is produced is controlled by hormones.

Adrenal gland

Right kidney

Inside the left kidney

Major artery and vein

Renal artery and vein

Ureter

Urethra

Bladder

▸ *The urinary system controls the balance of water in the body.*

● Excretion and digestion

About one-fifth of the blood pumped out by the heart *(see pg163 [i25])* goes to the two kidneys. Inside each kidney are about 1 million tiny filters called nephrons. These take waste substances from the blood, along with excess water, to form urine. The urine flows down a tube, the ureter, to the bladder in the lower body. The bladder usually needs to be emptied, through the urethra, when it contains about 400 ml of urine. The solid wastes are removed from the end of the digestive tract through the anus. They contain mainly rubbed-off bits of intestine lining and undigested parts of food.

▸ *Food takes about 48 hours to work its way through the digestive system.*

Liver

Stomach

Gall bladder

Pancreas

Small intestine

Large intestine

Anus

Read further ▸ digestion
▸▸ **pg164 (i13)**

Renal artery brings blood to the kidney

Renal vein takes filtered blood away from the kidney

Ureter takes urine to the bladder

Renal capsule (covering)

Outer layer or cortex containing nephrons (filters)

Inner layer or medulla

▴ *Inside the kidneys, the 1 million nephrons filter (clean) the blood.*

To scale
An adult kidney is about the same size as a small boxing glove – about 6 cm long

Adult kidney   Boxing glove

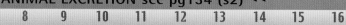

IT'S A FACT

• The kidneys receive more blood for their size than almost any other body organ – about 1.2 litres every minute.

• All the body's blood flows through the kidneys more than 300 times a day.

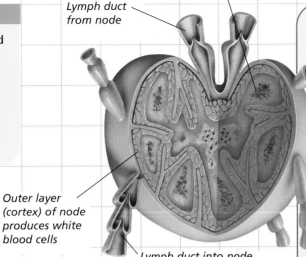

White and red blood cells

Lymph duct from node

Outer layer (cortex) of node produces white blood cells

Lymph duct into node

▲ *Lymph nodes are where most of the body's white blood cells are formed.*

Lymphatic system

Lymph is a pale yellow fluid in the tiny spaces between and around cells and tissues. It oozes into lymph ducts that carry it to lymph nodes. Lymph collects wastes of metabolism and the lymph nodes contain white blood cells *(see pg163 [f36])* that destroy harmful or unwanted substances, especially germs. The lymph ducts and vessels come together to pour lymph into the blood system. During infection, lymph nodes enlarge with extra fluid and white cells as 'swollen glands'.

▶▶ **Read further › white blood cells**
pg163 (b30)

Stress and the body

The adrenal glands above the kidneys make hormones that regulate how the body uses water and its reactions to stress. The main stress hormone is adrenaline. In a frightening or energetic situation, such as playing a sport, it makes the heart beat faster and the liver release glucose for extra energy. More blood flows to the muscles so that the body can take fast action.

▶▶ **Read further › sweating / pumping blood**
pg155 (b29); pg163 (b22)

BODY TALK

• In an average day (24 hours) the body produces about 1.5 litres of urine. But this amount varies hugely with activity and weather conditions.

• When the body is active in hot weather it sweats to keep cool, and water is lost in the sweat – sometimes 3 litres or more.

• Sweat is part of the excretory system, as is breathing out. Both remove unwanted substances.

Hormonal system

The hormonal or endocrine system consists of glands that make substances called hormones. These travel around in the blood and control internal body processes. For example, the thyroid gland in the neck makes thyroxine, which controls how fast cells use energy. The pea-sized pituitary gland, under the brain, is in overall control of the hormonal system. The amount of urine made by the kidneys is controlled by the hormone ADH (antidiuretic hormone). As water is lost in urine or through sweat during strenuous activity, it must be replaced by water in drinks.

▶▶ **Read further › substances in blood**
pg163 (b30)

Check it out!
• http://infozone.imcpl.org/kids_kidny.htm

Sight and sound

IT'S A FACT

• Each eye's retina has more than 130 million light-sensitive cells, rods and cones, in an area slightly larger than a thumbnail.

• Each ear's cochlea has 25,000 auditory cells, with a total of more than 2 million micro-hairs to detect sound vibrations.

MORE INFORMATION about the outside world enters the body through the eyes and ears – from pictures, noises, words on paper and everyday sounds – than through all the other senses combined. All the body's sense organs work in the same way. They detect changes or features, and produce patterns of tiny nerve signals that are sent to the brain. The eye detects light as rays of different colours and brightness. The ear detects vibrations of sound that reach it as invisible air waves.

▸ *Light enters the eye through the pupil. It then travels through the cornea and lens to form an image on the retina at the back of the eye.*

Optic chiasma where signals from each eye partly cross over

Retina – the lining of light-sensitive rods and cones

Choroid layer

Sclera (covering)

Ligaments supporting the lens

Iris

Lens

Optic nerve which carries the signals to the brain

Cornea

Tear fluid gland

Muscles that turn the eye

Pupil

Iris

Tear duct in to nose

Outer sheath of eyeball (sclera)

BODY TALK

• The level of a sound, whether high or low, is called its pitch and is measured in Hz (Hertz or vibrations per second). Most people can hear a range of sounds from about 20 Hz, such as the deep rumble of thunder, to 18,000 Hz, such as the shrill squeaks of a bat.

• However, as the body gets older, its ears and other sense organs work less well. The ears detect less high-pitched sounds.

Read further › eye colour
▸▸ pg169 (k22)

Inside the eye

The eyeball, about 2.5 cm across, has a tough outer cover, the sclera. At the front is a transparent window, the dome-shaped cornea, which lets in light rays. These pass through the lens that bends (refracts) them to shine a clear image of the world on to the retina lining the eyeball. Here, millions of light-sensitive cells change the patterns of light into nerve signals. The eye's retina has two kinds of light-sensitive cells. Rods are tall and slim, and number about 125 million. They detect shades of light and work well in dim light but cannot see colours. The 7 million cones are shorter and wider and clustered at the rear where the central part of the image falls. They see colours and fine details in bright light.

Check it out!
• http://www.kidinfo.com.health/ Human_Body.html

◀◀ LIGHT see pg31 (b29) ◀◀

1 2 3 4 5 6 7 8 9 10 11 12 13 14 15 16 17 18 19

Inside the ear

Sound waves pass into a slightly S-shaped tube, the outer ear canal, and hit the small, flexible eardrum at the end. The vibrations pass along three tiny bones – the hammer, anvil and stirrup – and into the fluid inside the snail-shaped cochlea. The vibrations cause ripples that are sensed by microscopic hairs on auditory cells, and then changed into nerve signals.

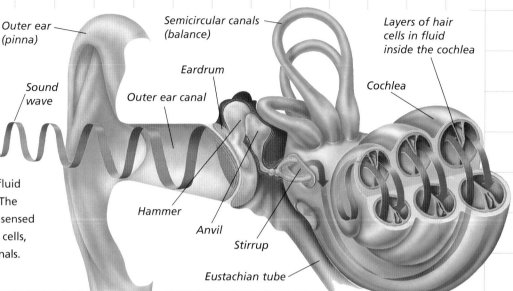

Outer ear (pinna)

Sound wave

Semicircular canals (balance)

Eardrum

Outer ear canal

Hammer

Anvil

Stirrup

Eustachian tube

Layers of hair cells in fluid inside the cochlea

Cochlea

Read further › nerve signals
pg173 (b22)

Eye colour

The coloured part of the eye is the iris – a ring of muscle seen through the clear cornea. The dark hole in the middle of the iris is the pupil, where light passes to the inside of the eye. Nearly all babies are born with blue eyes. After a few months the colour may change to a shade of brown, green or grey, then it stays the same. This colour is inherited from parents. If the mother and father are both blue-eyed, their child will almost certainly have blue eyes. However, if one or both parents are brown-eyed, then their child may have brown or blue eyes.

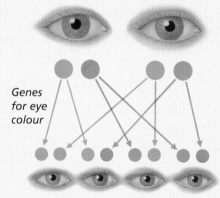

Parents' eye colour

Genes for eye colour

Possible colours for children

Read further › babies' genes
pg175 (k22)

Three ossicles

The three ear bones known as the ossicles are the hammer, anvil and stirrup. These are the smallest bones in the body. Surrounding muscles tense to hold them firmly so that they vibrate less when very loud sound waves hit them. These muscles prevent too-loud sounds damaging the ear. The eustachian tube controls the air pressure inside the ear by letting air in and out. The eustachian tube can be opened up by yawning or swallowing.

Laser surgery

A narrow beam of high-power laser light can be shone accurately into the eye, to carry out treatment for various eye disorders. The heat from the beam can seal a leaky blood vessel, or sculpt and reshape the lens (see pg168 [l18]) and cornea (see pg168 [m19]) to make vision clearer.

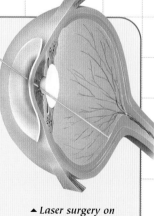

▲ Laser surgery on the retina can mean that spectacles or contact lenses are no longer needed.

Read further › inside the eye
pg168 (o13)

Smell, taste and touch

BOTH SMELL and taste are chemo-senses. They detect tiny particles of chemical substances – odorants floating in the air, and flavorants in foods and drinks. The two senses work separately, but they usually both send messages to the brain at the same time, when we eat and drink. So does the sense of touch, as the lips, tongue, gums and cheeks detect the temperature and hardness or consistency of the food. Smell, taste and touch are all closely linked or associated in the brain – especially when we eat. What we imagine as the 'taste' of a meal is really a combination of these three senses.

IT'S A FACT

• The nose can detect more than 10,000 different scents, smells and odours, using 25 million olfactory or 'smell' cells inside the nose.

• The tongue and inside of the mouth have up to 10,000 taste buds, but these sense only four main flavours: bitter, salty, sour and sweet.

Olfactory bulb

Olfactory tract to brain

Scent-sensitive cells of olfactory epithelium

Mucus lining (inside nose)

Hard palate (roof of mouth)

Nostril

▲ Scent particles dissolve in the mucus lining. The cells at the top of the nose then send signals along the olfactory nerve to the brain.

Read further › types of cells
pg153 (g22)

Inside the nose

The sensory parts for smell are two patches called olfactory (smell) epithelia. They are in the roof of the nasal chamber, inside the skull bone behind the nose. Each patch contains millions of olfactory cells (see pg171 [s25]), which have bunches of micro-hairs, cilia. These detect certain odorant particles from the air that float into the nose and land on them.

Epidermis

Keratin layer

Pain sensors

Light touch sensors

Heavy pressure sensors

Skin and touch

The sense of touch uses microscopic sensors at the ends of nerve fibres in the dermis, just under the surface of the skin (see pg154 [r12]), to detect a range of physical contacts. These include light touch and heavy pressure, heat and cold, and movements or vibrations. In the fingertips there are 10,000 micro-sensors in every square millimetre of skin.

Read further › dermis layer of skin
pg154 (i11)

▲ Some of the microscopic sensors found within the skin.

◄◄ ANIMAL SENSE OF SMELL see pg137 (b22) ◄◄

1   2   3   4   5   6   7   8   9   10   11   12   13   14   15   16   17   18   19

Tongue and taste

The front, sides and rear of the tongue have thousands of taste buds set into the surface, scattered between the larger 'lumps' called papillae. Each taste bud is one-tenth of a millimetre across. It contains about 25 gustatory (taste) cells, which have tufts of micro-hairs called cilia. These detect chemical flavouring particles in food. The tip of the tongue is most sensitive to sweet tastes, the front sides to salty, the rear sides to sour, and the middle rear to bitter tastes.

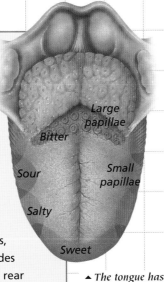

Large papillae

Bitter

Sour

Small papillae

Salty

Sweet

▲ The tongue has many taste buds to detect different flavours but its main upper surface has no taste buds.

Smaller papillae

Large papillae

Taste buds

Inner tongue layers

Read further › chewing food
pg164 (i13)

BODY TALK

• The body has five main senses: sight (visual), hearing (auditory), smell (olfactory), taste (gustatory) and touch (somato-sensory), but there are millions of other tiny sensors inside the body too.

• Sensors in the inner parts of the ear detect the head's position and movements, while those in muscles and joints bring information about the position of the body and limbs. This helps us to keep our balance and posture.

• Other micro-sensors detect internal body conditions such as temperature and blood pressure.

▼ Smells are scent molecules which are taken into your nose by breathed-in air. A particular smell may be noticeable even when mixed with millions of air molecules.

Smell cells

Olfactory cells have micro-hairs or cilia facing down into the nasal chamber, which detect smell particles landing on them. These particles drift into the nose with breathed-in air and move into the nasal chamber.

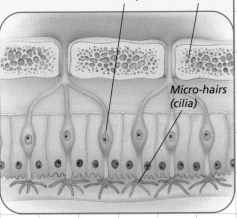

Olfactory cell

Bone

Micro-hairs (cilia)

Sensing smells and tastes

It is not clear how the micro-hairs, or cilia, on smell and taste cells respond to chemical particles. It is possible that the surfaces of the cilia have tiny pits in them of different shapes. A certain odorant or flavorant particle fits into one shape of pit, but not the others – like a key into its lock. Only when the particle fits properly, is a nerve signal sent to the brain.

Read further › nerve signals
pg173 (b22)

a b c d e f g h i j k l m n o p q r s t u v w

Nerves all over

THE BODY consists of many different organs and tissues. These must work together in an organized way for the whole body to stay healthy and active. The main system that controls and co-ordinates all these parts is the nervous system. Like a computer network, it sends tiny electrical signals to and fro, carrying information from one part of the body to another. The electrical signals are called nerve messages and they travel along wire-like nerves, which spread in a vast network through the entire body. Central control of the whole nervous system and the whole body comes from the brain.

Brain · Cranial nerve · Spinal cord · Brachial plexus (nerve junction) · Intercostal nerve · Lumbar nerves · Sacral nerve · Radial nerve · Ulna nerve · Sciatic nerve · Tibial nerve · Peroneal nerve · Lateral plantar nerve

IT'S A FACT

• The spinal cord is about 45 cm long and 31 pairs of main peripheral nerves branch from it.

• The thickest peripheral nerve is the sciatic nerve in the lower hip and upper thigh – almost as wide as a thumb.

▶ The spinal cord is the bundle of nerves running down the middle of the backbone.

Spinal cord · Backbone

The nervous system

The nervous system has three main parts: brain, spinal cord and peripheral nerves. The brain consists of billions of nerve cells and other tissues in the top half of the head. Its lower end merges into the spinal cord, the body's main nerve. The spinal cord is inside a tunnel formed by the row of holes inside the vertebrae of the backbone or spine. Peripheral nerves branch out from the spinal cord and brain to reach every body part.

▶▶ **Read further › bones and joints pg157 (b34; m22)**

Check it out!
• http://ghs.gresham.k12.or.us/science/ps/sci/ibbio/Anatomy/nervous/neuron.htm

Nerve cells

The nervous system is built up of billions of very specialized cells called nerve cells or neurons. Each has many spider-like branches, called dendrites, that receive signals from other nerve cells. The signals pass out along the nerve fibre, or axon, to other nerve cells. Nerve fibres are too thin to see with the unaided eye. But some nerve cells are more than 30 cm in length, making them some of the longest cells in the body.

Read further > waste removal
pg166 (m2)

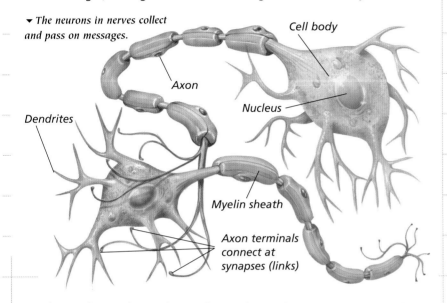

▼ *The neurons in nerves collect and pass on messages.*

Cell body

Axon

Nucleus

Dendrites

Myelin sheath

Axon terminals connect at synapses (links)

How the brain works

Nine-tenths of the brain consists of the cerebrum, composed of two large, dome-shaped, wrinkled parts called cerebral hemispheres. At the lower rear is a smaller wrinkled part, the cerebellum. It makes muscle-powered movements smooth, skilful and co-ordinated. The central parts of the brain, such as the thalamus, are involved in awareness, memories and emotions. The lowest part is the brain stem, which is responsible for automatic body processes such as digestion and heartbeat.

Thalamus affects sensory levels, awareness and alertness

Limbic system affects body functions and emotions

Hippocampus, linked to mood, willpower, learning and memory

Cerebellum controls co-ordination

Cerebrum is the site of mental activity such as thinking and learning

Hypothalamus controls body heat, water and hunger, and wakes you up

Brain stem controls heartbeat and breathing

Read further > digestion
pg166 (m2)

Inside a nerve

A nerve has a tough, shiny, greyish covering, called the epineurium. Inside are bundles, or fascicles, of nerve fibres that carry the tiny electrical pulses of nerve signals. A thick nerve has hundreds of thousands of fibres, while the thinnest nerves, as fine as a human hair, have just a few. Also inside the nerve are small blood vessels *(see pg163 [u30])* to bring nourishment and take away wastes. Nerve signals travel so fast that we can sense a situation and react to it in less than 0.2 seconds.

▼ *Nerves allow us to have split-second reactions – essential for sports such as snowboarding.*

Read further > types of cells
pg153 (g22)

BODY TALK

• Different types of nerve fibres carry signals at different speeds. The fastest signals travel at more than 120 m per second.

• The slowest signals travel at 1–2 m per second.

▶▶ CONSCIOUS THOUGHTS see pg225 (i22) ▶▶

Making babies

E VERY SECOND, another three human beings enter the
world. They are new babies, born after nine months of
growing and developing inside their mothers. The parts of the
body that produce new human beings are known as the
reproductive system. The reproductive parts are the only body
system that is not fully formed and working at birth. The
reproductive system completes its development around the
ages of 11 to 13 in girls, and 14 to 16 in boys, which is
the time known as puberty. The process of
reproduction begins with the joining
of two single cells – the egg from
the mother, and the sperm
from the father.

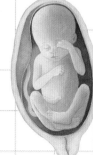

▼ Babies grow inside the womb for around 40 weeks (9 months), before they are born.

8 weeks

12 weeks

16 weeks

20 weeks

24 weeks

Female reproductive parts

The egg cell is relatively large, 0.1 mm across. The main female sex organs, the ovaries, contain many thousands of egg cells. Every month one egg becomes ripe and is released into the oviduct or egg tube (fallopian tube) in a process called ovulation. It passes along the tube, where it may meet a sperm cell (see pg175 [r24]) and be fertilized (see pg175 [j29]).

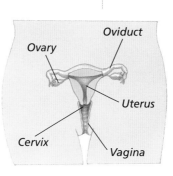

▲ Female reproductive parts.

Ovary
Oviduct
Uterus
Cervix
Vagina

▶▶ Read further › sperm cell
pg174 (q13)

BODY TALK
• During the first nine months of development, a baby's weight increases 5 billion times.

• In the nine months after birth, body weight increases by about three times.

Male reproductive parts

Compared to the egg cell, the sperm cell is tiny, just 0.05 mm long. The main male sex organs, the testes, make millions of them each day and they live for about 1 month. If the sperm cells do not pass along the ductus deferens or sperm tube, and then out of the body through the penis, they gradually die and break apart as new ones form.

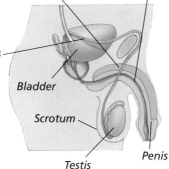

Erectile tissue
Urethra
Vas deferens
Bladder
Scrotum
Testis
Penis

▲ Male reproductive parts (side view).

▶▶ Read further › egg cell
pg174 (m2)

◀◀ ANIMAL BREEDING see pg146 (b30) ◀◀

▸ *Between 32 and 36 weeks, the baby usually turns in the womb, ready to be born head first.*

Umbilical cord

36 weeks

32 weeks

Placenta

28 weeks

40 weeks

Cervix (neck of the womb)

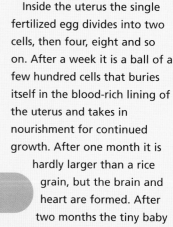

Read further › organs
pg150 (j14)

In the womb

Inside the uterus the single fertilized egg divides into two cells, then four, eight and so on. After a week it is a ball of a few hundred cells that buries itself in the blood-rich lining of the uterus and takes in nourishment for continued growth. After one month it is hardly larger than a rice grain, but the brain and heart are formed. After two months the tiny baby is still smaller than a thumb, yet all its main parts and organs have formed.

Egg cell's outer coat

Sperm

Egg cell cytoplasm

Getting together

The egg cell is only able to join with a sperm for a few days when a woman is ovulating (when an egg has been released from the ovary). Thousands of sperm cells swim near to the egg in the oviduct, but only one can join with or fertilize it. Both the egg and sperm contain sets of the body's genetic material, made of DNA *(see pg153 [n33])*. At fertilization the sets combine to form a unique set of genes for the new baby.

Egg cell nucleus

Read further › DNA
pg153 (b30)

▲ *An ultrasound scan shows the baby growing inside the womb.*

Nucleus with genetic material

Sperm head

Sperm tail

▲ *Only one sperm can fertilize the released egg.*

▸ *A newborn baby is carefully checked by a doctor to ensure it is healthy.*

New life

In the womb it was warm, wet and quiet, and oxygen and food came direct from the mother into the baby's blood. At birth a baby is pushed and squeezed into the fresh air, lights and sounds of the outside world. The baby takes its first gasps of air, often crying as it does so. This is a good sign, since it opens up the baby's airways and lungs *(see pg160 [m11])*. These were not used in the womb, but now the baby must breathe to get oxygen for itself. It also needs food and soon the baby takes a first meal of its mother's milk. The milk provides all the nourishment it needs for the first months of its life.

Read further › nourishment
pg164 (d2)

◀◀ ANIMAL BIRTH see pg146 (d2) ◀◀

22 23 24 25 26 27 28 29 30 31 32 33 34 35 36 37 38 39

Machine power

MACHINES MAKE it easier to perform tasks that would otherwise be very difficult or even impossible. Machines carry out tasks more efficiently by changing the strength or direction of a force. A machine can be as simple as a door handle or as complex as a spacecraft but all include types of six basic machines: the ramp or inclined plane, the wedge, the lever, the screw, the pulley, the wheel and axle. But most machines, even the complex ones, work because of the link between force and distance.

Effort

First-class lever

Load

Effort

▲ Prizing the lid from a can of paint: the tool acts as a first-class lever with the wrist doing the effort.

Fulcrum

How levers work

A lever is a bar or rod that is supported by a fulcrum (central pivot). Effort or force is needed to move one end of the lever to move a load at the other end. The closer the fulcrum is to the load, the less effort is needed to lift it. There are three classes of lever. In first-class levers, such as a seesaw, the fulcrum is in the middle. Second-class levers, such as a wheelbarrow have the fulcrum at one end, the effort (pushing) at the other end and the load in the middle. In third-class levers, such as a hammer, the effort is between the load and the fulcrum (the hand).

'Driver' cog is larger with more 'teeth'

Gearing up

Gears are used in machines such as clocks and cars, which have a rotating mechanism (parts that go round). Gears can alter the power from an engine so that it moves at the right speed and force, and goes in the right direction. Gears are usually sets of wheels called cogs with teeth that 'mesh' and turn together (see pg184 [u8]). A big cog turns a smaller cog with less force but faster. A small cog turns a bigger cog slower but with more force.

'Driven' cog has fewer teeth and turns slower but more powerfully

Wheel power

A heavy load is very hard to drag uphill on its own but rolling it in a wheelbarrow is much easier. The wheel reduces the friction (resistance) so that the load can be moved more easily. A ramp makes a task easier by enabling the load to be pulled or pushed up a slope rather than lifted.

Wheel and axle

Load

Effort

Fulcrum

Ramp or inclined plane

▶▶ Read further > cars / gears
pg184 (b15; p8); pg185 (l22)

▶▶ Read further > wheels
pg185 (b22)

▲ Three simple machines: a wheelbarrow (lever), wheel and axle, and ramp (inclined plane).

▶▶ WHEEL see pg201 (t22) ▶▶

● Weight lifters

A pulley is the best machine for lifting heavy loads. It can be as simple as a rope or chain flung over a bar. Usually, though, the rope runs over a number of grooved wheels. A single pulley wheel helps by changing the direction of the force because pulling down is easier than lifting up. If the rope is looped round and back over several pulley wheels, the load is spread over a great length of rope, and is thus reduced, making the object easier to lift. Pulley 'blocks' have many sets of pulleys and can lift very heavy loads for quite a small effort.

▼ A simple set of pulleys allows a person to lift a heavy weight using distance to increase the force.

Effort

More pulleys give a greater force for the person pulling

Load

Read further › weights
pg179 (b22)

▼ This seesaw is a first-class lever, as the fulcrum is between the load and effort.

Load

Read further › weight of loads
pg180 (d2)

● Moving staircase

Escalators – moving staircases – carry people up or down using the power of a pulley. The escalator's pulley is like a bicycle chain wrapped round a cog-like pulley at either end of the staircase. The stairs go round in a loop, moving down on top and coming back up from underneath, in reverse. The weight of the descending stairs pulls the ascending stairs upwards. So the escalator's drive motors only have to lift the weight of the passengers, not the weight of the stairs, too.

Read further › elevators
pg179 (b32)

Ascending or descending stairs

Motor-driven pulley

Stairs are fixed to the pulley with brackets

◄ Corkscrews are a type of turning wedge.

▲ An escalator's steps swivel past each other at either end of the pulley system.

Read further › propellers
pg186 (i13)

● WORK IT OUT

• Many bones in the human body work like levers. For example, the forearm pivots at the elbow, acting as a type of third-class lever to give extra lifting or pushing power.

• Bicycle gears help cyclists pedal between 60 to 90 turns a minute, reducing the effort needed.

● Simple machines

Two ramps (inclined planes) back to back form a wedge, for separating or splitting items, as in an axe. A wedge wrapped around a pole or rod forms a screw, which changes a turning force into a slow, steady, pulling force.

● **Check it out!**

• http://www.howstuffworks.com/pulley.htm
• http://www.fi.edu/qa97/spotlight3/spotlight3.html
• http://www.galaxy.net:80/~k12/machines/index.shtml

◄◄ FORCE see pg25 (b22) ◄◄

a b c d e f g h i j k l m n o p q r s t u v w

Construction

IN THE past, most big buildings such as cathedrals were built of stone, and their strength lay in the thick walls. Today, buildings such as skyscrapers get their strength from a framework or 'skeleton' of steel girders, beams and concrete columns, forced into the ground by heavy machinery such as pile-drivers. The skeleton supports the roof, walls and floors so the walls can even be made of glass, if designed to carry no weight. Tunnels and arches are different types of construction with their strength in curved walls or arches.

To scale

Two of the world's tallest structures
1 square = 100 m high

452 m high

300 m high

Petronas Twin Towers (Kuala Lumpur, Malaysia)

Eiffel Tower (Paris, France)

● Scraping the sky

Skyscrapers are dramatic buildings, often towering many hundreds of metres into the air. To support such a huge structure, every skyscraper must have deep foundations (the part below ground) made of massive concrete or steel piles sunk into the ground. Above these, the walls and floors are attached to a skeleton of steel girders and beams. When a skyscraper is over 40 storeys (levels) tall, the weight of a strong wind blowing against the side of the building is greater than the weight of the actual building. So architects must make the building strong horizontally as well as vertically.

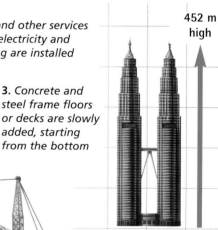

5. *Cladding of glass and concrete walls are added*

4. *Lifts and other services such as electricity and plumbing are installed*

3. *Concrete and steel frame floors or decks are slowly added, starting from the bottom*

2. *Heavy steel girders are lifted into position by tall cranes as the building rises*

1. *Foundations are dug and piles are set in the ground*

▶▶ Read further > steel girders pg181 (k22)

Pile-drivers

Buildings or bridges erected on soft ground are supported by posts called piles. Usually made of steel or concrete, the piles are driven firmly into the ground by pile-drivers. Pile-drivers wind up a heavy weight called a pile hammer inside a frame, then drop it on the head of the pile to bash it into the ground. In 1847, Scottish engineer James Naysmith invented a steam-driven version that could raise and lower a 7-tonne weight 80 times a minute. Today, pile-drivers use compressed air to raise the hammer, and the drop is precisely controlled by computers.

Read further › compressed air pg187 (b29); pg189 (b31)

Building an arch

Arches are usually made of stone or brick and built up from wedge-shaped blocks called voussoirs. While the arch is being built, a wooden frame the same shape as the arch supports the structure. When the frame is removed, the arch is supported by the pressure of each side of the arch against the keystone (centre block).

Keystone block in upper centre of arch 'locks' structure in place by balancing pressure from each side

Brick or stonework sides prevent the arch collapsing under the weight of structure above

◀ *The world's biggest free-standing arch is the 192 m-high Gateway to the West arch in St Louis, Missouri, USA.*

Read further › arch bridges pg180 (s8)

WORK IT OUT

• The first skyscrapers were built in New York and Chicago, USA. The 10-storey Home Insurance building in Chicago, was completed in 1885.

• The invention of the safety elevator by Elisha Otis in the 1850s made skyscrapers possible. Today, elevators in skyscrapers can travel at speeds of up to 10 m/sec.

Going underground

Tunnels just below the surface can be built by the 'cut-and-cover' method. This means simply digging a large, long ditch, then covering it over to make the tunnel. But deeper tunnels must be bored out. Tunnels through hard rock are often blasted out using explosives. Tunnels through soft rock or soil are dug with a powerful cutting machine called a shield, which is a large drum with disk cutters on the front. As the shield bores forward, debris is scooped out the back. Ring-shaped steel and concrete supports are put in place to prevent the tunnel caving in.

▸ *The shield's rotating cutting head is kept on a straight course by lasers.*

Read further › bridges pg180 (d2)

▶▶ STEAM see pg204 (l2) ▶▶

Bridging the gap

Central tower has two cantilever 'arms'

Steel beams span length of bridge

Piers on piles support weight of main towers

B RIDGES ARE vital links, carrying traffic – people, animals and vehicles – over rivers, roads, railways or ravines. To be safe, a bridge must be strong enough to bear the weight not only of the load moving across it, but also its own weight. This strength can be achieved in a number of ways, but every bridge has massive supports at either end called abutments that are embedded in solid ground. In between there are often extra supports called piers, linked by short sections of the bridge called spans. There is usually a long, middle span over the deepest water.

LONGEST SUSPENSION BRIDGES

Bridge, Country	Length
• Akashi–Kaiko, Japan	1990 m
• Great Belt, Denmark	1624 m
• Humber Estuary, Britain	1410 m
• Jiangyin, China	1385 m
• Tsing Ma, China	1377 m

Types of bridge

Traditionally, bridges were simple wooden or stone arches. Modern bridges are built of concrete and steel, and the type of construction depends on the heaviest load it has to carry and the nature of the place where it is to be built. For example, for wide spans over water, suspension or cable-stayed bridges are usually best. To carry a very heavy load over a short distance, a beam bridge may be built. To carry a heavy load over a greater distance, a cantilever bridge is often used.

Read further › construction pg178 (k2)

▼ Cable-stayed bridges, such as the Queen Elizabeth II Bridge, Dartford, hang from steel cables.

▶ Suspension bridges, such as the Golden Gate Bridge, San Francisco, have spans that hang on steel wires from a cable between two tall towers.

▼ Lifting bridges, such as Tower Bridge, London, use hydraulic power to swing a section of the bridge up to allow tall ships to pass underneath.

▶ Arch bridges, such as London Bridge, are very strong because the weight is pushed outwards to the abutments, rather than downwards.

▲ Cantilever bridges, such as the Forth Railway Bridge, Scotland, balance the load on two piers.

▲ Beam bridges, such as most city road bridges, rely on the strength of the material – usually steel or concrete – to support a beam between the spans, strengthened by a framework underneath.

Check it out!

- http://www.pbs.org/wgbh/ buildingbig/bridge/challenge/ indexp.html
- http://www.howstuffworks. com/ bridge.htm

◀◀ EFFORT AND LOAD see pg25 (b22) ◀◀

| 1 | 2 | 3 | 4 | 5 | 6 | 7 | 8 | 9 | 10 | 11 | 12 | 13 | 14 | 15 | 16 | 17 | 18 | 19 |

Cantilever bridges

Cantilever bridges are built from sections, each with two rigid steel beams on either side of a central tower. Each pair of beams balance each other so that each section of the bridge is an independent cantilever, standing without support from the others. The towers support the weight of the beams with a downward force, so there is no need for central supporting columns.

Supporting tower carries weight of link to bank

Read further > beams pg178 (d2)

▸ *In a bascule or lifting bridge, the half-spans are supported only at one end. The middle tilts up out of the way.*

Swinging around

If the banks of a river or canal are very low, one way to ensure that boats can pass underneath without colliding with the bridge is to move the actual bridge. Bascule bridges are built to lift up in the middle. Swing bridges are mounted on a central pier and pivot sideways out of the way, turned by powerful hydraulic (fluid-driven) systems.

Read further > boats pg186 (d2); pg187 (m32)

Read further > pumping water pg186 (o16); pg187 (b25)

Building bridges

The first step in bridge-building is to build the piers and abutments. To erect piers in the water, a steel wall or shuttering is built on the riverbed. The water is then pumped out while the pier is built, before the walls can be removed, and the spans laid between the piers.

Steel wall (shuttering)
Water
Collar
Space to accept pier or tower
Footings
River bed

IT'S A FACT

• The largest tilting or lifting bridge is in Michigan, USA. It has a 102-m opening.

• The world's longest arch is the 550 m-long Lupu steel arch in Shanghai, China.

Support tower
Main suspension cable
Vertical stay cable
Support pier
Deck

Suspension

For wide or deep channels, a suspension bridge, with a span of up to 1200 m, is often used. The deck (such as a roadway) is held up by steel cables hanging between tall towers. These cables are held in concrete blocks at both ends of the bridge. The deck may be supported by a framework to stop it swaying too much in the wind. The weight of the deck is transferred to the vertical cables, over the towers and to the concrete blocks at either end.

Read further > frameworks pg178 (d2; k2)

On the rails

A SINGLE TRAIN may carry 200,000 tonnes of iron ore, while many passenger trains have many carriages that can carry thousands of people. Railways can carry much heavier loads than road vehicles because they use steel wheels, guided by lips or 'flanges' that run along the inside of steel rails, which are tough enough to bear tremendous weight. However, not all rail transport runs on the rails – monorails often run underneath the track and maglevs actually float above it. Because they travel at great speeds, trains must be safely controlled by switches and signals.

One-track trains

Monorails are railways with a single rail. The track is made from steel or concrete sections and the carriages either hang beneath the rail or balance on top of it. When the cars run on top of the rail, they must be stabilized by guide wheels and gyroscopes – devices that rotate – to stop them falling over. Monorails are over a century old – the first was built in Wuppertal in Germany in 1901. Both Tokyo and Seattle have monorail systems in operation.

Read further › underground tunnels pg179 (g33)

▸ Monorail tracks can be held up above city streets, avoiding the need to dig deep tunnels.

IT'S A FACT

• The longest train ever was a 660-truck goods train 7.3 km long that ran from Saldanha to Sishen in South Africa on 26 August 1989.

• The longest passenger train ever was a 70-coach train 1732 m-long that ran from Ghent to Ostend in Belgium on 27 April 1991.

Check it out!
• http://travel.howstuffworks.com/maglev-train.htm
• http://www.csrmf.org/

Gyroscope sensors

Stabilizing side wheels

Monorail section

Weight-bearing drive wheels made of rubber for less noise and vibration

◀◀ STEEL see pg19 (e28) ◀◀

1 2 3 4 5 6 7 8 9 10 11 12 13 14 15 16 17 18 19

Signalling

Signals warn train crews of hazards on the track. Track controllers use a 'block' system to stop a train entering a block of track that already has a train on it. Some routes in Europe and Japan use Advanced Train Protection (ATP), where the cab picks up signals from the track telling the driver what speed to travel. If the driver fails to respond, the train slows automatically. In the US, they are developing Advanced Train Control Systems (ACTS) that will rely on satellites and other high-tech links.

▲ Signal lights are usually red for stop or danger, yellow for warning and green for all clear.

Read further › satellites pg193 (k22; p26)

Lifting by magnets

When the same poles of two magnets are placed together, they repel (push each other apart). Magnetic levitation (maglev) trains use this magnetic repulsion to lift the train clear of the track. Very powerful electromagnets lift the entire train so that it floats a few centimetres above the track. This cuts the friction so much that maglev trains can reach speeds of more than 480 km/h smoothly and almost silently. Plans are underway to build fast maglev lines from Anaheim in California to Las Vegas, and from Tokyo to Osaka in Japan, but they are costly to build and still not totally reliable. So most maglev systems have been short distance, low-speed train systems, such as the system at Shanghai Airport in China.

Read further › magnets pg187 (h22)

Track electromagnets

Concrete T-section track

Support pillar

Train electromagnets

▲ Maglev trains operate in many countries such as China, Japan, Germany and the United States.

Frog to carry train across old track

Old track direction

Switch rail pivots

Guard rail

New track direction

Slider moves switch rails across

Switch rails

◄ Switches are used to automatically change the direction of a railway train.

Points and junctions

Occasionally, a train must change tracks in order to change direction. As a train cannot steer, the track branches in two at 'turnouts'. Here a switch changes the train from one track to another by moving a pair of rails for the new track direction up against the old. The two switch rails pivot at one end and are moved sideways by a slider under them at the other end. The slider is usually moved by an electromagnet.

Read further › steering wheels pg185 (v30)

On the road

THERE ARE now more than half a billion cars in the world, and on average two new ones are built every second. There is a huge variety of motor transport, from 'saloon' cars with separate boots or trunks, to 'all-terrain' vehicles that can be driven across country, and motorbikes that can reach great speeds. However, all motor vehicles are built in a similar way. They all need brakes, are all driven by an engine or motor and most need gears to control the 'drive' of the engine.

Brake caliper

Brake fluid under pressure in brake pipe pushes on piston

Brake piston

Piston presses two brake pads together

Brake pads press on brake disc to create friction, thus slowing down wheel

● Putting on the brakes

Stopping a fast-moving car demands great force. When the driver presses the brake pedal, brake fluid is forced through narrow pipes to cylinders on each wheel. The pressure of the fluid presses special pads – brake pads – against the brake discs on the wheels, which slow it down by friction. Many cars have ABS (Anti-lock braking systems) where a computer applies the brake automatically within a split second and prevents the car's wheels from locking up and the car from skidding to a halt.

▶▶ **Read further › brake pads**
pg185 (v26)

▶▶ **Read further › gears**
pg176 (n2)

● Geared up

Most cars need gears between the engine and the wheels because engines only work well when running faster within a narrow range of speed. Gears change the drive – the link between engine and wheels – so the wheels turn at different speeds for the same engine speed. Slowing the drive increases the engine's force, enabling a small, fast-running engine to power a heavy car. When accelerating or climbing hills, the driver selects the low gears for extra force. In cars with automatic transmission, the right gear is automatically selected.

● WORK IT OUT

• The world's longest car was specially built for American, Jay Ohrberg. At over 30 m long, it has 26 wheels – and a swimming pool with a diving board!

• In 1997, the British jet-powered *Thrust SSC* car broke the sound barrier, travelling across the Nevada desert at over 1220 km/h.

▲ *Simple cogs reverse the direction of rotation.*

▲ *Rack and pinion change the rotation to a sliding motion.*

▲ *Bevels move the direction of rotation through a right angle.*

▲ *Worm gears slow the rotation down to a slower, stronger rotation at right angles.*

▶▶ WHEEL see pg201 (t22) ▶▶

a
b

Leaning into it

To go round corners, motorbikes' front wheels turn like cars do. Motorcyclists also lean the bike over on to the slanting edges of its tyres. If a motorcyclist tried to turn a corner with the bike in an upright position the force called momentum, which makes the bike carry on in a straight line, would tip it over onto the outside of the curve. So the rider leans the motorbike when turning the corner to counteract the outwards force pushing against the bike.

Petrol power

Petrol engines burn a mixture of fuel (petrol) and air inside cylinders in the engine. The mixture expands (increases in volume) when it is ignited (set alight) by an electric spark, from the spark plug. This forces a piston down the cylinder to push the crankshaft round to turn the car's wheels through the gearbox. Four cylinders (two- or three-cylinder engines exist) give these power strokes, each at a different time.

Valves

Cylinder

Piston

Crankshaft

▲ *Induction stroke – inlet valve opens and the descending piston sucks in the fuel and air mixture.*

c
d
e
f
g
h
i
j

◄ *The faster the bike corners, the greater the outward forces become and the more the biker has to lean over to counter them.*

▸ *Four-stroke cycle: commonly known as 'suck, squeeze, bang and blow'.*

Read further ▸ cylinders / gears ▸▸ pg184 (k2; p8)

▲ *Compression stroke – inlet valve closes and the rising piston squeezes the fuel.*

Read further ▸ wheels ▸▸ pg176 (s8)

Electrical system powers lights and instruments, such as temperature gauge and fuel gauge, on instrument panel

Exhaust at back of car carries away waste gases from engine

Gears in gearbox change the speed engine turns the wheels to suit different conditions

Ignition system gives an electrical spark to ignite the fuel

Engine burns fuel to provide power

Car transmission takes power from engine to wheels via the gearbox

Cooling system circulates water to stop engine overheating

Suspension softens bumps in road for passengers and keeps wheels in contact with road

k
l
m

Spark plug

n
o

▲ *Power stroke – spark ignites fuel and expanding gases push down the piston.*

p
q
r
s
t

▲ *Exhaust stroke – the exhaust valve opens and the rising piston pushes or blows out the burned gases.*

u
v

Check it out!
- http://www.auto.howstuff works.com/engine.htm
- http://auto.howstuffworks.com/ brake.htm

Steering gear controls direction by turning front wheels

Wheels are attached to brakes, which slow them down

w

◄◄ MOMENTUM see pg24 (l2) ◄◄

On the water

L IGHT MATERIALS such as wood and cork float because they are not as dense (heavy) as water. Ships can be built from heavy materials such as steel, yet still float. This is because the air inside the hull or body of the ship makes the ship lighter than the water it displaces (pushes out of the way). Water transport relies on many methods to move through water. Sailing ships use the power of the wind to travel along. Hydrofoils use 'wings' to travel on top of the water. Submersibles and submarines actually let in water to sink, before travelling underwater.

Metal blades or screws slice through water, propelling boat forward

Rudder steers boat left or right

Thrust and drag

Most ships are driven under the water by a screw propeller with slowly turning blades to force (thrust) the ship forward. This system is powerful, but the resistance of the water slows down the boat (drag). Small powerboats use high-speed jets of water instead to push themselves along faster.

Read further › propeller blades pg188 (j12)

IT'S A FACT

• The heaviest ship ever built is the oil tanker, *SeaWise Giant*, launched in 1976, weighing over 585,015 tonnes when laden.

• The world water speed record is 511.11 km/h set by Kenneth Warby's *Spirit of Australia* on 8 October 1978, using a 'hydroplane' designed to skim across the water.

How ships float

When launched, a ship pushes water away, but the water pushes back, causing 'upthrust'. The more water is pushed out of the way, the harder it pushes back. The hull of the ship is hollow, making the density – weight – less than water, so the ship keeps sinking until its weight is matched by the push of the water, then it can float.

Check it out!
• http://oceanexplorer.noaa.gov/technology/subs/subs.html

◄◄ MATERIALS see pg16 (d2) ◄◄

a
b
c
d
e
f
g
h
i
j
k
l
m
n
o
p
q
r
s
t
u
v
w

▼ *The first range of submersibles appeared in the 1960s and 1970s. Today's craft are much smaller and more advanced but still work in the same way.*

● Underwater explorer

Submersibles are used mainly for research into the ocean depths and undersea wrecks. Remote Operated Vehicles (ROVs) are small robot submersibles, controlled by operators using cameras and virtual reality systems *(see pg190 [o12])*. Submersibles alter their buoyancy – ability to float – to work.

▶▶ **Read further › magnets / virtual reality**
pg183 (b30); pg190 (m2)

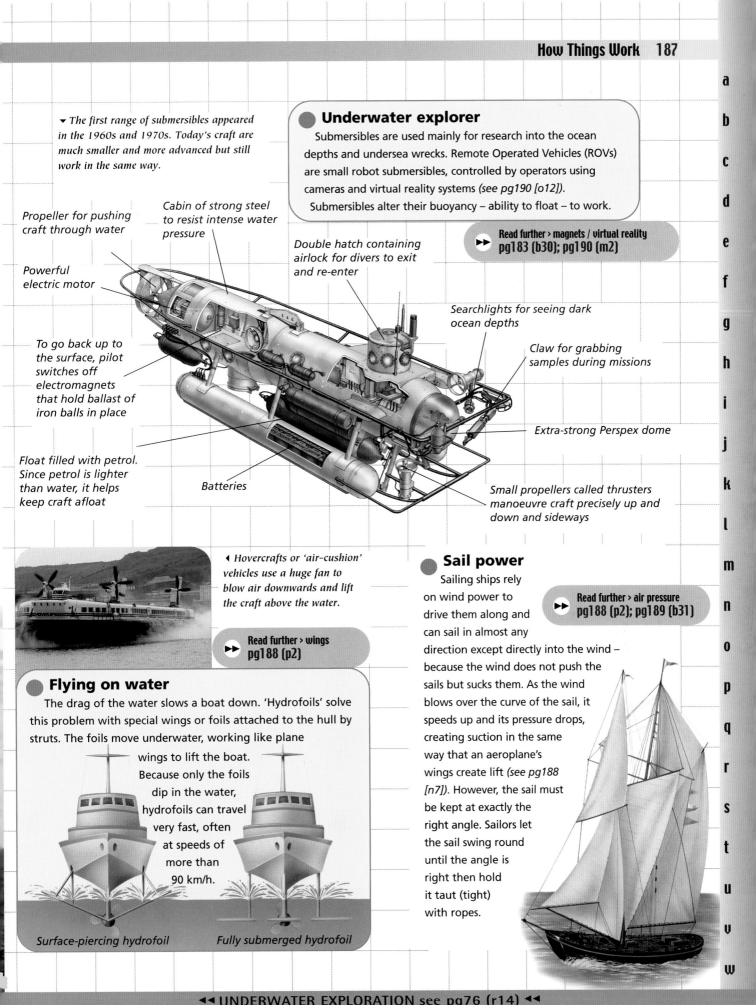

Propeller for pushing craft through water

Powerful electric motor

Cabin of strong steel to resist intense water pressure

Double hatch containing airlock for divers to exit and re-enter

Searchlights for seeing dark ocean depths

To go back up to the surface, pilot switches off electromagnets that hold ballast of iron balls in place

Claw for grabbing samples during missions

Float filled with petrol. Since petrol is lighter than water, it helps keep craft afloat

Batteries

Extra-strong Perspex dome

Small propellers called thrusters manoeuvre craft precisely up and down and sideways

◀ *Hovercrafts or 'air-cushion' vehicles use a huge fan to blow air downwards and lift the craft above the water.*

▶▶ **Read further › wings**
pg188 (p2)

● Flying on water

The drag of the water slows a boat down. 'Hydrofoils' solve this problem with special wings or foils attached to the hull by struts. The foils move underwater, working like plane wings to lift the boat. Because only the foils dip in the water, hydrofoils can travel very fast, often at speeds of more than 90 km/h.

Surface-piercing hydrofoil   *Fully submerged hydrofoil*

● Sail power

Sailing ships rely on wind power to drive them along and can sail in almost any direction except directly into the wind – because the wind does not push the sails but sucks them. As the wind blows over the curve of the sail, it speeds up and its pressure drops, creating suction in the same way that an aeroplane's wings create lift *(see pg188 [n7])*. However, the sail must be kept at exactly the right angle. Sailors let the sail swing round until the angle is right then hold it taut (tight) with ropes.

▶▶ **Read further › air pressure**
pg188 (p2); pg189 (b31)

◀◀ UNDERWATER EXPLORATION see pg76 (r14) ◀◀

In the air

AEROPLANES ARE the fastest means of transport, able to make journeys in just a few hours that would take days by road or sea. Most modern aeroplanes are powered by jet engines that can propel some military craft along at speeds of more than 3000 km/h, three times the speed of sound. Helicopters rely on their rotor blades to hover in the air. Not all air transport needs an engine – hot-air balloons use hot air and gas to stay up.

Swashplate controls angle of blades

Jet turbine engine

Rotor blade

To fly up or down, pilot alters angle or 'pitch' of main rotor blades with 'collective pitch' control. When blades cut through the air almost flat, they give no lift and helicopter sinks. To climb, pilot steepens pitch to increase lift

To fly forwards or backwards, pilot uses 'cyclic pitch' control to vary rotor pitch as blades go around from one side to the other

▲ The Sikorsky UH-60 Blackhawk can carry up to 12 soldiers and has two crew members.

Taking to the skies

Helicopters are able to take off vertically or hover in the air for long periods. They owe their versatile flying ability to big rotor blades, which are like long, thin wings that whirl around at high speed, slicing through the air and providing lift. The blades also act like huge propellers (see pg186 [i13]), hauling the helicopter upwards or backwards.

▶▶ Read further › propellers
pg186 (i13)

Lift

Drag

Thrust

Weight

Flap

Trailing edge

Rib

Spar

Aileron

Tip

Leading edge

On the wing

An aircraft's wings are lifted by the air flowing above and beneath them as they slice through the air. Because the top of the wing is curved, air pushed over the top is forced to speed up and stretch out, reducing its pressure and pulling from above. The curved shape is called an aerofoil. Under the wing, the air slows down and bunches up, and pressure here rises, pushing the wing up. How much 'lift' this creates depends on the angle and shape of the wing, and how fast it moves through the air.

▲ Thrust and lift are the main forces that enable aircraft to fly.

IT'S A FACT

• A jumbo jet, sucks in 1 tonne of air every second.

• In December 1986, the American experimental plane, *Voyager*, flew right round the world without landing once.

Check it out!

• http://travel.howstuffworks.com/airplane.htm
• http://travel.howstuffworks.com/airplane3.htm

▶▶ Read further › lifting
pg183 (b30); pg187 (p23)

◀◀ ANIMAL FLIGHT see pg128 (f2) ◀◀

1 2 3 4 5 6 7 8 9 10 11 12 13 14 15 16 17 18 19

Tail rotor drive shaft

FASTEST JETS

Jet, year flown	Speed
SR-71A Blackbird, 1976	3529 km/h
Mikoyan E-66, 1959	2387 km/h
F-100 Super Sabre, 1955	1323 km/h
F-86 Sabre, 1948	1080 km/h
Gloster Meteor, 1946	990 km/h

▶▶ **Read further › thrust** pg20 (p2)

● Hot-air balloon

Hot-air balloons get their lift by filling a huge bag of very light material with hot air from a gas burner. Because hot air is lighter and less dense than cooler air, the bag simply floats up, carrying the basket and passengers with it. As the air cools, the balloon begins to sink. To maintain height, the balloonist relights the burner to warm up the air in the bag again.

▲ *To descend quickly, the balloonist pulls a cord to let warm air escape through a vent in the top of the balloon.*

▶▶ **Read further › air pressure** pg187 (m32)

● How jets work

The simplest jets, called turbojets, work by pushing a jet of hot air out of the back to thrust the plane forward. Engines like these were used on the supersonic (faster than sound) airliner called Concorde, and some very fast military jets (see pg189 [r28]). Most airliners use quieter, cheaper turbofans that combine the hot-air jet with the draught from a whirling, multi-bladed fan to give extra thrust at low speeds.

Main shaft

Gases roar past exhaust turbines

'Bypass' air from main fan flows around engine core

Hot gases rush out of engine

Main fan sucks air in

Air is squashed by compressor turbines

Jet fuel is sprayed on to air, and continuous explosion happens

Afterburner burns leftover fuel in exhaust gases

▲ *In a typical turbojet, exhaust gases roar out of the back of the engine at more than 1600 km/h.*

Fin (tail)

Rudder turns plane left or right

Jet exhaust

Cockpit

Radar in nose cone to detect other aircraft in the air

Air intake for jet engine

▲ *The jet-powered American F-16 Fighting Falcon is used by more than 14 countries worldwide.*

Whole tailplane tilts as elevator to angle plane up or down

Fuel tanks in wing

Single jet engine within fuselage (main body of plane)

● Soaring forward

Today, nearly all military planes are powered by jet engines. The huge thrust of jet engines means wings can be smaller than on propeller-driven planes. They are swept back to allow the planes to fly fast with minimum air-resistance. The plane's path is directed by control surfaces – movable panels on the wings, tailplane and fin.

▶▶ **Read further › air-resistance** pg187 (m32)

Electronic brains

COMPUTERS HAVE entered our lives both at home and at work and can be used for anything from helping with homework to landing a spacecraft. Over the years, there has been a vast increase in the amount of data computers can store – and the speed with which they handle it. The advances in the computer world have even led to virtual reality – a way of creating artificial situations – being used for entertainment or business purposes.

WORK IT OUT

• In May 1997, IBM's Deep Blue computer beat the reigning World Chess Champion, Garry Kasparov.

• A 'byte' consists of eight on/off instructions or bits in a computer: 1024 bytes make 1 kilobyte (KB); 1024 kilobytes make 1 megabyte (MB); 1024 megabytes make 1 gigabyte (GB); 1 trillion bytes make 1 terabyte (TB).

Special eyepieces show slightly different views of an image to each eye to create illusion of real space

Sound effects are played in stereo through earphones, enhancing experience to make it seem even more realistic

Read further > undersea wrecks / data
pg187 (b29); pg191 (b22)

Is that for real?

Computers can sometimes fool our senses into thinking something is real using virtual reality (VR) systems. VR sends data (information) to our senses that closely mimic real scenes. A computer or robotic vehicle *(see pg187 [b29])* is sent to explore a situation such as an undersea wreck, or is programmed to show a fictional situation such as a tennis match. We can see what the computer sees by wearing a special headset.

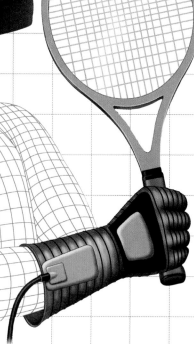

IT'S A FACT

• The world's most powerful computer is the Earth Simulator, built at Kanazawa in Japan to help predict earthquakes.

• IBM are planning to build the world's biggest computer, called Blue Gene, to research proteins.

Check it out!
• http://www.computer.howstuffworks.com/computer-memory.htm
• http://computer.howstuffworks.com/bytes.htm

▲ *A number of pressure and flex (bending) sensors in the glove pick up wrist, hand and finger movements and send these along the cable to the computer. The computer analyses these movements to determine if the player had moved in the correct way to hit the 'virtual' ball, which can only be seen through the eyepieces.*

Hardware and software

The actual material from which computers are made is called hardware. Equipment such as the keyboard, screen, mouse, printer, scanner and CD-writer are called peripherals – they sit outside the casing. The instructions or program that make the computer work is called the software. Software packages range from simple text and scanning images to the more challenging creation of graphics and special effects.

▶▶ Read further > storing data pg197 (m30)

101001001010

100010100101

010101010010

Zeros and ones

Since electronic circuits can only be switched on or off, computers store and handle data using a 'binary' system. This system turns all data into a code of 0s and 1s, or offs and ons. For example, the number five is 0101 in binary code, or off-on-off-on. Each 0 or 1 is called a binary digit or 'bit', and they are grouped together in 'bytes'. Electronic circuits store and process data in this way.

▶▶ Read further > electrical signals pg192 (l2); pg193 (b22)

101 010010010 01010100101010010

Chip

Plastic casing protects components

◀ The main part of a computer is the central processing unit, containing a microchip that is no bigger than a fingernail.

Wire 'feet' are connections that attach to other parts in computer

Microchips on circuit board

Main computer casing, to protect all components inside

'Read-only memory' (ROM) is computer's basic working instructions installed in computer at factory

Flat screen monitor

Inside central processing unit (CPU) is a powerful microchip – a tiny block of complex electronic circuits – that is 'brain' of computer and carries out main tasks

Digital camera or Webcam to record images and send messages or photos over Internet

Random-access memory (RAM) temporarily stores data as it is being used

Data can be stored as laser guided pits on a CD or DVD that can be inserted into computer in CD or DVD drive (Reader)

Roller sensors

Moving mouse rolls the ball that turns sensors so on-screen cursor moves

Keyboard to type on or control computer functions

▶▶ INVENTION OF COMPUTERS see pg207 (h22) ▶▶

a b c d e f g h i j k l m n o p q r s t u v w

22   23   24   25   26   27   28   29   30   31   32   33   34   35   36   37   38   39

Instant contact

IT'S A FACT

• The Internet grew during 2002 at the rate of 300 new pages or screens of information being added every minute.

• Some mobile phones include a digital camera for sending live video pictures.

TELECOMMUNICATIONS MAKE it possible to see and talk to people almost anywhere in the world. Some communications such as phone calls, faxes or e-mail can be one-to-one. Radio and television *(see pg195 [f33])* programmes are broadcast to millions of people. Cable TV and web-casting (Internet broadcasting) combine both elements. Yet all these forms of communication work in much the same way.

Phones on the move

Mobile or cell phones use low-power radio waves to send messages. Areas across the world are divided into many small sectors called cells, each with an antenna *(see pg193 [s24])* that picks up signals from phones and sends them out. Because there are so many antennae spread across the world, millions of people can use mobile phones at once.

Small loudspeaker in earpiece

Mode or function keys

Small microphone in mouthpiece

Numerical keys

Land lines

Telephones convert sound into an electrical signal. When you speak into a phone, the vibrations of your voice move a tiny microphone that alters an electrical current in strength. This creates an electrical signal, which is sent to the receiving phone. In the receiver the varying signal works a loudspeaker, which vibrates the air and recreates the sound of your voice. Today, many signals are sent as pulses of laser light along special glassy fibres called optical fibres. Signals are also sent as radio waves or microwaves through the air – bouncing off satellites *(see pg192 [p18])* in space.

▶▶ **Read further › signals**
pg183 [b22]

Many communications, such as mobile phone calls and e-mails, are sent on or relayed by satellites in space

Signals from individual transmitters are sent on from a telephone exchange or a service provider

Computer data is translated by a modem into signals that can be carried along phone lines

▶▶ **Read further › electromagnet**
pg183 [b30]

TV and radio signals are either broadcast as pulses of radio waves, sent direct via cables or broadcast from satellites

a
b
c
d
e
f
g
h
i
j
k
l
m
n
o
p
q
r
s
t
u
v
w

Instant letter

Fax is short for 'facsimile', which means 'copy'. A fax machine scans a document under a light past a line of sensors. The white parts of the document reflect light so switch on the sensors; the dark parts do not reflect light so switch off the sensors. Thus, a pattern of ons and offs is created and sent to the receiving fax. The receiving fax machine uses heat sensors that pick up the pattern of electrical signals coming through and creates the same pattern on the heat-sensitive paper. More modern machines print on plain paper, using charges of static electricity to attract the toner powder to the paper.

Telephone

Dial pad for typing in fax number

Phone socket that enables fax to connect to a phone line and send and receive messages

Image received is printed on paper from internal roll

Image to be sent is fed through a scanner

Drive rollers, to run document under scanner

Scanner sensors

Read further > on / off patterns
pg191 (b32)

Bouncing signals

Any telecommunications message needs a transmitter such as a phone; a communications link such as an antenna or satellite; and a receiver or destination, such as an e-mail address or receiving telephone number. The message can travel through electrical or optical (fibre-optic) cables, as microwaves or as radio waves, to arrive at its destination.

WORK IT OUT

• A third of the 45 million mobile phones in use in the UK are thrown away or lost each year. If you stacked them one on top of the other, the pile of lost mobile phones would be 250 times higher than Mount Everest!

• Most of the 5000 satellites circling the Earth in space are used for telecommunications. Communications satellites use a special orbit, called a geo-stationary orbit, which keeps them in the same place above the Earth constantly.

Read further > telephones
pg192 (k2)

Communications travel via satellites and are beamed up and down from antenna dishes on ground

Electronic letters

A fast and convenient form of contact today is electronic mail or e-mail. The message is typed up on a computer or even on some mobile phones and is sent to another e-mail address along a phone line, via a modem, to the central computer of the ISP (Internet Service Provider). The message is stored here until the recipient connects or 'logs in' to a computer to receive it.

Read further > computers
pg191 (b22)

Telephones link into phone network by a direct cable link. Mobile phones link through the air to local relay towers by radio waves

►► INTERNET see pg209 (l30) ►►

22   23   24   25   26   27   28   29   30   31   32   33   34   35   36   37   38   39

Super vision

MICROSCOPES THAT magnify objects too tiny for our eyes to see and telescopes that magnify things that are far away have been used since the 1600s. Photography has been recording accurate pictures for more than 160 years. Today, microscopes can show fantastic pictures of minute micro-organisms or even atoms and telescopes can reveal the most distant galaxies in the universe. Cameras take better quality photographs than ever, and digital technology enables pictures to be scanned into a computer to be enhanced and even sent across the world instantly via e-mail (see pg192 [s5]).

Read further › pixels pg196 (q2)

IT'S A FACT

• The world's largest optical telescope is the four-part VLT (Very Large Telescope) on Cerro Paranal in Chile.

• Many ground-based astronomic telescopes use computers to alter how we see the twinkling of stars caused by Earth's atmosphere.

Eyepiece lens

Pentaprism turns image right way round for eyepiece

Zoom ring

Objective lenses gather light rays of scene together and make them converge so that image is smaller

Aperture (hole for incoming light)

Light from scene

Lenses

Focus ring

Mirror reflects light up to pentaprism

▲ Single-lens reflex (SLR) cameras and simpler compact cameras use a different technology than more recent digital cameras, which record images electronically on a microchip.

Snap happy

The lens inside a camera is a disk of glass or plastic, specially shaped to focus (bring together) all the light from the scene and create a tiny image (picture) inside the camera. In most cameras, the image is recorded on film coated in chemicals that react to the light that comes in through a hole (aperture). The mirror reflects the light up to a prism and then to the eyepiece for the photographer to see the image. To take the picture, the mirror swings out of the way so that light falls on to the photographic film behind it for a split second.

WORK IT OUT

• A microscope's magnification is limited by the smallest wavelength of light, which is about 4000 angstroms (a millionth of a centimetre). The wavelength of electrons used in electron microscopes is just 0.5 angstroms.

• Individual atoms can be seen with the scanning tunnelling microscope (STM), which scans the surface of materials by tunnelling an electric charge into them.

1 2 3 4 5 6 7 8 9 10 11 12 13 14 15 16 17 18 19

a
b
c
d
e
f
g
h
i
j
k
l
m
n
o
p
q
r
s
t
u
v
w

Farsighted

Telescopes help you see distant things better by focusing (concentrating) the light onto a small area, then magnifying the focused image so you can see it. In 'refracting' telescopes, a large lens focuses the image by bending or refracting the rays, then a smaller lens, called the eyepiece, magnifies it. In 'reflecting' or mirror telescopes, the image is focused by a large dish-shaped mirror onto a smaller mirror and through the eyepiece. Astronomers now use amazingly powerful telescopes to see galaxies billions of light-years away. The image from these galaxies is picked up by light-sensitive pixels and fed into a computer, where it can be electronically enhanced.

Read further › computers
pg190 (b22)

◀ Telescopes allow astronomers to see stars not visible to the naked eye.

▼ Reflecting telescopes have a curved main mirror.

Eyepiece lens

Incoming light

Secondary mirror

Flat mirror

Reflected light

Main mirror

Incoming light

Focused light

Objective (front) lens

Eyepiece lens

◀ Refracting telescopes use only lenses, not mirrors.

Seeing microbes

Powerful 'electron' microscopes work differently from optical microscopes. Instead of using lenses to magnify light, they fire streams of particles – electrons – at the specimen (the object being studied) and show the result on a monitor. In a transmission electron microscope (TEM), the specimen is so thinly-sliced – usually less than one-hundredth of a millimetre – that electrons can pass through to give a shadow, which is picked up by detectors under the image. Chemicals are added to partly block the electron beam and make the shadows stand out more strongly. TEMs can magnify things up to 1 million times.

▶ A scanning electron microscope (SEM) scans across the surface of the bug to get a very detailed, almost three-dimensional surface view.

Check it out!
• http://www.rmcain.com/mcama/adv/advidxkids.mv
• http://electronics.howstuffworks.com/digital-camera.htm

Read further › television
pg197 (b22)

Round lenses

Glass lenses are shaped to bend light rays in a particular way. Sometimes they are made dish-shaped or 'concave' – thin in the middle and thick round the rim. Light rays passing through a concave lens are bent outwards, so spread. This means when you see something through a concave lens it looks smaller than it really is. Other lenses bulge outwards or are 'convex' – fat in the middle and thin at the rim. Light rays passing through a convex lens bend inwards, so come together or converge. This means that things look bigger when viewed through a convex lens. The point where the converging light rays meet is called the focus.

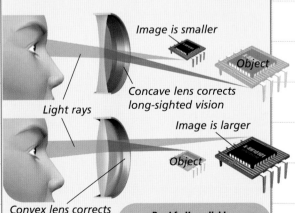

Image is smaller

Object

Concave lens corrects long-sighted vision

Light rays

Image is larger

Object

Convex lens corrects short-sighted vision

Read further › light
pg194 (o2)

◀◀ LIGHT RAYS see pg31 (b22) ◀◀

Sound and vision

TELEVISION BRINGS pictures and sound from all around the world right into our homes, letting us watch events such as top sports games as they happen live across the world. Not only can we watch such events on television, but we can also record many of our own events, using personal camcorders. These recordings can be saved on video tapes or disks to play back later. Other recordings such as music or films can be stored on CD or DVD to be played many times.

▼ A camcorder records images on a small reel of magnetic tape (videotape) or in microchip memory circuits.

Objective lenses

CCD (charge-coupled device) has an array of pixels that detect light

Electric motors and gears to move lenses for focusing (making the image sharp and clear) and zooming (bigger or smaller)

Eye piece

Eyepiece display screen

Monitor screen showing what is being viewed or recorded

Control buttons

Camcorders

Digital camcorders have a lens for projecting a picture that can be recorded using a tiny patch of light-sensitive cells, or pixels. Where the light in the picture is bright, the cell sends out a brief electrical pulse; where it is dark, the cell stays off. As the picture changes, this creates a pattern of electrical pulses. This pattern can then be stored in the camera's memory for playback later, or be sent instantly to the camcorder's viewer or a TV screen to be watched as it is viewed or recorded.

▶▶ Read further › animated film
pg199 (b25; k27)

WORK IT OUT

• The spiral of bumps on a CD are less than half a millionth of a metre wide. The bumps are just 125-billionths of a metre deep.

• Because there is a limit to the resolution (sharpness) of conventional 'analogue' TV, more and more broadcasters are switching to digital pictures like those on computer screens, which can be up to 10 times sharper.

▶▶ INVENTION OF DVD see pg212 (t16) ▶▶

1 2 3 4 5 6 7 8 9 10 11 12 13 14 15 16 17 18 19

● On the tube

Older televisions have a slightly curved screen, which is the front end of a device called the tube – like a giant light bulb. Inside the rear of the tube are 'guns' that create the picture by firing nonstop streams of electrically-charged particles, called electrons, at the back of the screen. Where they hit the screen, they make it glow by heating up its coating of phosphor dots. When we look at the screen, we see thousands of these glowing spots of phosphor in the form of a picture. The broadcast or recorded signal controls where the beams target the screen, making it glow and creating the picture.

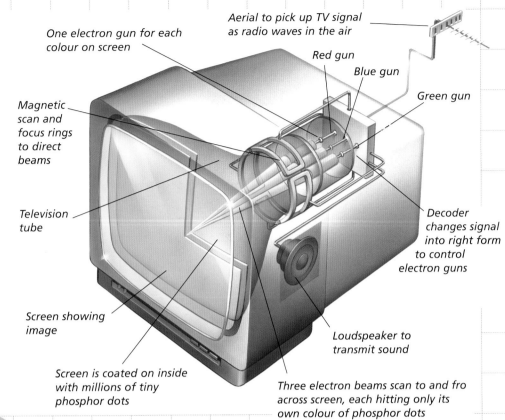

One electron gun for each colour on screen

Aerial to pick up TV signal as radio waves in the air

Red gun

Blue gun

Green gun

Magnetic scan and focus rings to direct beams

Television tube

Decoder changes signal into right form to control electron guns

Screen showing image

Loudspeaker to transmit sound

Screen is coated on inside with millions of tiny phosphor dots

Three electron beams scan to and fro across screen, each hitting only its own colour of phosphor dots

▶▶ **Read further › electrical particles**
pg195 (k22)

● DVDs

Digital Versatile Discs (DVDs), are an efficient way of storing all kinds of data, from music and films to video games. Made of plastic, coated with acrylic and sprayed with aluminium, DVDs store data as a spiral track of tiny pits pressed into the otherwise flat (land) surface. When the DVD is played, a laser beam 'reads' these pits by scanning the underside of the disc. As light hits land it is read as a binary 1. Light that hits a bump is read as a binary 0.

▼ DVDs and CDs work in the same way but a CD holds about one-seventh of the data of a DVD.

Slider carries laser unit across DVD

Spinning disc

Laser beam focused by prism

Laser

Beam bounces off DVD

Reflected beam detected by sensor

Laser beam bent by prism

Spin motor and disc gears

● Check it out!
- http://www.howstuffworks.com/tv.htm
- http://electronics.howstuffworks.com/camcorder.htm

▶▶ INVENTION OF TELEVISION see pg206 (g15) ▶▶

Mass media

MANY KINDS of different media are used for communicating with large numbers of people, whether for entertainment, information or advertising. Newspapers, books, magazines, films, cartoons and the Internet are just some of the many media available to the public. The printing press has enabled written media to reach more people, faster than before. Computers now combine different media to create 'multimedia'. This combination can be used to create video games, CD-Roms, interactive TV and computer-animated films that are more realistic and ambitious than ever.

▲ *Animatronic models such as dinosaurs are usually filmed against a blue screen, while a background such as a wood is filmed separately. The blue screen is later replaced by the real background.*

● IT'S A FACT

• The light sabres in the *Star Wars* movies are filmed using aluminium dummies, which are then replaced by light on a computer, frame by frame.

• Repeat print-runs of books can be made by simply inserting electronic 'smart cards' into the printing machine's computer.

● Straight off the press

Computer technology has revolutionized printing. In the past, pages were printed by wiping ink over metal type (words and letters), which had to be made from scratch using hot metal, or even assembled painstakingly from a store of letters. Now an exact picture of all the text and illustrations can be created on a computer screen. This computer picture is then used either to make a film that can set up the printing photographically, or directly control lasers or jets of ink as they print on to the page.

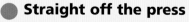

▶▶ Read further › photography pg194 (o2)

▼ *The full-colour lithoprinter makes coloured images out of four colours of ink – cyan (C), magenta (M), yellow (Y) and black (K) – as tiny dots on the page. Four-colour or CMYK printing is used to produce most magazines, books and newspapers. The fifth press contains a special mix of colour or 'text black' for printing words.*

Reel of paper can be changed while printing press is still running so no time is lost during printing

Inking rollers make sure ink is spread evenly on paper. Surfaces of roller can be made from rubber or metal

'Paper web' is a very long, continuous piece of paper that runs through press to be cut into separate sections at end of the press

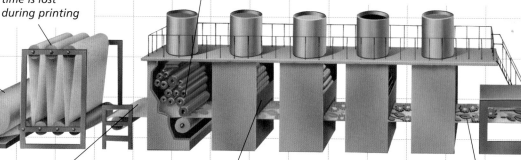

Transfer roller holds paper tightly in place to ensure everything is printed in the right place and that paper does not move between printing presses

Image that needs to be printed comes from a plate that is placed in press and transferred to rubber blanket roller, which rolls image over paper evenly

Drier's heated plates dry ink so that it does not smudge when paper is folded

▶▶ PRINTING PRESS see pg208 (k10) ▶▶

Bringing dinosaurs to life

Dinosaurs died out 65 million years ago, but amazingly lifelike recreations in films, on TV and in museums enable us to see what they were really like. These are called 'animatronics' and are basically mechanical puppets. From walking to breathing, each movement is created by electric motors and hydraulics, controlled remotely by a team of operators. The initial designs are hand-drawn and then reproduced by computers, which in turn guide the machine to make a mould. This mould is used to make a body shell from stiffened foam rubber.

▶▶ Read further > hydraulics
pg181 (f32)

▶▶ Read further > printing
pg198 (k2)

A world in three colours

Almost every colour can be printed by combining just three 'primary' colours of ink. Three 'separations' – versions of the picture in terms of its red, green and blue content – are created. Layers of yellow, magenta and cyan inks then soak up the right amounts of blue, green or red from the light falling on the page.

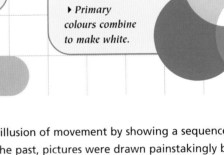

▶ Primary colours combine to make white.

▶▶ Read further > camcorders
pg196 (q2)

Living pictures

Animation means creating the illusion of movement by showing a sequence of subtly-changing still pictures. In the past, pictures were drawn painstakingly by hand, which could take a long time. The use of computer-generated animations has sped up the process and enabled a startling amount of realism by scanning real movements into the camera to act as a base for the animation. Since the computer can store a complete three-dimensional image of all the characters and the way they move, the animator only has to drag the character into position on screen to make a new frame (scene).

▲ The model of a character such as a monster is photographed in one pose. A computer scans the photograph and plots the positions of each tiny part of the model's surface into its memory.

◀ The model is moved into another position and photographed again. The computer scans this new image, compares it with the first, and 'fills in' the in-between images so that they differ only slightly from each other.

Folding unit folds paper so it can be taken off press and packaged straight away

Folded pages are cut to right size and stapled or stitched to hold batches together for easy transportation out to retailers

● WORK IT OUT

• For the movie *Jurassic Park III*, a life-sized animatronic of Spinosaurus – one of the largest meat-eating dinosaurs that ever lived – was made measuring 13.3 m long and weighing more than 12 tonnes.

• The first movie to be made entirely with computer-generated animation was Disney's *Toy Story* in 1995.

▶▶ ANIMATION see pg207 (q27) ▶▶

22 23 24 25 26 27 28 29 30 31 32 33 34 35 36 37 38 39

Early inventions

P EOPLE HAVE been inventing things for about 2.5 million years to make their lives easier and more comfortable. Writing was not invented until about 5000 years ago, so the origins of the earliest inventions were not written down. We only know about them from archaeological discoveries. The first inventions were stone tools and weapons made by early hunters and gatherers. Later, they carved needles from bones to sew clothes for warmth. When people began to settle in one place about 10,000 years ago, they invented wheels, ploughs and irrigation devices to water their crops. They made jars and pots to store food, and better weapons to defend their settlements. However, labour-saving devices were not developed, possibly because work was often carried out by slaves.

● Digging made easy

The earliest known picture of a plough dates from about 5500 years ago in the ancient city of Ur (present-day Iraq). The first plough was wooden and developed from simple digging sticks used to make holes for planting seeds. Its wedge-like blade made long furrows in the soil as it moved forward. After the discovery of iron about 2500 years ago, farmers used iron blades on their ploughs, which were stronger than wooden blades and cut deeper into the soil. The first all-iron plough was invented in 1785 by Robert Ransome in Britain.

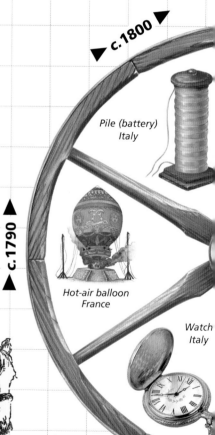

▼ c.1800 ▼

Pile (battery)
Italy

▲ c.1790 ▲

Hot-air balloon
France

Watch
Italy

▼ c.1450 ▼

◄ Farmers used horses to pull the heavy ploughs while they walked behind, steering the blade through the soil.

▶▶ Read further › seed drills / harvesting
pg202 (o2; r10)

Reading the past

We know about ancient civilizations, such as those of the Sumerians (who lived in part of modern Iraq) and the Egyptians because of the picture writing they left behind. About 5250 years ago the Sumerians were the first people to write down their language properly, using pictures to represent words. They developed this into wedge-shaped signs on clay tablets called cuneiform writing (cuneiform means wedge-shaped). The Egyptians developed a form of picture writing known as hieroglyphics *(see pg208 [t6])*.

Read further › picture writing
pg208 (m2)

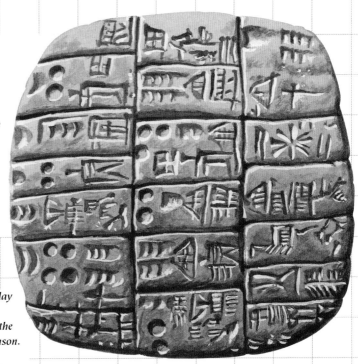

▸ *The cuneiform writing on clay tablets, dating from the 6th century BC, was translated in the 19th century by Henry Rawlinson.*

▲ **3000 BC** ▲

*Abacus
Middle East*

*Glassware
Egypt*

▼ **2000 BC** ▼

*Spectacles
Italy*

▲ **AD 1290** ▲

▲ *The wheel was first invented over 5000 years ago. Early wheels were made from wooden planks. Around 2000 BC spoked wheels, used for chariots and carts, were invented.*

Lifting water

Archimedes (*c.*287–212 BC), an ancient Greek mathematician and inventor from Sicily (then ruled by Greece), invented the water-screw. This is a mechanical device used for raising water from a lower to a higher level. Known as the Archimedean screw, it is still used to irrigate fields in the Middle East. The same principle is used in the grain loader of a combine harvester.

▸ *A large screw is set at an angle in a tube that is open at both ends. When the screw is turned, water fills the air pockets between the twists and gradually travels upwards until it pours out of the top.*

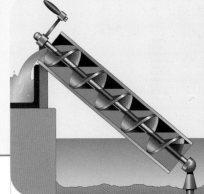

Read further › combine harvesters
pg202 (r10)

INVENTIVE

• By about 1450 BC, the Egyptians were making glass bottles, shaping the glass by blowing it into moulds. Glassblowing (using air to shape very hot glass) was probably invented in Syria about 10 BC.

• To build the city of Jericho in Jordan about 8000 years ago, bricks were made from clay baked in the sun. About 5500 years ago, bricks were fired in a kiln to make them harder and waterproof.

Check it out!

• http://www.enchantedlearning.com/inventors

▸▸ ARCHIMEDES see pg214 (m15) ▸▸

Food and farming

PEOPLE HAVE been inventing ways of growing, cooking and preserving food for centuries. But after the invention of ploughs (*see pg200 [t9]*), there was little advance in farm machinery until the 18th century in Britain – a period known as the Industrial Revolution – when new machinery began to develop rapidly, leading to such inventions as the combine harvester. Food and drink, such as sugar and tea, have been available for centuries, but burgers, crisps and bubble gum are more recent inventions, dating from the 19th century.

Seed stored in hopper

◄ *Jethro Tull's seed drill made harvesting easier as seeds were sown in rows.*

Seeds fall down tubes into holes in soil

Drill digs holes

● Sowing seeds

Three thousand years ago, people living in Babylonia (present day Iraq) used a simple device for sowing seeds, which dropped them down a tube on top of a plough. In 1660, Taddeo Calvani invented the first seed drill, which consisted of a container with holes in the bottom mounted on a cart. The vibrations of the cartwheels shook the seeds out through the holes. In 1701, English farmer Jethro Tull invented a much more efficient version. The seeds dropped down tubes into furrows in the soil and were sown in regular rows. This made it much more likely that seeds would take root, because they had plenty of room in the soil to grow.

▶▶ Read further › ploughs
pg200 (j8)

● Harvesting

A combine harvester combines the two stages of harvesting: cutting the crop and separating the grain. The first combine harvester was designed in 1836 by Americans Hiram Moore and John Hascall. It was pulled by horses.

▼ *The first motorized combine harvesters, produced in 1961, increased the speed at which crops are harvested.*

▶▶ Read further › harvesting
pg201 (k28)

a
b
c
d
e
f
g
h
i
j
k
l
m
n
o
p
q
r
s
t
u
v
w

▶▶ **Read further › wheels**
pg201 (u22)

Shopping on wheels

Sylvan Goldman of Oklahoma, USA invented the shopping trolley in 1936 to persuade people to buy more in his grocery store. He had noticed that people stopped shopping when their hand-held baskets were full. His first design, based on a folding chair with wheels on the legs, one basket on the seat and another just above the wheels, was a simple idea, but very effective. Goldman's invention came at the right time because supermarkets were starting to be built in America. His invention made him a millionaire.

From pots to burgers

In 1904 Fletcher Davis invented the hamburger. He was a potter by trade and became involved in the burger business by cooking at pottery shows. He also ran a small café in east Texas. His burgers were the classic burger made from ground beef, served on toasted bread and garnished with salad, mustard and mayonnaise.

▸ *The word 'cheeseburger' was patented in 1944 by Louis Ballast, after he grilled a slice of cheese on top of a burger at his Colorado drive-in.*

INVENTIVE

• The popsicle was invented by 11-year-old American Frank Epperson in 1905 after he left a fruit drink out overnight (with a stirrer in it) and the drink froze. The popsicle was originally called the Epsicle, after its inventor.

• Inventors are trying to grow square tomatoes, which would be much easier to stack in boxes for shipping.

Double bubble

Bubble gum is extra-strong gum that can be blown into bubbles. First invented in 1906 by American Frank Henry Fleer, it was called Blibber-Blubber. It was too sticky – when it popped it was very difficult to peel off the face – and therefore unsuccessful. In 1928, Walter E. Deimer invented a better mixture for bubble gum, which he called 'Dubble Bubble'.

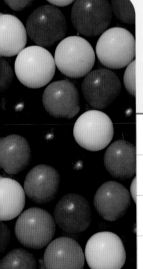

◂ *Bubble gum is made in all sorts of shapes, colours and sizes, from simple, round spheres to novelty shapes, such as cigars.*

◂ *Farmers across the world seek ways to increase their produce: GM is one way they can do this.*

Genetically modified

One of the most controversial scientific discoveries of the 20th century is the genetic modification (GM) of foods. The genes of every living organism can be altered to change its characteristics. For example, farmers can add anti-pest genes to crops, which enables them to survive longer or grow unusually large.

Check it out!

• http://www.ideafinder.com/history/inventions/story026.htm

▶▶ **Read further › genes**
pg212 (b15)

▶▶ GENETIC MODIFICATION see pg234 (p2) ▶▶

22 23 24 25 26 27 28 29 30 31 32 33 34 35 36 37 38 39

Power it up

INVENTIONS THAT use sources of natural power have been developed over thousands of years to make our lives easier. The ancient Greeks and Romans used water mills to grind grain and olives more than 2000 years ago. The invention of the steam engine and ways to control gas and create electricity revolutionized mechanical movement and power. Today, coal and oil is burnt in power stations to make electricity and to power engines for transport, but these sources of energy will eventually run out. We need therefore to utilise natural energy – solar, wind and water power are everlasting sources.

▶ *Before automatic timers were installed in the early 1900s, gas lamps were lit using long torches.*

Gas lighting

In 1792, Englishman William Murdock invented a lighting system based on heating coal in a closed vessel and piping the gas it made to make light. He later developed a system for producing and storing gas. In the 19th century, coal gas provided many towns with energy for lighting and heating. In 1885, Austrian Carl Auer invented the gas mantle: this was a mesh of carbonized cotton that glowed brightly when heated and was used in street lamps.

First engines

The first practical steam engine, invented by Englishman Thomas Savery in 1698, pumped out water from flooded coal mines. Savery's engine cooled and condensed steam (a gas) into water, leaving a vacuum (no gas), which sucked up the flood water (a liquid). In 1712, Englishman Thomas Newcomen built an improved steam engine. The steam and the vacuum moved a piston up and down, which rocked a crossbeam, which in turn worked a water pump. In 1765, James Watt made improvements to Newcomen's engine. He added a chamber to cool and condense the steam to change it back into water so that the engine did not have to be heated and cooled all the time.

▶▶ Read further › pumping water pg201 (k28)

◀ *James Watt made the piston on the steam engine move like a wheel, using gears and a connecting rod.*

Check it out!
• http://www.bbc.co.uk/history/historic_figures/newcomen_thomas.shtml

◀◀ STEAM see pg27 (b26) ◀◀

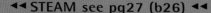

1 2 3 4 5 6 7 8 9 10 11 12 13 14 15 16 17 18 19

Water power

The oldest known dam, made of soil and stones, was built across the Garawi valley in Egypt about 5000 years ago. Modern arch dams were invented in the 1850s by French scientist François Zola. They resist the pushing force of the water because their shape pushes the water down. In a gravity dam, the great weight of the material they are built from stops the water from pushing its way through.

▲ Water falling from inside a gravity dam can push turbine wheels around to generate electricity. This is called hydro-electric power (hydro means water).

▶▶ **Read further > use of water**
pg213 (r27)

▶▶ **Read further > electricity**
pg205 (j32)

▼ In 1882, Thomas Edison's factories made 100,000 light bulbs. By 1900 over 45 million were needed in the US alone to light towns and cities.

Power of the Sun

The Sun beams a vast amount of energy to the Earth. This energy can be collected and concentrated by photovoltaic (solar) cells to generate electricity. The manufacture of photovoltaic cells was only possible from the mid-1900s when American scientists G.L. Pearson, D.M. Chapin and C.S. Fuller developed a solar battery made of tiny solar cells. Solar power is safe and environmentally friendly because it does not cause pollution of any kind.

▶ Solar cells can turn about 15 per cent of the sunlight that falls on them into electrical energy. Scientists hope to improve this percentage.

▼ Oil refineries produce enough oil to fuel about half the energy we use.

Electric city

Before gas and electricity were used, people relied on oil and gas lamps and candles to provide artificial light. The electric light bulb, invented by American scientists Thomas Edison and Joseph Swan in about 1879, was air-tight so that it could burn for longer. Inside a light bulb, a tiny, thin coiled wire called a filament gets so hot that it glows brightly, giving off light when electricity tries to squeeze through it. The flow of electricity causes the wire filament to glow brightly inside the airless bulb. Made of a type of metal called tungsten, the filament can get very hot without melting.

▶▶ **Read further > gas lamps**
pg204 (i14)

Drilling for oil

The Chinese first drilled for oil 2000 years ago using bamboo and bronze pipes. In 1844, Englishman Robert Beart introduced rotary drilling using steam engines. A drilling bit on the end of a hollow steel pipe forced up the rock (and oil) by pumping water down the pipe. The first offshore oil well was built off the American coast.

INVENTIVE

• In 1867 Alfred Nobel invented dynamite (named after the Greek word for power, *dynamis*). In his will, he requested that it should not be used in war.

• Five prizes (Nobel Prizes) are awarded each year for: physics, chemistry, medicine, literature and the promotion of peace.

◀◀ FILAMENT see pg15 (b29) ◀◀

22 23 24 25 26 27 28 29 30 31 32 33 34 35 36 37 38 39

a b c d e f g h i j k l m n o p q r s t u v w

Electronic media

ELECTRONIC DEVICES such as radios, televisions and computers change electrical signals into sounds and pictures. Inside these devices are electronic components that control the way electricity flows around a circuit, making it perform particular tasks. Early radios and televisions used valves to switch tiny electrical signals, but these were large and used up lots of electricity. In the 1940s American scientists invented transistors that worked like valves but were smaller and more efficient. By the 1960s, transistors and other electronic components were all placed in one chip of silicon 5 mm square. Today microchips control computers and many other devices.

Televisions

The first televisions relied on the cathode ray tube, invented in 1897 by German physicist Karl Braun. These fire streams of electrons – tiny particles that are parts of atoms – at a specially coated screen to make it glow. The first television was presented in 1926 by John Logie Baird. In a colour television there are three electron streams: red, blue and green. These light up phosphor dots on the screen, which blend to form a full colour image.

▲ Some flat screen TVs invented in Japan in the 1980s, use liquid crystal displays instead of cathode ray tubes.

Early computers

In 1823, English mathematician Charles Babbage invented the first type of computer – the 'difference engine'. It proved too complex to complete and in 1834 Babbage began constructing his 'analytical engine' in which data was fed into the engine by punched cards. The results were designed to be printed out. Though it was never built in full, as it would have been the size of a small train, Babbage's idea helped others to invent the first computers.

◄ The engine had a memory that was able to retain up to 100 40-digit numbers and a central processor to make calculations.

To scale
1 square across = 16 cm

Personal Digital Assistant
8 cm in length

Early computer
90 cm across

Radio revolution

In 1895, Italian inventor Marchese Guglielmo Marconi was the first person to send signals without wires. Marconi produced invisible radio waves from an electric current that changes direction thousands of times a second. In 1901 he sent radio messages across the Atlantic, from England to the USA. In 1906 people first heard voices over the radio. Today radio waves are also used in mobile phones.

▲ Early radios were called wirelesses as they used only waves, not wires or cables, to carry sound.

◄◄ COMPUTERS see pg191 (b32) ◄◄

1 2 3 4 5 6 7 8 9 10 11 12 13 14 15 16 17 18 19

a b c d e f g h i j k l m n o p q r s t u v w

Video games

The first successful video game was invented in 1972 by American computer programer Nolan Bushnell. It was a form of electronic table tennis called *Pong*. A video game is controlled by the memory on a silicon chip computer circuit. Most systems are based on the central processing units (CPUs) used in many computers. Video games are controlled using a user control interface, such as a key pad. All game consoles use a video signal that is compatible with television.

▶ **Read further › light**
pg205 (j32)

▶ *In this game called* Ape Man, *a graphics processor provides texture, colour and other functions and a chip handles the sound.*

Clever computers

The first home computer was produced in 1975 by Altair in the USA, and the Apple Macintosh followed in 1984. When computers were first developed in the 1940s they filled entire rooms. The ENIAC (Electronic Numerical Integrator and Calculator), built in 1946, weighed 30 tonnes. Using 805 km of wire, it carried out 100,000 tasks per second. Computers are smaller since the invention of the transistor (electronic switch that detects electric current) in 1948 and integrated circuits in 1957. The latest iMacs are flat-screened.

▶ **Read further › early computers**
pg206 (m2)

▲ *A liquid crystal display (LCD) produces images on a flat screen by using electric current to control the path of light through liquid crystals and coloured filters.*

INVENTIVE

• In 1926 the first moving television picture was made by John Logie Baird, using a spinning disc with holes, invented in 1884 by Paul Nipkow.

• Baird's system was later replaced by an electronic system invented by Vladimir Zworykin in the 1920s.

Moving pictures

Animated films create the impression of movement using a rapid series of still pictures of cartoons or puppets. The first animated films of the 1900s were cartoons. These were drawn on transparent sheets of celluloid before being photographed over a fixed background.

▶ **Read further › video games**
pg207 (b22)

▶ *Today, computers are programed to draw the images, made from thousands of shapes in a structure called a wireframe, where colour, texture, shading and perspective is added to make the image appear three-dimensional.*

Check it out!
• http://www.computerhistory.org
• http://www.jonesencyclo.com/trends.cfm
• http://www.greatachievements.org

◀◀ ANIMATION see pg199 (k27) ◀◀

22 23 24 25 26 27 28 29 30 31 32 33 34 35 36 37 38 39

Keeping in touch

U NTIL PEOPLE learned to write they were only able to communicate when speaking face to face. Information was passed verbally through the generations, often through story-telling. About 5000 years ago the Sumerians and ancient Egyptians invented writing. Then about 4000 years later, the Chinese invented printing by hand. The mechanical printing press was invented about 500 years ago in Europe by Johannes Gutenberg. Other communication methods, such as Braille and Morse code, were invented in the 1800s. Today e-mails, telephones and fax machines connect people all over the world, and because of the Internet, information is easier to access than ever before.

▼ The printing press enabled newspapers and books to be read by more people.

Clues to the past
The ancient Egyptians used written pictures and symbols, called hieroglyphics, instead of words. They used these hieroglyphics for 3500 years until about AD 400 when Greek became their written language. The Rosetta Stone, discovered in 1799, written in both hieroglyphics and Greek, provided the key to translating hieroglyphics.

Printing
Before printing was invented, books were copied by hand. Invented in China before AD 868, 'letterpress' printing used letters and pictures carved from blocks of wood, clay or ivory, which were covered with ink so that when paper was pressed on them they printed the raised carving. Peking blacksmith Pi-Sheng invented movable type (individual letters on reusable blocks). In 1436 German Johannes Gutenberg invented typecasting, which made large amounts of movable type quickly and cheaply. In 1886, the linotype machine automatically cast complete lines of type from molten metal. Today, computers are used to input and print type and images.

▶▶ Read further › writing pg201 (b22)

▶▶ Read further › writing pg201 (b22)

◀ Each hieroglyph (symbol or picture) represents an object or a sound. In total, there are about 700 different hieroglyphs.

COMMUNICATION

Invention	Year first used
Writing	about 3500 BC
Paper	AD 105
Numbers 0 to 9	about 500
Mechanical clock	1000s
Printing press	1400s

◀◀ PRINTING see pg198 (k2) ◀◀

1 2 3 4 5 6 7 8 9 10 11 12 13 14 15 16 17 18 19

Dot writing

In 1829, Frenchman Louis Braille invented a six-dot coded system of raised dots that could be used by the blind to read. Louis Braille was accidentally blinded at the age of three. When he was ten, he was shown a way of writing messages with raised dots, designed for soldiers to use at night. Braille simplified it so it was easier to read with the fingertips. Braille is still used worldwide today.

▼ *Braille is made up of different patterns of six dots, each pattern representing a letter and some short words such as 'the'.*

▶▶ Read further › symbols
pg201 (b22)

Dots and dashes

In 1838 Samuel Morse and Alfred Vail stopped and started an electric current along wires (or telegraphs) to communicate. Named Morse code, the short (on) bursts were the dots, and the longer (off) bursts were the dashes. In 1844, the first telegraph line opened between Baltimore and Washington, DC, enabling messages that would normally take weeks by post, to be sent instantly. Within 30 years, telegraphs covered the globe. Morse code is still used by the Navy today.

Long and short bleeps tapped into telegraph machine

Electric current

Message travels along telegraph wires to recipient

▲ *As an electric current running along a wire is stopped and started, the on and off bursts form coded messages.*

▶▶ Read further › radio
pg206 (q11)

The Internet

The Internet is a worldwide network of computers. Developed in the 1970s by American computer scientist Vinton Cerf and American engineer Robert Kahn, it connects, using phone lines, local networks of computers to special computers called gateways. Cerf and Kahn defined the Internet Protocol – the software that controls the Internet. Then, in 1989, English computer scientist Tim Berners-Lee invented the World Wide Web to share information over the Internet. At the beginning of the 21st century, more than 25 million computers were linked to the Internet, and this number continues to rise.

▶ *Internet phones allow people to 'surf' (browse) the Internet from all over the world.*

▶▶ Read further › computers
pg207 (h22)

Telephones old and new

Telephones were invented by Scottish-born American Alexander Graham Bell in 1876. Bell discovered how to change sound vibrations in the human voice into electrical signals, which he sent along wires to a receiver. Today, pulses of light send telephone calls down fibre optic cables, and electrical signals are sent along copper cables. The word 'telephone' comes from the Greek words for 'far' and 'sound'.

◀ *Mobile phones, invented in the 1980s, send digital radio signals to base stations, which send the signal around a network until it reaches the right phone.*

▶▶ Read further › electricity
pg205 (j32)

To scale

1 square across = 6 cm

20 cm across

Bell's first telephone

Check it out!
- http://www.bbc.co.uk/arts/books/historyofbooks
- http://www.worldalmanacfor kids.com/explore/inventions.html

◀◀ COMMUNICATION see pg192 (I2) ◀◀

22 23 24 25 26 27 28 29 30 31 32 33 34 35 36 37 38 39

a b c d e f g h i j k l m n o p q r s t u v w

Medicine

FROM STETHOSCOPES and vaccinations to contact lenses and forceps, many of the medical inventions of the 19th century are still used today. Before this, there was little understanding of germs or the importance of keeping wounds clean to avoid the spread of infection. Without anaesthetics to numb the pain during surgery, patients sometimes died from shock. Patients often had to be cut open to find out what was wrong with them, until instruments such as endoscopes, invented in the 1950s, were able to see inside the body. Body scanners, heart pacemakers and plastic contact lenses have since been invented.

Magnifying lenses enable surgeons to see small details

Sharp scalpel for cutting through skin, organs and blood vessels

EEG machines monitor patient's heartbeat during operation

● Fighting infection

Vaccinations protect the body against diseases, such as smallpox, tetanus and tuberculosis. Two forms of vaccination are used today: 'active' immunization is a weak but harmless form of the disease that tricks the body into producing antibodies to fight it. 'Passive' immunization uses antibodies that are already able to fight the disease. When disease affects someone who has been vaccinated, the antibodies are ready to fight.

◀ *The first vaccine was developed by Edward Jenner, about 200 years ago, to fight smallpox.*

▶▶ **Read further › treatment**
pg211 (j29)

▶▶ **Read further › operation**
pg211 (b22)

● Ancient surgical tools

About 5000 years ago, the first saws for cutting off limbs were made from wood, bone or flint, shaped into rows of sharp teeth. Flakes of flint were fixed into straight handles of wood or bone with sticky tree resin or pitch. Bronze-age patients suffered under a sharp saw to remove limbs without anaesthetic. Forceps are metal pincers that can be used to deliver babies. A hook knife was used to extract organs from a patient's body during an operation.

Iron forceps

Hook knife

Bronze Age saw

▶▶ MEDICAL DEVELOPMENTS see pg224 (d2) ▶▶

| 1 | 2 | 3 | 4 | 5 | 6 | 7 | 8 | 9 | 10 | 11 | 12 | 13 | 14 | 15 | 16 | 17 | 18 | 19 |

a
b
c
d
e
f
g
h
i
j
k
l
m
n
o
p
q
r
s
t
u
v
w

● Operation

Before an operation, patients are given anaesthetics, which either cause a loss of feeling in the body, numbing the pain, or send them to sleep temporarily. In 1799, English chemist Humphrey Davey described the benefits of nitrous oxide (laughing gas). It was later used by Horace Wells in 1844.

▶▶ **Read further › ancient tools**
pg210 (q10)

◀ *An operating theatre is kept extremely clean to prevent the spread of infection. Surgeons wear masks, hats and coats to avoid spreading infection through breathing and from any cuts on the skin.*

Very bright lights help surgeons to see clearly during operations

● Contact lenses

Contact lenses are tiny lenses that are worn on the eye to help people see clearly. First thought of by Leonardo da Vinci around 1503, glass contact lenses were not actually made until 1887 when Adolf Eugen Fick made heavy, brown glass lenses for animals. Then in 1948, Californian optician Kevin Tuohy invented plastic lenses. In the 1970s, soft, gas-permeable lenses (that let oxygen pass through the lenses to the eyes) were made from a soft, plastic material. These float on the surface (cornea) of the eye and so can be worn for longer periods.

▶▶ **Read further › spectacles**
pg201 (r22)

▲ *The eye has to be held wide open when putting in contact lenses.*

● Medicine

Drugs are used to treat and prevent disease and pain. The oldest list of drugs came from ancient Babylonia about 3700 years ago. Today most drugs are chemicals mixed together, or made from plants and other natural sources.

▶▶ **Read further › Babylonians**
pg202 (o2)

INVENTIVE

- The two parts of a hypodermic syringe – the needle and the plunger – were invented in 1853 by two people in two different countries: Scotland and France.

- In 1972 Godfrey Hounsfield developed a Computerised Tomography (CT) scanner, to take pictures of the inside of the body.

● Pacemaker

A person's heart normally beats at about 60 to 100 times per minute but sometimes the rate becomes too fast or too slow. The rhythm can be corrected or steadied by a pacemaker, which was invented in 1958 by Swedish doctor, Ake Senning.

▶ *The battery-operated pacemaker is connected to the heart and sends it timed electrical impulses to help it beat with a regular rhythm.*

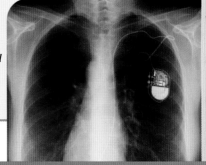

 Check it out!

- http://www.worldalmanacforkids.com/ explore/inventions.html
- http://www.enchantedlearning.com/ inventors/medicine.shtml

◀◀ EYES see pg168 (o13) ◀◀

Into the future

TODAY THE pace of new technology moves very quickly, and we take for granted machines that have been invented recently. Future inventions could be more amazing than ever before. Virtual reality, flat-screen televisions and computer animation have changed the entertainment world. Robotic space explorers may pave the way for human exploration of other planets in the 21st century. Advances in gene therapy and cloning may have huge influences on the living world. Inventions, such as personal flying machines and ways to live at sea or on other planets could change our lives forever.

● IT'S A FACT
• The first successful gene therapy – replacing faulty genes with new ones – took place on a four-year-old girl who was unable to fight infections.

• The first robot programed to respond to commands was an artificial duck created in 1738.

• In 2002, a South African millionaire paid $20 million for a 10-day 'holiday' in space.

● House robots
The invention of the microchip in 1952 enabled the movement of machines, such as robots, to be controlled by computer. In the future, robots, such as this vacuum cleaner, may assist humans in many ways, such as doing the housework.

▶▶ Read further > robots
pg213 (c33)

▼ *This robot vacuum cleaner contains sensors to stop it bumping into things or getting stuck in corners.*

▶ *The Solo Trek XFV is a compact aircraft with vertical take-off and landing. It has a potential 240-km range and a top speed of 129 km/h.*

● Flying machine
In 2001, Michael Moshier and Robert Bulaga and their team invented a personal flying machine that straps on to a person's back: the Solo Trek XFV. On the test flight, Moshier hovered above the ground for only 19 seconds at an altitude of just 0.6 m, but this could indicate the start of a new method of flying.

▶▶ Read further > flight
pg200 (o16)

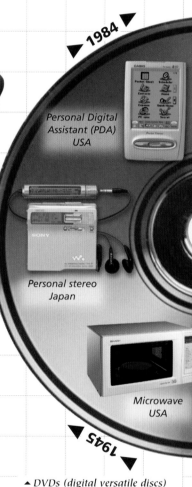

▲ 1984 ▼

Personal Digital Assistant (PDA) USA

▲ 1980 ▲

Personal stereo Japan

Microwave USA

▼ 1945 ▼

▲ *DVDs (digital versatile discs) store information such as music and films. DVD players use lasers to 'read' the information. DVDs are similar to CDs but they have the capacity to store much more information and have excellent sound and picture quality.*

Living in space

Over the next couple of centuries, explorers may be able to set up colonies on Mars. Future NASA missions are planned to land Mars rovers and mobile laboratories with instruments for drilling below the surface, and detecting and analysing minerals and water samples. NASA is also developing technology to turn Martian resources into rocket fuel for the trip back.

▶▶ Read further › NASA
pg57 (b22)

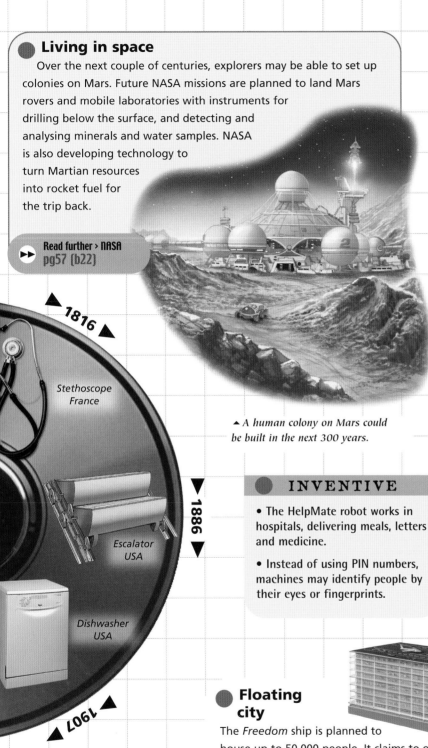

1816

Stethoscope
France

▼ 1886 ▼

Escalator
USA

Dishwasher
USA

1907 ▲

▲ *A human colony on Mars could be built in the next 300 years.*

▶▶ Read further › computers
pg207 (h22)

Intelligent robots

Robots have only been possible since computers were invented, which enabled robots to follow instructions. Robots were first patented in 1961 by American scientists George C. Devol and Joseph F. Engelberger. Today, thousands of robots go to places where people cannot go, such as the deep ocean or other planets. They do tedious and even dangerous jobs, such as handling hazardous, radioactive material. Robots have been used to explore the surface of other planets.

▼ *The robot* Sojourner *was a space probe sent onto the surface of Mars in 1997 to investigate the rock type.*

INVENTIVE

• The HelpMate robot works in hospitals, delivering meals, letters and medicine.

• Instead of using PIN numbers, machines may identify people by their eyes or fingerprints.

Floating city

The *Freedom* ship is planned to house up to 50,000 people. It claims to offer a solution to the problem of overcrowding on land. The ship is planned to contain a school, a hospital, yacht marinas, one of the largest shopping malls in the world, sports facilities, theatres, nightclubs, restaurants and a golf range.

▲ *The* Freedom *ship will recycle much of its waste, rather than dumping it into the ocean.*

▶▶ Read further › hospitals
pg211 (b23)

◀◀ MARS see pg47 (n22) ◀◀

a b c d e f g h i j k l m n o p q r s t u v w

Great Greeks

THE NATURAL world was studied by many ancient peoples, but it was in ancient Greece that science really began, in about 2500 BC. Ancient Greek thinkers began to look at the world logically – to work out how natural events occurred by reasoned argument instead of looking for mysterious spiritual forces. Great thinkers such as Plato, Aristotle, Socrates, Euclid and Archimedes made profound insights into the world around them. Their studies included natural forces, mathematics, the nature of matter and how the body works. These studies laid the foundations of modern science.

▼ *Archimedes discovered the principle of liquid displacement as he saw the water level in his bath rise as more of his body became immersed. He is said to have jumped out of the bath and run naked through the streets shouting 'Eureka!' – Greek for 'I've got it!'*

● **Ancient scholars**

The ancient Greeks called their thinkers and scholars 'philosophers', which means lovers of wisdom. Today we think of philosophy as studies based on thoughts and theories about human existence. But Greek philosophers, often whilst living and studying in Athens, studied all kinds of subjects, including science and mathematics. A temple – the Museion, or Museum – was built in Alexandria in Egypt to celebrate the Greek 'muses' said to inspire ideas and art. The museum had a famous library where scholars from many parts of the world – particularly Greek-speaking countries – came to work.

▼ *Greek scholars, such as Plato and Aristotle, developed the idea of intellectual debate.*

● **Eureka!**

Greek scientist Archimedes (c.287–c.212 BC) who lived in Syracuse in Sicily (then ruled by the Greeks), was the first to apply mathematics to science. He worked out how effective levers and other machines could be. One of his best ideas was the Archimedean screw, still used today, for pumping water. Archimedes showed that objects float because of the weight of water they displace (push away). This idea is now called Archimedes' Principle.

▶▶ **Read further › mathematics**
pg226 (d2); pg227 (c22)

▶▶ **Read further › House of Wisdom**
pg226 (q2)

● **Check it out!**

• http://www.utm.edu/research/iep/a/aristotl.htm

◀◀ ARCHIMEDEAN SCREW see pg201 (k28) ◀◀

1   2   3   4   5   6   7   8   9   10   11   12   13   14   15   16   17   18   19

Early medicine

The ancient Greek doctor Hippocrates (460–379 BC) is often called the father of medicine. He lived during a time when many believed that illness was caused by evil spirits or magic. Hippocrates showed that disease has physical causes, such as poor diet or dirt. Today, doctors still practise under an updated version of the 'Hippocratic oath' undertaking to provide good care for their patients.

▸ *Hippocrates recorded people's reactions to certain treatments and so established medicine on a practical basis.*

▶▶ **Read further › medicine**
pg224 [d2; g15]; pg225 [i22]

Covering the angles

Though the ancient Egyptians had a good knowledge of angles and triangles to enable them to build the pyramids, the ancient Greeks created the first systems of geometry – the study of lines and the angles between them. The Greek mathematician Euclid (c.330–260 BC) who studied and lived in Alexandria in Egypt, wrote *Elements of Geometry*, which gave a clear and thorough analysis of geometric principles. Even today, mathematicians refer to the geometry of flat surfaces – lines, points, shapes and solids – as Euclidean geometry.

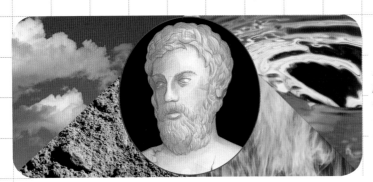

◂ *Aristotle developed Empedocles' idea of four elements (earth, air, fire and water) into a coherent and logical argument.*

Aristotle

Ancient Greek thinker Aristotle (384–322 BC) studied many areas of science and philosophy at Plato's academy in Athens and helped pioneer the study of animals (zoology) and plants (botany). He established a basic approach to science, showing how scientists must observe things closely, classify these observations, and use logical arguments to understand them. He opened, and directed for 12 years, the Lyceum school in Athens. His ideas remained a key part of university education in Europe for more than 2000 years.

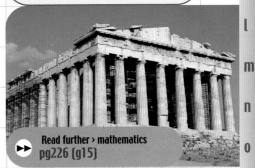

▶▶ **Read further › mathematics**
pg226 [g15]

▴ *Classic principles of geometry were put into practice in temples such as the Parthenon in Athens, built between c.447–c.432 BC. It has two adjoining square forms topped with a triangular gable.*

▶▶ **Read further › classification**
pg223 [m22]

GENIUS GENES

• The Greek geographer Eratosthenes (c.285–c.194 BC) measured the Earth's circumference with astonishing accuracy 1800 years before European explorers showed that the world is round.

• The Greek scholar Xenophanes realized, thousands of years before Victorian scientists developed the idea, that fossils were rocks containing the remains of dead plants and animals.

OTHER KEY FIGURES

Date	Name, nationality	Achievements
c.582–c.497 BC	Pythagoras, Greek	Discovered basic mathematical rules
c.390–c.340 BC	Eudoxus, Greek	Worked out the mathematics of spheres (ball-shapes)
c.265–c.190 BC	Apollonius, Greek	Discovered circles that can be cut from cones, such as parabolas
1st century AD	Hero of Alexandria, Greek	Discovered several uses for steam, such as opening temple doors

◂◂ CONSTRUCTING BUILDINGS see pg178 [l2] ◂◂

Inside the body

FOR 1500 years medicine was based on the writings of Greek physician Claudius Galen (AD *c.*130–*c.*200) who studied animals to support his theories on human medicine. Galen's ideas remained unchallenged until the 15th and 16th centuries when physicians such as Andreas Vesalius and artists such as Leonardo da Vinci began to look at real bodies by dissecting (cutting up) dead human bodies to investigate their structure. This new approach began in Italy at the University of Padua where the great anatomist Vesalius was professor. It spread throughout most of Europe, and later pioneers such as William Harvey and Marcello Malpighi made crucial breakthroughs.

GENIUS GENES

• In the 1820s, Edinburgh medical students needed a lot of bodies to dissect in order to learn about anatomy. So Irishmen William Burke and William Hare began to provide the extra corpses – first by stealing them from graves, then by murdering people!

• When William Harvey suggested that blood circulated, many people thought he was mad. When he demonstrated blood flowing through a weightlifter's veins, doctor Caspar Hoffman (1572–1648) said, 'I see it, but I don't believe it!'

Knife master

Flemish physician Andreas Vesalius (1514–1564) began the first systematic study of human anatomy – the composition of the human body. Whilst lecturing in surgery at Padua University in Italy, Vesalius saw Galen's books as inaccurate, based as they were on studies of animals. So Vesalius began to carry out his own dissection, though he was not the first. Vesalius dissected the corpses himself, often in front of a large audience of students. His findings were published in *De Humani Corporis Fabrica* – 'On The Structure of the Human Body' – the first great book of anatomy, which was illustrated by Flemish artist Jan van Calcar.

▶▶ Read further › anatomical drawings
pg217 (d22)

▸ *About 30 years before Vesalius, artists such as Italian Raffaello Sanzio (1483–1520) (better known as Raphael) began to observe skeletons to make anatomically accurate drawings of the bones.*

Check it out!

• http://www.knowitall.org/kidswork/hospital/history/

a
b
c
d
e
f
g
k

▶ *Leonardo da Vinci dissected corpses to find out how bodies worked. His drawings were revolutionary in their accuracy.*

Drawing the body

Crucial to our understanding of the human anatomy was the development of accurate anatomical drawings. One of the first great anatomical artists was Italian Leonardo da Vinci (1452–1519). Leonardo had a great mind and contributed to science in countless ways. Human dissection allowed him to produce detailed anatomical drawings to learn how bones and muscles work and how babies grow inside the mother's womb. Accurate drawings enabled physicians to record the results of dissections, and pass on the results to students and other researchers.

▶▶ **Read further › recording results** pg215 (b22); pg218 (p11)

Body pump

English physician William Harvey (1578–1657) was the first to show that the heart pumps blood. Physicians already knew that blood moved around the body through veins but thought it moved backwards and forwards like tides. Harvey showed that valves in the blood vessels allow blood to continually circulate the body in one direction, flowing from the heart through branching arteries and back through converging veins. However, he could not see how blood moved from arteries to veins.

▶▶ **Read further › Malpighi** pg217 (n22)

▶ *In describing the circulation of the blood, Harvey labelled veins and arteries to try to understand how blood circulated through the body.*

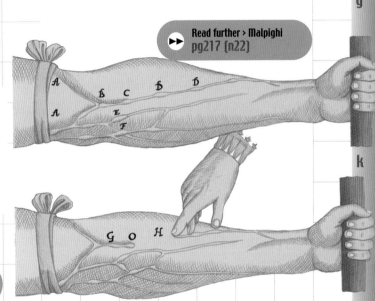

The final link

In 1661, Italian physician Marcello Malpighi (1628–1694) showed how arteries and veins are linked. Using the newly invented microscope, Malpighi saw that arteries and veins are linked by minute blood vessels called capillaries, far too small to see with the naked eye. He also used the microscope to study organs such as the lungs, kidneys, brain and skin.

▶▶ **Read further › DNA** pg234 (r8); pg235 (p22)

◀ *Microscopes reveal things in the body too small for the eye to see, such as tiny blood cells that float in the blood.*

o
p
q
r
s
t
u
v
w

OTHER KEY FIGURES

Date	Name, nationality	Achievements
c.335–c.280 BC	Herophilus, Greek	Began the science of anatomy
c.304–c.250 BC	Erasistratus, Greek	Began the science of physiology
AD c.130–c.200	Claudius Galen, Greek	Collated all the existing knowledge of medicine and the human body
1523–1562	Gabriello Fallopio, Italian	Discovered tiny structures in the ear and female reproductive system
1561–1636	Sanctorius, Italian	Designed a clinical thermometer and studied the body's metabolism
1809–1885	Friedrich Jacob Henle, German	Discovered kidney tubules
1821–1902	Rudolf Virchow, German	Led our understanding of how disease affects body cells
1868–1943	Karl Landsteiner, Austrian-American	Discovered blood groups

◀◀ HEART see pg163 (b22) ◀◀

22 23 24 25 26 27 28 29 30 31 32 33 34 35 36 37 38 39

Star gazers

ASTRONOMY IS one of the oldest sciences. It dates back to the earliest days of humankind when hunters gazed into the night sky to work out which night would give them a full Moon – and more light to hunt by. When people began to form settlements and farm the land, astronomers told farmers when the seasons would come and go. Ancient Egyptians, such as Imhotep, who designed the first pyramid 4500 years ago, were known for their astronomy so it was already an ancient art by the time Greek astronomer Hipparchus began to study the sky.

IT'S A FACT

• The Greek astronomer Aristarchus (c.310–c.230 BC) suggested that the Earth revolved around the Sun more than 2000 years before Copernicus released his theory on this subject.

• In 1918, an unknown American astronomer showed that the Earth is on the edge of our own local Galaxy, not at the centre.

GENIUS GENES

• In 1593, Galileo invented what could be called the first thermometer – a glass bulb in which coloured water moved up and down as the temperature changed.

• When Edwin Hubble (1889–1953) showed that the universe is expanding, Belgian astronomer George Lemaitre (1894–1966) suggested that this was because the universe was originally tiny, before bursting into existence with a mighty explosion called the Big Bang.

◀ As well as plotting the position of about 850 stars, Hipparchus invented trigonometry, which is used to mathematically calculate the angles and lengths of the sides of triangles.

● Early star

The ancient Greek astronomer Hipparchus of Rhodes lived during the second century BC. His amazingly accurate observations laid the foundations of astronomy for more than 2000 years. Using the naked eye and astronomical instruments that he had invented himself, Hipparchus plotted the positions of all the stars in the sky visible to the naked eye. He used them to work out the length of one year to within less than seven minutes. He also assigned Magnitudes (a measure of brightness) to all the stars. He called the brightest, the Dog Star Sirius, a First Magnitude star and the faintest he could see, a Sixth Magnitude. Astronomers still use this system today.

▶▶ Read further › Copernicus
pg219 (b22)

Moving the Earth

Until the 16th century, most people believed that the Earth was at the centre of the universe, and that the Moon, Sun, planets and stars all revolved around it. But the Polish astronomer Nicolaus Copernicus (1473–1543) thought that the occasional backward loops in the movement of some planets through the sky did not support this theory. From his observations, Copernicus developed the revolutionary new theory that the Sun, not the Earth, was at the centre of the universe. This idea was so shocking that it was more than 100 years before it was widely accepted.

▼ *Copernicus discovered that the Earth and other planets move around the Sun. He also observed that the Earth takes one year (365 days) to travel around the Sun and revolves on its own axis once in every 24-hour period (a day).*

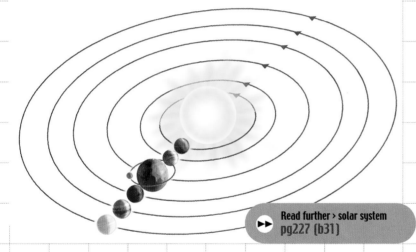

> ►► Read further > solar system
> pg227 (b31)

◄ *Copernicus' book,* De Revolutionibus orbium coelestium *– 'On the Revolutions of the Heavenly Spheres' – published in 1543, was placed on the 'Index', a list of books banned by the Roman Catholic Church, until 1835.*

Seeing the universe

Less than 100 years ago it was thought that the universe was little bigger than our local Milky Way Galaxy. Then in the 1920s, American astronomer Edwin Hubble (1889–1953) began to study the Andromeda Galaxy. Astronomers had previously thought this was just a cloud of gas called a nebula. But with a very powerful telescope Hubble saw that it was another galaxy full of stars. Soon many other galaxies were discovered and it became clear that the universe is gigantic. In 1927 Hubble made another discovery – that all the galaxies are zooming away from us. He realized that the universe is actually expanding (getting bigger) all the time.

> ►► Read further > telescope
> pg221 (b22)

▲ *Hubble showed that the fuzzy patches of light once thought to be nebulae were in fact other galaxies far beyond the milky way.*

OTHER KEY FIGURES

Date	Name, nationality	Achievements
c.2600 BC	Imhotep, Egypt	First known astronomer
270–190 BC	Eratosthenes, Greek, born in Cyrene (now Libya) and lived in Egypt	Made the first accurate measurement of the Earth's circumference
AD 90–170	Ptolemy, Egyptian-Greek	Wrote a guide to astronomy that was the standard textbook for 1400 years
1546–1601	Tycho Brahe, Danish	First to spot an entirely new star
1571–1630	Johannes Kepler, German	Discovered that planets move not in circles but oval-shapes called ellipses
1738–1822 1750–1848	Sir William Herschel, Caroline Herschel, German-British	Worked together to discover the planet Uranus and over 300 different stars

 Check it out!

● http://space.about.com/library/weekly/ aa103102a.htm

◄◄ GALAXIES see pg52 (d2) ◄◄

Three greats

UNTIL THE 17th century, much of our view of the natural world was based on superstition. Then three of the greatest scientists of all time developed our understanding and perceptions of the world around us. Italian astronomer Galileo Galilei laid the foundations of our understanding of how things move. Englishman Isaac Newton showed that all things move according to three simple rules, and realized that gravity is a force. Dutchman Christiaan Huygens suggested that light travels as waves.

The great Newton

Born in England, Isaac Newton (1642–1727) was one of the greatest scientists. His greatest achievement was his discovery of gravity and three fundamental laws of motion, which he described in his famous book published in 1687, *Philosophiae naturalis principia mathematica* – 'The Mathematical Principles of Natural Philosophy' – usually called just *The Principia*. But he made many other important discoveries, including the fact that white light is a mixture of all colours. He found that by shining it through a prism (wedge of glass), white light could be split into a spectrum – an array of all seven colours. He also invented the mirror telescope to prevent coloured edges on the image. This design is still used in manufacturing many modern telescopes.

▶▶ Read further › telescopes
pg219 (d33); pg221 (b22)

Gravity

Before Newton, no one knew why things fall to the ground or why planets go around the Sun. Newton said that the idea came to him one day while sitting in an orchard. As an apple fell nearby, Newton wondered if the apple was not simply falling but was actually being pulled down by an invisible force. From this simple idea, Newton developed his theory of gravity – a universal force that tries to pull all matter together.

▶▶ Read further › gravity
pg232 (q12)

◀ As Newton showed, a glass wedge or prism bends different colours of light different amounts, so white light is split into all seven colours of the rainbow (red, orange, yellow, green, blue, indigo, violet).

Check it out!
- http://www.infoplease.com/ce6/people/A0835490.html
- http://www.imahero.com/hero history/galileo_herohistory.htm

◀◀ FORCE see pg24 (d2) ◀◀

1 2 3 4 5 6 7 8 9 10 11 12 13 14 15 16 17 18 19

Yet it does move!

Galileo (1564–1642) helped us to understand how things move, by proving that nothing changes, stops or starts, goes faster or slower unless a force is applied. He also found that if something moves faster, the rate it accelerates at depends on the strength of the force. Galileo also used the newly-invented telescope to discover that Jupiter has four moons and that Venus goes through phases like our Moon. His observations led to the proof that Copernicus (see pg219 [b28]) was right: that the Earth is not at the centre of the universe and that it does move around the Sun.

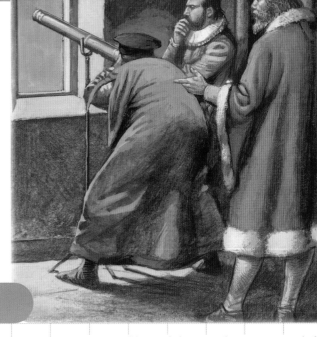

▲ In 1609, Galileo made his own telescope. It magnified objects up to 30 times, so that he was able to observe the rings of Saturn and see how many stars there were in the solar system. The scholars he showed it to thought that it was a cheat and that he had painted magnified views on the lens.

▶▶ Read further › Copernicus
pg219 (b22)

▲ Galileo is said to have muttered 'eppir si muove' – 'yet it does move' – after the Catholic Church, who were so horrified by his theory, made him deny it under threat of torture.

Light waves

Born to a wealthy Dutch family, Christiaan Huygens (1629–1695) was a brilliant scientist who developed Galileo's idea – of using a swinging weight or pendulum to keep a clock in time – to make the first accurate clocks. Like Galileo, Huygens also made his own telescopes to study the night sky and discovered that vague blurs around the edge of the planet Saturn were actually Saturn's rings. Perhaps his most brilliant insight was the theory that light travels in waves and spreads like ripples when a stone is dropped into water.

◀ Huygens developed the pendulum clock, which enabled time to be measured accurately.

▶▶ Read further › light waves
pg228 (h15); pg229 (d22)

GENIUS GENES

• Galileo is said to have proved that all objects fall at the same rate, by dropping a wooden ball and a cannon ball from the Leaning Tower of Pisa. In fact it was one of his students who carried out the experiment, because Galileo already knew what the result would be.

• Huygens was the first scientist to write about extraterrestrial (alien) life, in a book called *Cosmotheoros*.

IT'S A FACT

• In 1699, Newton was asked to look after the Royal Mint in England, where coins are made, to try to stop counterfeiting.

• Galileo is said to have got the idea for the pendulum clock by watching a swinging bell rope in the cathedral at Pisa in Italy, the town where he went to university.

a b c d e f g h i j k l m n o p q r s t u v w

Evolution

NOWADAYS WE take for granted all kinds of things about the natural world that would have surprised, or even shocked, our ancestors. For example, it was only about 350 years ago, that Dutch scientist Anton van Leeuwenhoek discovered that the world is teeming with many forms of life too small for the naked eye to see. About 200 years ago, naturalists realized that species of living organisms do not always remain the same but, as Charles Darwin showed, they constantly evolve (change) through time. Even the classification of species dates back only 250 years to the discoveries of Swedish naturalist Carolus Linnaeus.

GENIUS GENES

• Linnaeus made reproduction and mating the core of his classification system. He liked to talk of the 'marriage' of plants, with the stamen of the flower, the groom, and the pistil, the bride.

• After each day's teaching, Linnaeus' students would stand around his house shouting 'Long live Linnaeus' – in Latin.

Nature hunters

Our knowledge of the natural world comes from both the work of the great naturalists, and the diligence and interest of countless millions of others – from farmers who learned how to turn wild plants to their own use to early hunters who studied the ways of creatures in order to catch them better. But the twin sciences of botany and zoology were further developed in the 18th and 19th centuries, when naturalists, professional and amateur, began to study plants and animals out of pure interest. Some studied the wildlife just a short walk from home. Others, like Charles Darwin, went all round the world to bring back exotic species from faraway places to study.

▶▶ Read further > Aristotle and Darwin
pg215 (m22); pg223 (g29)

IT'S A FACT

• In 1683, Dutch scientist Anton van Leeuwenhoek made the first drawing of bacteria – though he had no idea what they were.

• When Linnaeus invented his system, botanists knew of 7700 plants. Now we know of 275,000.

▶ About 2 million years ago, humans learned how to hunt large animals for food. They chipped flakes off stones to make sharp-edged tools.

Check it out!
• http://www.aboutdarwin.com/

▸ *Hooke invented the compound microscope, which had several lenses. This enabled scientists to see tiny microbes and other living things.*

The tiniest creatures

People never suspected that there were organisms too small for the eye to see – let alone living things – until the microscope was invented around 1590. In the 1670s Dutch scientist Anton van Leeuwenhoek (1632–1723) became fascinated with what could be seen through the microscope. For 50 years he used his home-made, single-lens microscopes to find microscopic creatures in water, which he called 'animalcules', from protozoa to bacteria. In 1665, Englishman Robert Hooke (1635–1703) developed a new version of the microscope to study the form of plants.

▸▸ Read further › microscopes
pg217 (n22)

OTHER KEY FIGURES

Date	Name, nationality	Achievements
c.372–c.287 BC	Theophrastus, Greek	Father of botany
AD 1665–1721	Rudolf Camerarius, German	Showed how plants reproduce sexually
1823–1913	Alfred Wallace, English	Developed theory of evolution
1825–1895	Thomas Huxley, English	Established humankind's link to other mammals

Life-changing

▸▸ Read further › Church
pg219 (b22); pg221 (b22)

By 1837 naturalists realized that many extinct species, such as dinosaurs, had lived in the past. By studying creatures on his worldwide voyage aboard the HMS *Beagle*, English scientist Charles Darwin (1809–1882) developed the theory of natural selection. This showed that creatures are all born slightly different; those with a natural advantage, such as being suited to their environment, are more likely to survive and pass on their advantage to their offspring. Darwin showed that some species evolve while some weaker species cannot and so die out. Darwin published these findings in his book *The Origin of Species* in 1859 but it caused uproar because it contradicted the Bible about the origin of human life on Earth.

▾ *Discoveries of bones have shown how our ancestors evolved over millions of years, learning to walk upright, to use tools and eventually light fires.*

Organizing nature

The identification of animals and plants was confusing until Swedish botanist Carolus Linnaeus (1707–1778) devised a system for naming and classifying them all by giving two-part names to every species. The first part is for the genus or group of species with similar characteristics; the second part is its own species name. So every plant and animal had its own name – and its own place in the overall scheme.

◂ *Capsella* (genus) *bursa-pastoris* (species).

◂◂ ANIMAL KINGDOM see pg103 (m32) ◂◂

22 23 24 25 26 27 28 29 30 31 32 33 34 35 36 37 38 39

Medical matters

D ISEASE AND ill-health were not always understood and so were often untreatable. People died younger on average than they do today. In the 11th century, Persian doctor Avicenna wrote the *Canon of Medicine*, a medical textbook used across the Arab Empire for centuries. In the late 18th century, Englishman Edward Jenner found a way to protect people against some diseases by a vaccine – a small, harmless dose of the disease, often given by injection. Pasteur's realization in the 1860s that germs caused disease was a huge medical breakthrough, opening the way to the discovery of medicines, such as antibiotics in the 1920s.

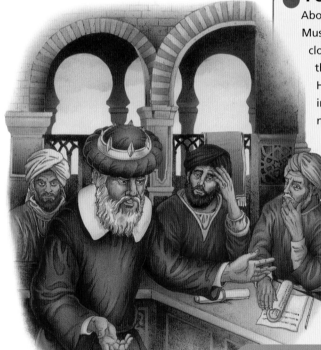

▲ *Avicenna's book* Canon of Medicine *was based in part on the ideas of Aristotle and Galen about how the body works and included information on anatomy and his observations as a doctor.*

IT'S A FACT

• In 1945, Fleming, Florey and Chain shared a Nobel Prize for their work developing antibiotics.

• The antibiotic streptomycin – the first effective drug against tuberculosis – was discovered in soil fungi by American Selman Waksman (1888–1973).

Persian medicine

About a thousand years ago, Muslim physicians began to closely study the work of the ancient Greeks such as Hippocrates and Aristotle in order to develop many new ideas on medicine. Persian doctor Avicenna or Ibn Sina (980–1037) worked for Persian rulers and wrote more than 200 books on many subjects, including *Canon of Medicine* which became the standard medical textbook for centuries.

▶▶ Read further › Hippocrates / Aristotle pg215 (b22; m22)

Antiseptic spray

English surgeon Joseph Lister (1827–1912) was appalled at the number of deaths caused by infection after surgery. After reading of Pasteur's discovery that bacteria can be air-born, he developed the carbolic steam spray. This produced a fine mist of mild carbolic acid in the operating room, which killed bacteria thus reducing the risk of infection.

▶▶ Read further › bacteria pg225 (b33)

▶ *By using carbolic steam spray, the death rate among Lister's patients fell from 50 to 5 per cent.*

Check it out!

• http://www.pbs.org/wgbh/aso/ databank/entries/bmflem.html
• http://ambafranceca.org/HYPE RLAB/PEOPLE/_pasteur.html

GENIUS GENES

• Pasteur famously exclaimed *'Tout est trouvé!'* ('All is found!') when he discovered isomers – mirror image chemicals.

• When we accidentally say a wrong word that reveals our true desires, it is known as a 'Freudian slip', because Freud suggested it was our unconscious mind that caused the mistake.

a
b
c
d
e
f
g
h
i
j
k
l
m
n
o
p
q
r
s
t
u
v
w

OTHER KEY FIGURES

Date	Name, nationality	Achievements
936–1013	Albucasis (Al-Zahrawi), Spanish Arab	Compiled a 1500-page surgical encyclopedia and described 200 surgical instruments
1749–1823	Edward Jenner, English	Discovered a vaccine for smallpox
1813–1878	Claude Bernard, French	Discovered how sugars give the body energy
1843–1910	Robert Koch, German	Proved germs cause disease
1854–1915	Paul Ehrlich, German	Developed chemical drugs for diseases
1881–1955	Alexander Fleming, Scottish	Developed a mould – Penicillin *notatum* – that kills bacteria
1898–1968 1906–1979	Howard Florey, Australian Ernst Chain, German	Worked together to develop the first antibiotic, penicillin

The germ of an idea

French scientist Louis Pasteur (1822–1895) discovered that liquids turn sour because they contain tiny organisms. He found that these organisms can be killed by heat in a process now known as 'pasteurization' whereby a substance, such as milk, is heated to a certain temperature then rapidly cooled. Pasteur's greatest breakthrough was to find that germs, such as bacteria and viruses, carry disease from one person to another. He showed how vaccination works by using a tiny amount of the germ to build up the body's defences.

◀ *Pasteur discovered a vaccine for cattle and sheep against anthrax, as well as a life-saving cure for rabies.*

Thoughts and feelings

Few scientists have had such an impact on our way of thinking about ourselves as Austrian psychologist Sigmund Freud (1856–1939). Freud suggested that we have 'conscious' thoughts, which we know about, and 'unconscious' thoughts, which we do not – but which both influence our behaviour. Freud believed that our childhood experiences play an important role in shaping our unconscious thoughts and that our behaviour as adults is affected by these thoughts.

▶▶ **Read further > Freudian slips** pg224 (s14)

▶▶ **Read further > bacteria** pg224 (p2)

▶ *Freud believed in talking to his patients about their problems to find out if any past experiences in their lives affected their behaviour as adults.*

Maths masters

THE FIRST mathematics was undertaken entirely for practical purposes. Early tax officials – people who collect money for the government – helped develop arithmetic as they worked out tax sums. Ancient Sumerians and Egyptians developed geometry to help build the pyramids and other buildings. Gradually, people became interested in the theory of mathematics and many of the great mathematicians through the ages worked on theoretical problems. The achievements of these theorists were less well known than the work of other scientists, as few people could realise the uses of mathematics.

Pythagoras

Greek mathematician Pythagoras (c.582–497 BC) developed a mathematical rule regarding the lengths of the sides of triangles. This rule, called Pythagoras' theorem, states that the square of the lengths of the two shorter sides of any right-angled triangle add up to the square of the length of the longest side.

Read further > geometry pg215 (b34)

Mathematical letters

Algebra is a branch of mathematics that solves problems by substituting letters and other symbols for different quantities. The name comes from the Latin name for the book where it was first properly described – *Al-jabr* – the full name meaning 'The Compendious Book on Calculation by Completion [or Restoring] and Balancing'. This is one of the most famous mathematics books of all time, written by Arabic mathematician Al-Khwarizmi in about 830.

▲ *Al-Khwarizmi taught algebra in the House of Wisdom – a mathematical school in Baghdad (now in Iraq). He wrote his influential book on algebra between 813 and 833.*

Read further > mathematics pg214 (m15); pg215 (b34)

GENIUS GENES

• In 1796, Laplace suggested 'the attractive force [gravity] of a heavenly body [an object in space] could be so large that light could not flow out of it' nearly 200 years before astronomers showed this was so in black holes.

• Descartes suggested that it made sense to think of our body and mind as entirely separate. Our bodies and senses are solid, material things; but our minds are something entirely different.

◄◄ GRAVITY see pg24 (m12) ◄◄

1 2 3 4 5 6 7 8 9 10 11 12 13 14 15 16 17 18 19

▶ *For more than 2000 years, Euclid's textbook was used in schools to teach children the basics of geometry.*

Muslim scholars

Greek thinkers such as Euclid achieved much in basic mathematics, but more advanced mathematics was mostly developed by Arab scholars. In the 9th century, the caliph (Muslim leader) Al-Ma-mum turned Baghdad (now in Iraq) into a centre of learning. The focus was the Bayt al-Hikma (House of Wisdom). Al-Uqlidisi gave us decimal fractions; Abu'l-Wafa developed the idea of tangents (special angles in right-angled triangles); mathematician and poet, Omar Khayyam made advances in ways to solve complex equations.

▶▶ **Read further › Euclid** pg215 (b34)

Saving the world

French mathematician and astronomer Pierre Laplace (1749–1827) calculated the mathematics of the orbits of the planets and their gravitational pulls in a way that not even Newton had been able to do. In 1773 he showed how one planet would not be thrown off course by the gravity of another as they passed nearby – an effect Newton had feared might lead to the end of the world. Laplace was also the first to suggest that the Solar System was created from a cloud of gas.

▶ *Laplace showed how Saturn does not wobble even when Jupiter passes close by.*

▶▶ **Read further › Solar System** pg219 (b22)

Graphic answers

French philosopher and mathematician René Descartes (1596–1650) is best known for his ideas on the nature of human existence. He is most famous for arguing that everything should be doubted before being believed, and for stating that proof that he existed was his ability to think. From this came his famous quote, '*Cogito ergo sum*' – 'I think therefore I am'. He also developed a kind of maths called co-ordinate or analytical geometry. This enables scientists and mathematicians to show statistics using lines of geometry on a graph, so that the statistics can be understood easily.

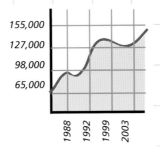

155,000
127,000
98,000
65,000

1988 1992 1999 2003

▲ *Co-ordinate or analytical geometry allows scientists to analyse how fast things change using Cartesian co-ordinates or graphs to plot statistics.*

Accurate reflections

English friar Roger Bacon (1214–1292) made many discoveries in the geometry of reflections from mirrors and the angles of light rays passing through lenses. Bacon also believed that the world was round. This idea was ridiculed and even caused him to be imprisoned.

▶▶ **Read further › light** pg220 (l2)

▼ *Bacon showed that light rays bounce off and hit a mirror at the same angle.*

OTHER KEY FIGURES

Date	Name, nationality	Achievements
c.1170–c.1250	Leonardo Fibonacci, Italian	Introduced the Arabic numeral system we use today in Europe
1561–1630	Henry Briggs, English	Simplified the idea of logarithms
1601–1665	Pierre de Fermat, French	Introduced probability theory and number theory
1707–1783	Leonhard Euler, Swiss	Developed trigonometry
1777–1855	Karl Gauss, German	Developed theory of numbers
1781–1840	Siméon-Denis Poisson, French	Developed probability theory
1854–1912	Jules Poincaré, French	Invented chaos theory

 Check it out!

- http://www.bbc.co.uk/education/maths file/index.shtml

Bright sparks

W E DEPEND on electricity so much today it is hard to imagine a world without it. Yet about 250 years ago almost nothing was known about it. Electricity is one of the basic forces of the universe, and it exists everywhere. Yet people knew it only as a tiny spark made by rubbing amber or glass against silk. In the 1750s, Benjamin Franklin showed that lightning is electric and soon after electricity became a practical reality. Soon scientists made dramatic discoveries about its properties. About 50 years later, Joseph Henry and Michael Faraday discovered how to generate huge quantities of electricity, and our modern electrical world was born.

IT'S A FACT

• In attempts to repeat Franklin's experiment with a kite in a thunderstorm, many scientists were electrocuted – harmed by the force of electricity.

• Michael Faraday's scientific demonstrations were the top shows of the time, attracting enormous audiences.

Flying a kite

There is no more dramatic sign of the presence of natural electricity in the world than lightning. Yet no one realized just what lightning was until the mid-1700s. At that time, scientists were learning how to make big sparks for the first time by rubbing together materials such as glass on sulphur. American statesman and scientist Benjamin Franklin (1706–1790) wondered if lightning consisted of these same sparks. He conducted an experiment that proved that electricity is produced by lightning. This discovery led to the development of the lightning conductor or rod.

Read further › electricity
pg229 (d22)

◄ To test his idea, Franklin flew a kite in a thunderstorm, attaching a metal key to the string on a short silk thread. Electricity from the lightning flowed down the wet string to the key and made a huge electrical spark. Franklin had proved his point – but he was lucky to be alive.

▶ *In 1826 Faraday started the Christmas lectures at the Royal Institution, London. In these lectures he explained his ideas and discoveries clearly to the public.*

Magnetic electricity

Chemical batteries such as Volta's *(see pg229 [p38])* gave a steady flow of electricity, but only in small quantities. In the 1820s, scientists discovered a link between electricity and magnetism. Then in 1830, Joseph Henry (1797–1878) in America and Michael Faraday (1791–1867) in England discovered that moving a magnet could create an electric current. Engineers were soon able to build machines that used moving magnets to generate huge quantities of electricity for the first time. This paved the way for the development of modern electrical appliances, from light bulbs to computers.

▶▶ **Read further › appliances** pg231 (h25)

◀ *Faraday built a dynamo – used to convert mechanical energy into electric energy – by winding coils of wire around a piece of iron and passing electricity through the iron to create a magnet. He then created a hollow coil, moving the magnet in and out to make the current flow.*

GENIUS GENES

• In the 1780s, Italian physicist Luigi Galvani (1737–1798) experimented with a dead frog's leg hung on a brass hook and a piece of iron. The frog's leg twitched as the iron touched it, and many people believed it was 'animal electricity'.

• Following Galvani's idea of animal electricity as a life force, scientists around 1800 tried to bring corpses back to life by electrifying them – a practice made into a vivid story in Mary Shelley's novel *Frankenstein*.

The first battery

In the 1790s, Italian scientist Alessandro Volta (1745–1827) realized that electricity can be made by mixing the right chemicals. The chemical reaction caused by the mix makes electricity. By building up alternate layers of copper and zinc and putting them in a jar of salt water, Volta made the first battery. The chemical reaction created, for the first time in history, a steady supply of electricity.

▶▶ **Read further › electricity** pg228 (d2)

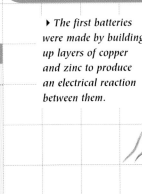

▶ *The first batteries were made by building up layers of copper and zinc to produce an electrical reaction between them.*

OTHER KEY FIGURES

Date	Name, nationality	Achievements
c.1666–1736	Stephen Gray, English	Showed that some substances conduct electricity and others do not
1698–1739	Charles Dufay, French	Discovered positive and negative electrical charges
1775–1836	André Ampere, French	Found how to measure electric current
1777–1851	Hans Christian Oersted, Danish	Discovered that an electric current is magnetic
1789–1854	Georg Simon Ohm, German	Showed that the flow of electricity in a wire depends on the wire's resistance
1856–1943	Nikola Tesla, Serbian–American	Invented alternating current generators that supply most of our electric power

Check it out!

• http://www.pbs.org/benfranklin/
• http://www.bbc.co.uk/history/historic_figures/faraday_michael.shtml

◀◀ INVENTION OF BATTERY see pg200 (k17) ◀◀

a b c d e f g h i j k l m n o p q r s t u v w

Atom experts

IN THE first half of the 19th century, it became clear that gravity is not the only invisible force in the universe. Scientists soon began to realize that all matter in the universe is held together by the invisible forces of electricity and magnetism. A string of brilliant scientists, such as James Clerk Maxwell in the 1860s and the Curies in the 1900s, showed that these forces get their energy from atoms – or from the various particles that make up atoms. On the way, scientists learned all about radiation and nuclear power – and atomic bombs.

● Rutherford and Bohr

By the end of the 1800s, scientists knew that everything is made from tiny, invisible bits or 'particles' called atoms. In the 1890s, Englishman J.J. Thomson (1856–1940) showed that there were even smaller particles called electrons. Then New Zealander Ernest Rutherford (1871–1937) showed that an atom is mostly empty space – with a tiny, dense blob at the centre called the nucleus. By the 1930s, Rutherford was working with Danish physicist Niels Bohr (1885–1962) and together they created a picture of the atom – with tiny electrons circling a dense nucleus made from particles called protons and neutrons. We now know that atoms are much more complex, and that there are many particles even smaller than atoms.

►► **Read further > atoms**
pg235 (b22)

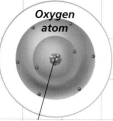

Chlorine atom · *Electron*

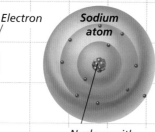

Sodium atom

◄ *Atoms are formed with a nucleus at the centre. Each atom has an equal number of electrons and protons. Electrons have a negative electrical charge and move around the nucleus. Protons have a positive electrical charge and cling to the nucleus.*

Nucleus with 17 protons

Nucleus with 11 protons

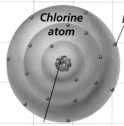

Oxygen atom

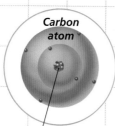

Carbon atom

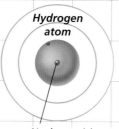

Hydrogen atom

Nucleus with 8 protons

Nucleus with 6 protons

Nucleus with single proton

GENIUS GENES

• As well as discovering radioactivity, the Curies found two entirely new radioactive elements: radium and polonium.

• It was first thought that the atom nucleus was made of just one kind of particle – a proton. But in 1932, James Chadwick (1891–1974) found another particle, later called a neutron.

OTHER KEY FIGURES

Date	Name, nationality	Achievements
1857–1894	Heinrich Hertz, German	Discovered radio waves
1878–1968	Lise Meitner, Austrian	Worked together on the
1879–1968	Otto Hahn, German	chemistry of radioactivity
1902–1980	Fritz Strassman, German	to discover nuclear fission

◄◄ ATOMS see pg13 (i22) ◄◄

1   2   3   4   5   6   7   8   9   10   11   12   13   14   15   16   17   18   19   2

Fields of force

In the 1840s, the great scientist Michael Faraday suggested the idea of field of force – a region where the effect of an electric current or a magnet is felt. About 20 years later, young Scottish scientist James Clerk Maxwell (1831–1879) showed that these electromagnetic fields spread out or 'radiate' in invisible waves, like ripples around a stone dropped in a pond. He also showed that these waves travel at the speed of light – and deduced that light is in fact an electromagnetic wave.

Read further › light waves / Faraday's dynamo
pg221 (n22); pg229 (d22)

▼ Röntgen's X-ray invention allowed doctors to diagnose, for example, lung diseases.

Inside view

German scientist Wilhelm Röntgen (1845–1923) discovered X-rays while experimenting with electron beams. He saw that material glowed while the electron beam was on. This was caused by the X-rays that were produced as the electrons made the material fluorescent. Röntgen received the Nobel Prize for physics in 1901.

Atomic radiation

In 1897 French scientist Henri Becquerel (1852–1908) found that the new kinds of radiation being discovered did not always come from electricity. They seemed to appear around uranium atoms. His work influenced Polish–French scientist Marie Curie who, with her husband Pierre, showed that the radiation was coming directly from the atoms themselves. The Curies called this atomic radiation 'radioactivity'. Tragically, Marie Curie died from blood cancer brought on by her exposure to radioactive substances during her research.

▸ For their research, the Curies, together with Becquerel, won the Nobel Prize for physics in 1903.

Read further › radiation
pg233 (i31)

Atomic bomb

Holding the nucleus of atoms together requires an enormous amount of energy. In 1939 scientists split the nuclei of uranium atoms – these are among the biggest and easiest atoms to break. During World War II, American (Italian-born) Enrico Fermi (1901–1954) made particles that flew off, splitting uranium nuclei which then split other atoms. This set off a 'chain-reaction' of splitting that could release huge amounts of nuclear energy.

▲ In 1942, a team under Robert Oppenheimer (1904–1967) in New Mexico used the 'chain reaction' to make the first atomic bomb.

Check it out!
• http://www.chem4kids.com/index.html

Read further › Einstein
pg233 (b22)

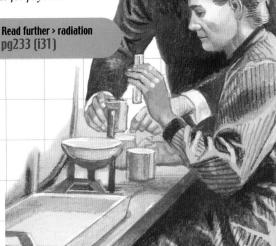

◄◄ ELECTROMAGNETIC RADIATION see pg22 (f2) ◄◄

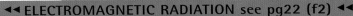

Time and space

A CENTURY AGO, our idea of the way the world worked was straightforward. It seemed obvious that things happen, one after another. But two extraordinary scientific ideas – quantum science and relativity – have shown that it is not as simple as that. Quantum science shows that effect does not inevitably follow cause. Relativity overturns our common sense view of time, with time running identically everywhere in the universe. While these ideas have only a limited impact on our everyday lives, they have revolutionized science – from the study of our vast universe to the study of minute atoms.

OTHER KEY FIGURES

Date	Name, nationality	Achievements
1644–1710	Ole Roemer, Danish	Discovered that the speed of light can be measured
1838–1923	Edward Morley, American	Worked together to show that the speed of light is the same in all directions
1852–1931	Albert Michelson, American	
1902–1984	Paul Dirac, British	Developed quantum physics

▸ *Hawking's research into black holes, relativity, cosmology and gravitation has gained him numerous scientific awards and honorary degrees. His work provides a strong base for proof that the universe began with a Big Bang, starting from one point and exploding outwards.*

Black holes

Einstein showed that gravity pulls things closer by shrinking the space and time between them. If gravity is incredibly powerful it will shrink space and time to the point where it disappears. In his book *A Brief History of Time*, English physicist Stephen Hawking (born 1942) suggests that this is what happens in the centre of a black hole – a place in space where gravity is so strong that it sucks everything in, including light.

Check it out!
• http://www.eclipse.net/
 ~cmmiller/BH/blkmain.html
• http://www.pbs.org/wgbh/
 nova/einstein

▸▸ Read further › Newton and gravity
pg220 (l2; n13)

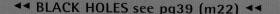

◄◄ BLACK HOLES see pg39 (m22) ◄◄

1 2 3 4 5 6 7 8 9 10 11 12 13 14 15 16 17 18 19

Everything is relative

It would seem to be the case that time is the same everywhere and moves in only one direction, from past to future. German physicist Albert Einstein (1879–1955) showed that this is not so. In his theory of relativity Einstein completely overturned this idea of time and was the first to show that time is relative. Time is not fixed but depends entirely on how you measure it – and you can only measure it relative to something else. Einstein showed that time does not run one-way, but is a dimension, just like length, breadth and depth, and that it can run backwards as well as forwards.

Read further › atomic bomb pg231 (n22)

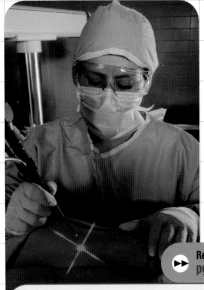

◄ *Advanced understanding of quantum mechanics has enabled scientists to develop more effective lasers. Because light does not travel in waves but in quanta, lasers focus the light precisely, allowing surgeons to carry out operations, such as removing birthmarks and treating skin disorders.*

Read further › light waves pg220 (l2); pg221 (n22)

Quantum world

Most scientists once thought light and other kinds of radiation travel in waves. But in the 1890s German scientist Max Planck (1858–1947) observed the range of radiation sent out by a hot object – and it did not support the theory that radiation travels in waves. Planck realized that the range of radiation made sense if it was emitted in chunks, or what he called 'quanta'. Quanta are very, very small. When lots are emitted together they appear like smooth waves; when they are emitted separately, they are like particles. Soon scientists realized the quantum concept applied to all kinds of particles smaller than an atom, and quantum mechanics became a whole new science.

▲ *Einstein's equation E = mc² showed just how much energy there was in an atom, and led to the development of the atom bomb.*

GENIUS GENES

• Black holes may be linked by tunnels through space and time called wormholes, to exactly opposite 'white' holes. Wormholes may make it possible to travel through time in the future.

• Teleporting may seem to have come straight from *Star Trek*, but scientists have succeeded in teleporting particles. Using a phenomenon called quantum entanglement, particles are destroyed in one place only to reappear instantly some distance away.

▼ *Minkowski used geometry to solve problems in number theory, mathematical physics and the theory of relativity.*

Four-dimensional

Hermann Minkowski (1864–1909) developed Einstein's theory of relativity to suggest that space and time were not separate things. Space has three dimensions – up, down and sideways. Minkowski suggested that time was just another dimension. So it made sense to talk of time as the fourth dimension, and join space and time together to create four-dimensional spacetime.

Read further › geometry pg215 (b34)

◄◄ TIME see pg37 (m22) ◄◄

Genetics

DNA's double spiral shape

Each base pairs up with one other base

THE GREAT biologists of the last few centuries have shown us that every living thing is made from thousands or even millions of tiny little packages called cells. Each cell carries with it not only its own instructions for life, but the complete instructions for the whole animal or plant of which it is part. These instructions, called genes, are coded in the structure of a chemical molecule called DNA (deoxyribonucleic acid). DNA works by passing on characteristics from parents to their offspring. Today scientists understand the function of DNA so well that they are beginning to take control of and alter the very materials of life, in what is called genetic engineering.

GENIUS GENES

• Crick and Watson's great discovery of the DNA double helix was based on the work of a young expert in microscopy called Rosalind Franklin (1910–1958).

• Some scientists think they may one day be able to duplicate ancient DNA samples from fossils to make dinosaurs live again, as in the film *Jurassic Park*.

Rungs made from four different chemical bases

◀ *DNA is structured in bundles called chromosomes. Humans have 46 chromosomes (23 pairs), which control our characteristics.*

Strands of DNA divide to form a template of instruction

IT'S A FACT

• Genetic engineers put fluorescent jellyfish genes in a rabbit, making it glow in the dark.

• In the future, scientists hope to use genetic engineering to make goats deliver spider's web silk in their milk for making ultra-light bullet-proof vests.

▶▶ Read further › blood cells / vessels pg217 (b32; n22)

The amazing spiral

Even under a powerful microscope, the DNA molecule inside every cell looks like little more than a tangled thread. In fact, its chemical structure is a double 'helix' or spiral – a bit like a twisted rope ladder. The sequence of the 'rungs' is the code that gives the cell instructions by telling it to make particular proteins. When a protein is to be made, the ladder unzips down the middle to expose the code of rungs. Discovering this structure was one of the scientific breakthroughs of the 20th century. It was achieved in 1953 by two young scientists working in Cambridge, England: Englishman Francis Crick (b.1916) and American James Watson (b.1928). Their work won Crick and Watson the 1962 Nobel Prize for medicine.

Check it out!
• http://gslc.genetics.utah.edu/
• http://www.dnaftb.org/dnaftb/1/concept/index.html

◀◀ DNA see pg153 (b30) ◀◀

1   2   3   4   5   6   7   8   9   10   11   12   13   14   15   16   17   18   19   2

Stitching DNA

One of the greatest scientific discoveries of the 20th century was the idea of genetic engineering or modification (GM). In 1972, American biochemist Paul Berg discovered how to snip a bit of DNA from one bacteria and chemically 'stitch' it into the DNA of another. This achievement, known as recombinant DNA, enables the genes for one characteristic to be moved from one kind of plant or animal into another. Biotechnology firms use this technique to add qualities, such as pest resistance or extra growth, to crops.

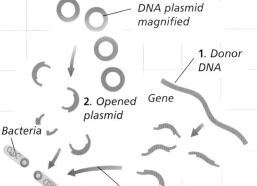

DNA plasmid magnified

1. *Donor DNA*

2. *Opened plasmid*

Gene

Bacteria

4. *Bacteria with altered DNA multiplying*

3. *Splicing the gene into the plasmid*

Altered DNA plasmid less magnified

Bacteria's ordinary DNA

◄ *This sequence shows the steps in gene splicing. 1. The bit of the donor DNA carrying the right gene is snipped out using restriction enzymes. 2. A special ring of DNA called a plasmid is then broken open. 3. The new gene is spliced into the plasmid, which is sealed up with DNA ligase and introduced into bacteria. 4. The bacteria reproduce.*

▶▶ **Read further › DNA**
pg234 (r8)

OTHER KEY FIGURES

Date	Name, nationality	Achievements
1877–1955	Oswald Avery, Canadian-American	Discovered DNA gave instructions
1905–	Erwin Chargraff, Czech-American	Discovered how DNA bases pair up
1908–1997	Alfred Hershey, American	Developed the idea that DNA gave instructions

Mendel's peas

The puzzle of how characteristics are passed on from one generation to the next, or even why some characteristics skip a generation, was solved by an Austrian monk called Gregor Mendel (1822–1884). Mendel grew peas, and studied their sizes and colours. By recording how these characteristics were passed on from one generation to the next, he worked out a set of the basic rules of genetic inheritance – how different characteristics are passed down through the generations.

▶▶ **Read further › offspring**
pg223 (g29)

Breaking the code

In 1967 two biochemists: American Marshall Nirenberg (b.1927) and Indian-American Har Khorana (b.1922) broke the genetic code. They showed that the genetic code depends on the sequence of four different chemical 'bases' down each strand of the DNA molecule. These bases are like letters of the alphabet, and the sequence is broken up into 'sentences' called genes. The code in each gene is the cell's instructions to make a protein.

◄ *Identical twins share the same characteristics as each other, caused by their genetic code.*

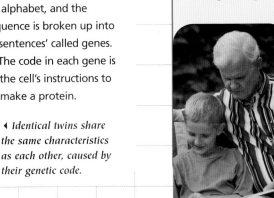

◄ *Scientists today use the rules of inheritance to determine if diseases are likely to be passed down through generations.*

a b c d e f g h i j k l m n o p q r s t u v w

Glossary

Abutment A solid structure that supports the end of a bridge or takes the load of an arch.

Abyssal plain Broad plain on the deep seabed, 5000 m down and covered in ooze.

Acceleration A change in speed or direction.

Acid A solution made when substances containing hydrogen dissolve in water. Some acids taste sour. Others are highly corrosive.

Acid rain All rain is slightly acidic, but acid rain forms when pollution by sulphur dioxide and nitrogen reacts in sunlight with oxygen and moisture in the air.

Aerofoil A curved surface such as an aircraft wing, which provides control in the air.

Algebra A branch of mathematics that uses letters to represent numbers when making calculations.

Alkali A base that dissolves in water.

Allergy A condition some people experience when they come into contact with a substance such as pollen.

Allotrope One of various forms in which an element occurs. For example, diamond and graphite are allotropes of carbon.

Alloy Metal mixed with another metal or substance. Steel is a tough alloy made from iron, carbon and traces of other substances.

Alveoli Tiny air spaces or bubbles inside the lungs, where oxygen is taken into the blood from breathed-in air.

Anaesthetic A substance given by medical staff that stops the body from feeling pain, sometimes making a person unconscious.

Animation Making drawings appear to move, using a series of similar, but very slightly different, drawings one after the other.

Annual A flowering plant that completes its life cycle in one year.

Antenna A metal rod or wire for sending and receiving radiowaves or microwaves.

Antennae Long, slim parts on the head of animals, such as insects, often called 'feelers' that sense touch, movement and taste.

Antibiotic A medicine, such as penicillin, which works in the body to kill bacteria.

Antibodies Chemicals produced to attack a particular germ, known as an antigen.

Antiseptic A substance that helps to prevent infection by stopping the growth of germs.

Artery A large blood vessel that carries blood rich in oxygen from the lungs out to the rest of the body from the heart.

Arthropod Any invertebrate animal.

Asexual reproduction When a living thing produces offspring without a mate.

Asteroid One of many thousands of large chunks of rock that orbit the Sun.

Astronaut A person trained to be a crew member in a spacecraft.

Astronomer A person who studies the stars, planets and other bodies in space.

Atmosphere The thick layer of gases surrounding the Earth.

Atom The smallest particle of an element.

Aurora Colourful glowing lights seen in the sky in the far north and far south.

Bascule A bridge with a roadway that can be lifted to allow tall ships to pass through.

Base The chemical opposite of an acid. Weak bases taste bitter and feel soapy. Strong bases are corrosive.

Bases In the genetic material DNA, types of chemical subunits that carry information in the form of a chemical code.

Biennial A flowering plant that takes two years to complete its life cycle.

Big Bang The huge explosion-like expansion of the universe that may have occurred when it began some 15 billion years ago. At first, the universe was a minute, very hot ball of matter and radiation. The universe then expanded and swelled, and stars, galaxies and planets began to form.

Binary Consisting of two parts or numbers. A computer code of offs or ons, (0s and 1s).

Binary star A true binary is a pair of stars that orbit each other. An optical binary is a pair of stars that look close together in the night sky but are really far apart.

Black hole A point in space where gravity sucks everything in, including light.

Black smoker Small volcanic chimneys on the seabed that throw out black fumes of superheated water.

Brachiation Hanging while swinging with a pendulum-like motion, as when gibbons swing through tree branches.

Broadleaved tree A tree that grows leaves that are wide and flat. It may be an evergreen or deciduous tree.

Browser An animal that eats mainly leaves from taller plants such as trees and bushes.

Buoyancy How well something floats.

Cache A store of something, such as food, by an animal for later use, usually during winter.

Camouflage When an animal is shaped, coloured and patterned to merge or blend in with its surroundings.

Canines Long, sharp teeth near the front of the mouth used to stab and rip at prey.

Cantilever A bracket that supports a shelf or balcony, or a bridge with rigid arms projecting out from piers to meet in the middle.

Capillary Tiny blood vessel in the body that links veins to arteries.

Carbon An element found as coal, diamond and various other substances. Compounds that it makes are called organic chemicals.

Carnivore An animal that eats mainly meat, usually by catching other animals.

Cell The smallest part of a living thing that contains the chemicals of life, such as DNA, and which make up its tissues, organs and other parts.

Chain reaction Nuclear reaction that goes on gathering pace by itself.

Chelicerae Fang-shaped or pincer-like biting parts on the head of animals, such as spiders and scorpions.

Chlorophyll A green substance found in plants, which traps sunlight that falls onto the leaves. This helps the plant make food.

Chromosomes Lengths of the genetic material DNA that have been coiled up very tightly to resemble microscopic threads.

Chromosphere The lower layer of the Sun that burns at about 10,000°C, just below the photosphere. The colour of chromosphere is a pale red or pink.

Cilia Tiny flexible hairs, usually sticking out or projecting from a cell, that can bend or wave, or detect certain chemicals.

Circulatory system Parts of an animal – usually the heart, blood vessels (tubes) and blood – that spread nutrients around the body, and collect wastes and leftovers for removal.

Class The groups into which a phylum (main group) of animals is divided. For example, the phylum chordata is divided into classes such as amphibians, reptiles, birds and mammals.

Cloning Making an identical copy of an organism from one of its cells.

Cold-blooded Animals whose body temperature varies with their surroundings. The main group are warm-blooded animals.

Combustion When a chemical reacts with oxygen it creates heat, and often light.

Comet A 'dirty snowball' of rock, dust and ice orbiting the Sun. When its orbit brings it close to the Sun, it partially melts, sending out a giant, shining tail.

Compound Substances made by the atoms of two or more elements chemically bonding.

Compression Squeezing, especially of air or gas, inside a cylinder.

Concave Curved inwards like a dish.

Condensation The process by which a gas turns into a liquid, such as air to water.

Conduction The spreading of heat from hot areas to cold areas by direct contact.

Conservation Saving or preserving animals and their natural surroundings or habitats.

Constellation A group of stars that form a pattern in the night sky.

Continental drift The process whereby continents move slowly around the world.

Contraction When something gets smaller, usually as it gets colder.

Convection When warm air or liquid rises through cool air or liquid.

Convex Curved outwards like a ball.

Core The dense, hot centre of the Earth.

Cotyledon The food store that is contained in every new seedling.

Crust The solid outer shell of the Earth, varying from 5 to 80 km thick.

Cuneiform Cuneiform writing was made by making wedge-shaped signs in soft clay.

Decibel A measure of the loudness of sound.

Deciduous tree A tree that loses all its leaves at once, spends some time with bare branches, then grows new leaves.

Delta A flat piece of land, which has built up from material such as silt that has been deposited by a river as it flows to the sea.

Detritivore An animal that eats rotting bits of once-living things, such as the meat off an old carcass, or tiny edible particles in mud.

Dicotyledon A plant that has two cotyledons, for example a pea.

DNA De-oxyribonucleic acid, a chemical that makes up the instructions or genes for how the body grows and functions.

Drag The way in which air or water slows down an object moving through it. This is sometimes called air or water resistance.

Earthquake A brief, violent shaking of the Earth's surface, typically set off by the movement of tectonic plates.

Echolocation Method used by animals, such as bats, to find their way and locate objects in darkness, by sending out pulses of high-pitched sounds and listening to the echoes.

Eclipse When one space object blocks the view of another. When the Moon blocks Earth's view of the Sun, it is a solar eclipse. When the Earth blocks the Sun's light from the Moon, it is a lunar eclipse.

Ecosystem A local community of plants, animals and other living things interacting with their surroundings.

Effort The force to make something move.

Electric motor A device that changes electrical energy into movement.

Electrical charge The force of attraction between certain sub-atomic particles.

Electromagnet Powerful magnet that works when an electric current is passing through it.

Electron The smallest of the particles of an atom. Electrons circle round the atom's nucleus and have a negative electrical charge. Electricity is the movement of electrons.

Electronics The use of electronic components to control the flow of current around a circuit.

Element The simplest possible chemical made of one type of unique atom that cannot be broken down.

E-mail (electronic mail) A way of sending messages over the Internet.

Endoskeleton A skeleton inside the body, consisting of strong supporting parts, usually bones, to hold the body together.

Energy The power to make things happen.

Ephemeral A plant with a life cycle that only takes a few weeks to complete.

Era, geological One of the three major divisions of the last 500 million years of Earth's history: the Palaeozoic, the Mesozoic and the Cenozoic.

Evaporation When liquid turns to vapour as it gets warm.

Evergreen tree A tree that does not shed its leaves all at one time and so remains green in colour throughout the year.

Evolution The gradual changing of species of living things over time, in response to changing conditions.

Excretion The removal of wastes, by-products and other unwanted substances from the body – by the excretory or urinary system.

Exosphere The layer of the atmosphere above the thermosphere, beginning at about 500 km up.

Expansion When something gets bigger, usually as it gets warmer.

Extinct When a particular species of living thing has died out and disappeared for ever.

Extrasolar planet A planet outside the Solar System, not circling the Sun but another star.

Fault A fracture in rock where one block of rock slides past another.

Fertilization The process by which the nucleus of the pollen grain fuses with the nucleus of the ovule to make a seed.

Force Something that changes an object's shape or movement by pulling, pushing, stretching or squashing it.

Fossil The preserved remains of a creature or plant long dead, usually turned to stone.

Fulcrum The point at which a lever turns.

Fungi Living things, most of which have tiny hairs, that feed on dead plants and animals and decompose them.

Fuselage The tube-shaped body of an aeroplane, excluding the wings.

Galaxy A giant collection of stars in space containing millions of stars. Some are spiral shaped, some are elliptical (oval) and some are irregular in shape. The Sun is part of a local galaxy called the Milky Way Galaxy or just the Galaxy.

Gas A substance without shape or form.

Gastric To do with the stomach, for example gastric juices made in the stomach contain powerful chemicals for digestion.

Gears Wheels with teeth around the edge that fit together to change the speed or direction of movement.

Genes Instructions or information, in the form of the chemical DNA, for how the body develops, grows and functions.

Genetics The study of genes and DNA.

Genome The full set of genes for a human body, which number 35,000.

Geometry The mathematics of lines, angles, curves, surfaces and solid shapes.

Germ A microbe that can cause disease and grow into a new organism.

Germination The process that occurs when the seedling breaks out of its case, sending out its root and shoot.

Gills Body parts for breathing underwater. They are usually feathery or frilly and take in oxygen that has dissolved in the water.

Glaciation The moulding of the landscape by glaciers and ice sheets.

Gland A body part specialized to make a certain product, usually in liquid form, which can be released directly into the blood flowing through the gland.

Global warming The gradual warming of the Earth caused by pollution in the atmosphere, which traps the Earth's heat.

Glucose A type of high-energy sugar, often called 'blood sugar', that is broken down inside the cells of the body to release its energy, which powers the cell's life processes.

Gravity The force of attraction between every bit of matter in the universe. Gravity makes things fall, holds things to the ground, and keeps the Earth and other planets circling round the Sun.

Greenhouse effect The way certain gases in the atmosphere trap the Sun's heat like the panes of glass in a greenhouse.

Habitat Particular place with its own kinds of animals and plants, such as a pine wood, grassland, desert, seashore or deep seabed.

Heat The total energy a warm substance has due to the movement of its molecules.

Herbivore An animal that eats mainly plant foods, such as leaves, fruits and seeds.

Heredity The passing of characteristics, such as eye colour, through the generations.

Hibernation When an animal's body temperature falls very low, usually to less than 10°C, and the animal falls into a deep sleep to survive the long, cold season.

Home range An area where an animal usually roams and feeds, but which it does not defend, unlike a territory.

Hormones Natural body substances that control processes such as growth, how fast cells use energy, and the balance of water.

Hydro-electric power Electrical power generated by the force of falling water.

Hydrogen The lightest, most common gas in the universe, and the first to form. Stars are made mostly of hydrogen and another light gas called helium.

Ice age A long cold period when huge areas of the Earth are covered by ice sheets.

Igneous rock Rocks created as hot magma from the Earth's interior cool and solidify.

Incisors Teeth at the front of the mouth, usually shaped like chisels with sharp straight edges for gnawing and nibbling.

Inclined plane A slope that makes lifting easier by sliding or rolling things.

Induction The induction stroke in a car engine is the movement of the piston that draws new fuel into the cylinder.

Industrial Revolution The rapid development of the use of machines in late 18th and early 19th century British industry.

Internet A vast computer network linking computers all over the world via satellites, optical fibres and telephone wires.

Invertebrate An animal that does not have a backbone (vertebral column).

Involuntary In the muscle system, when a muscle works automatically without need for thought, rather than being controlled.

Irrigation Watering dry land to make it suitable for growing crops.

Keratin A tough substance that forms the horns, claws, hooves and nails of mammals, the feathers, beaks, claws and scales of birds, and the claws and scales of reptiles.

Knot A unit for measuring speed at sea or in the air. A knot is about 1.85 km/h.

Krill Shrimp-like animals that thrive in vast shoals (groups) in the ocean and are food for larger animals, such as penguins, seals and whales.

Larva The growing stage of a creature, such as an insect, that looks different to its parent, for example, the caterpillar of a butterfly.

Lateral line Line of tiny sensors along a fish's body, to detect movement in the water.

Lava Hot molten rock emerging through volcanoes, known as magma when underground.

Lift Force to lift an aircraft or hot-air balloon.

Light-year The distance light travels in one year – about 9.5 million million km. Distances to the stars are measured in light-years.

Liquid crystal display (LCD) A display made with liquid crystals. A passing electric current lines them up, blocking the light and so forming patterns.

Lithosphere The rigid outer shell of the Earth, including the crust and the rigid upper part of the mantle.

Lymph A pale fluid that collects between cells and oozes to collect in tubes and lymph ducts, and flow through lymph nodes.

Magma Hot molten rock in the Earth's interior. It is known as lava when it emerges to the surface of the Earth.

Magnetism The force of attraction or repulsion in substances such as iron, and around a moving electrical charge or current.

Mammary glands Parts on a female mammal's front that make milk for her young.

Mantle The warm layer of the Earth's interior below the crust. Every now and then parts of the upper mantle melt to form magma.

Marrow Soft, jelly-like substance in the middle of many bones, which makes new cells for the blood (red marrow) or stores energy and nutrients as fat (yellow marrow).

Mass The amount of matter in an object.

Matter Anything of physical substance in the universe.

Medula The inner or lower region of a body part such as the kidney or brain.

Melting The way a solid substance turns to liquid when it reaches a certain temperature.

Mesosphere The layer of the atmosphere above the stratosphere, beginning 50 km up.

Metabolism All of the body's internal chemical processes that involve changing and breaking down, such as digestion, respiration and excretion.

Metamorphic rock Rocks created by the alteration of other rocks by heat or pressure.

Metamorphosis When an animal changes its body shape greatly as it grows, instead of the same body shape just growing larger.

Meteor A meteoroid that crashes into Earth's atmosphere and burns up – often seen as a glowing streak in the sky called a shooting star.

Meteorite A small piece of space rock that flies into the surface of a planet or moon.

Meteoroid A piece of rock or debris from space, caused by asteroids and comets, that floats around space.

Microwave Radio waves with a short wavelength, which are used in cooking and telecommunications.

Mid-ocean ridge A ridge down the middle of the sea floor where tectonic plates meet.

Migration Long-distance journeys, usually carried out at certain seasons, there and back again each year.

Milky Way The faint band of light stretching across the night sky, made of billions of stars. This is the edge-on view of our own Galaxy, the Milky Way.

Mimicry When one animal looks like another (the model) to gain an advantage, for example pretending to be a poisonous animal when it is not itself poisonous.

Minerals Substances in the soil that a plant needs for healthy growth.

Model In animal mimicry, the creature that the mimic looks like or pretends to be.

Molecule The smallest bit of a substance that can exist by itself.

Momentum The force that makes an object move at the same speed and in the same direction.

Monocotyledon A plant with only one cotyledon, for example a grass plant.

Motor In the body, to do with muscles and movements, for example motor nerves carry signals from the brain to muscles to tell them when to contract and by how much.

Muscle Part inside an animal's body that gets shorter, or contracts, to move the body.

Myofibres Muscle fibres, which are bundled together inside a muscle – 'myo-' is to do with muscles.

Natural selection Strong features of living things are naturally selected because those possessing them survive to pass them on.

Nebula A cloud of dust and gas in space. Some glow because they contain young stars. Some glow because they reflect light from other stars.

Neurons Nerve cells, specialized to receive and pass on information in the form of tiny electrical signals called nerve impulses.

Neutrino One of the tiniest of all particles from which matter is made.

Neutron With protons, one of the two basic particles that make up an atom's nucleus.

Neutron star A very small and dense star formed when a large star explodes.

Nuclear energy Energy released by splitting or fusing the nuclei of atoms.

Nucleus (plural nuclei) The core of an atom, made from protons and neutrons.

Nutrients Substances in digested food that are useful to the body, such as providing energy for growth and repair of body parts.

Nymph The growing stage of an animal, such as an insect, which resembles its parent in general shape.

Ommatidia Tiny rod-shaped parts that together form the eye of an insect.

Omnivore An animal that eats a wide range of foods, both meat and plant matter.

Optical fibre Special glass cable that transmits signals using laser light.

Organelles The different parts inside a cell, such as the nucleus or control centre, and the folded sheets of membranes, which are called endoplasmic reticulum.

Organs Major parts of the body such as the heart, lungs or stomach, which are usually made of several different kinds of tissues.

Oxygen A gas making up one-fifth of air, which has no colour, taste or smell but is needed in continuing supplies by the body to break apart substances such as glucose.

Ozone layer A layer of gas called ozone (a form of oxygen) high up in the Earth's atmosphere that absorbs most of the Sun's harmful ultraviolet radiation.

Parasite A parasitic animal gains nourishment or shelter from another living thing, called its host, and in doing so, can damage or harm the host.

Parthenogenesis When a female animal can produce offspring without a mate.

Particle A tiny piece of matter.

Pasteurization Liquids, such as milk, are heated to a certain temperature and then rapidly cooled in order to destroy germs.

Patent The exclusive right to make, use or sell an invention for a set number of years. Inventors must apply for a patent.

Perennial A plant that lives for many years.

Period, geological One of the major periods of time into which the Earth's history is divided, each lasting many millions of years.

Periodic Table The table of chemical elements arranged in order of the number of protons in the nucleus of their atoms.

Pheromone A chemical substance produced by an animal, which affects the actions and behaviour of others of its kind.

Photon One of the tiny particles or 'packages' that light travels in.

Photosphere The surface of the Sun, which is made from churning, hot gases.

Photosynthesis The process by which plants make food using water, sunlight and carbon dioxide from the air.

Phylum The main groups into which the animal kingdom is divided, such as sponges molluscs, echinoderms and annelid worms. Each phylum is divided into various classes.

Planet A large world that revolves around the Sun or another star.

Planetary nebula A gigantic ring of clouds of gas emitted at speed that form around the outside of a supernova.

Planetesimal One of the small lumps of rock circling the early Sun which later clumped together to form the planets.

Plankton Tiny plants and animals that drift in seas, oceans and large lakes.

Plasma Special form of gas at very high temperatures, full of charged particles.

Plasma The liquid part of blood without the microscopic cells (red cells, white cells and platelets).

Pole, Magnetic The region of a magnet where the magnetism is strongest. Every magnet has north and south poles.

Pollen Tiny capsules made by the stamens. To reproduce, plants must pass pollen between flowers. Pollen is carried by the wind or other insects to other plants.

Pollination The process by which the pollen moves from the stamens to the stigma of the same flower or a different flower on the same kind of plant.

Pollution The introduction into an environment of substances harmful to living things.

Polymer Substance such as plastic made from long chain or branchlike molecules.

Positron A particle identical to an electron but with a positive electrical charge.

Predator An animal that hunts and catches other creatures, called prey, for its food.

Prey A creature that is hunted or caught as food by another animal, called the predator.

Prism Wedge of glass that splits white light passing through it into different colours.

Program Coded instructions telling a machine, such as a computer, how to work.

Proton With neutrons, one of the two basic particles that make up an atom's nucleus.

Pulley Wheel with a grooved rim that guides a rope to make it easier to lift things.

Pulsar A neutron star that spins rapidly sending out regular pulses of radio waves.

Pulse rate The number of times per minute that the heart beats and sends blood, causing pulsations (pressure waves) in the arteries.

Pupa A hard-cased, inactive stage in the life of an insect before becoming an adult.

Quantum (plural quanta) A tiny package of light, energy or matter.

Quasar A small, very distant object that looks like a star but is hundreds of times brighter than galaxies. Most quasars are billions of light-years away, the furthest things visible in the universe.

Radiation Energy emitted from particles as electromagnetic waves such as light and radio waves, or as radioactive particles.

Radio waves Electromagnetic waves with the longest wavelength and lowest frequency, including microwaves and those used for radio and TV broadcasting.

Radioactivity The break-up of atomic nucleus, sending out energetic particles that are very dangerous to animal life.

Reaction, chemical The joining of two or more chemicals when at least one of the chemicals changes.

Recombinant DNA The way scientists take DNA from one thing and add it to the DNA of another to alter its life instructions.

Recycling Using the same materials, such as newspaper, over and over again.

Red giant A huge red star at least ten times as big as the Sun, formed when a medium-sized star, such as the Sun, begins to burn out and swell up.

Red shift The change in colour as light from galaxies turns redder because the waves are stretching away from us.

Reflection The bouncing back of light or other waves when they hit a surface.

Refraction Light rays bend as they pass from one transparent substance to another.

Relativity The theory that you can only measure time relative to something else.

Renewable resources Materials that can be used and replaced naturally, without being used up. The sun, wind and water are renewable energy resources.

Respiratory system Parts of an animal that take in oxygen from the air.

Root The part of the plant that holds the plant in the soil and takes up water and minerals for the plant to use.

Satellite Any object orbiting a star, planet or asteroid. Man-made satellites orbiting the Earth are used to gather scientific data or receive and transmit radio signals.

Scales Small, hard parts, usually in overlapping rows, covering the bodies of animals such as reptiles and fish.

Seed A capsule, which forms from the ovule after fertilization and contains a tiny plant with a foodstore.

Sepal A small leaf that forms part of the covering of the flower bud.

Sexual reproduction When a living thing produces offspring with a mate.

Solar cell A cell that converts the Sun's energy into electricity.

Solar System The collection of planets, moons and smaller objects that orbit (circle) the Sun.

Solid Matter with a shape and form.

Solution Liquid in which a solid, a liquid or a gas is broken up and intermingled so it behaves as part of the liquid.

Space probe An unmanned spacecraft sent from Earth to investigate the Solar System and beyond.

Space station A spacecraft, big enough for people to live and work on, which orbits the Earth.

Species The groups into which animals are divided. All members of a species can breed together, but they cannot breed with members of other species.

Spectrum The range of colours created when light is split by a prism.

Spiral galaxy A rotating galaxy with a spiral shape like a giant Catherine wheel. The Milky Way is a spiral galaxy, and the Sun is on one of its arms.

Spore A tiny capsule made by non-flowering plants such as mosses and fungi. It contains a piece of the parent plant or fungus, which can break out and grow into a new plant.

Stamen The part in the flower that produces pollen.

Static electricity Electricity that builds up when things rub together but do not move.

Steam Gas formed by evaporating water.

Stigma The part of the flower on top of the ovary, which receives pollen.

Stomata Holes on the underside of a leaf that let air and water in and out.

Strata Layers of sedimentary rock.

Stratosphere The layer of atmosphere above the troposphere, beginning about 10 km up, where temperatures rise with height.

Sub-atomic particles Particles that are even smaller than an atom.

Subduction The bending of a tectonic plate beneath another as they collide.

Sunspot A dark spot that develops on the surface of the Sun, which interrupts the flow of gases.

Supernova A gigantic explosion caused when a giant star runs out of energy. It throws off its outer layers and burns as bright as billions of ordinary stars.

System Several parts such as tissues and organs that work together to carry out one major, vital function.

Tectonic plate The 20 or so giant slabs of rock that make up the Earth's surface.

Tendon A strong, rope-like part where the end of a muscle narrows to join to a bone.

Terrestrial An animal that lives on land.

Territory An area or place where an animal lives and feeds, and which it defends by chasing away others of its kind.

Testa The protective outer casing of a seed.

Theory A carefully thought out idea to explain a particular scientific phenomenon.

Thermosphere The layer of the atmosphere above the mesosphere, beginning 80 km up.

Thorax The name for the middle or chest region of the body in many kinds of animals. In an insect, the legs and wings join to the thorax.

Thrust The force to drive something along.

Tissues Parts of the body formed of many cells of the same kind, such as muscle cells (fibres) that make up muscle tissue.

Tropical rainforest A forest that grows where the weather is always hot and wet.

Troposphere The lowest layer of the atmosphere existing up to 10 km.

Vaccination Injecting a substance into the blood so that it produces antibodies, which provide protection against a disease.

Veins Main blood vessels or tubes that carry blood towards the heart.

Vertebrate An animal that has a backbone (vertebral column), usually as part of its inner skeleton of bones.

Virtual reality A computer recreates a three-dimensional space, so that it seems as if you are actually in the space.

Voluntary In the muscle system, when a muscle can be controlled at will or by thinking, rather than working automatically without the need for thought (involuntary).

Warm-blooded When an animal's body temperature stays the same, despite changing temperatures in its surroundings. The two main groups of warm-blooded animals are mammals and birds.

Warning colours Usually bright colours and patterns to warn other creatures that an animal is harmful, such as being poisonous.

Wavelength The length from the crest of one wave to the crest of the next.

Weathering The breakdown of rock when exposed to the weather.

White dwarf A small, dense star formed when a medium-sized star such as the Sun runs out of fuel.

Wood A material made by trees that contains large numbers of tiny fibres.

X-ray High energy electromagnetic radiation used to take pictures through the body of bones and other structures.

Index